The Color Line and the Assembly Line

AMERICAN CROSSROADS

Edited by Earl Lewis, George Lipsitz, George Sánchez, Dana Takagi, Laura Briggs, and Nikhil Pal Singh

For a full list of titles in the series, see the final pages of this volume.

The Color Line and the Assembly Line

MANAGING RACE IN THE FORD EMPIRE

Elizabeth D. Esch

UNIVERSITY OF CALIFORNIA PRESS

University of California Press, one of the most distinguished university presses in the United States, enriches lives around the world by advancing scholarship in the humanities, social sciences, and natural sciences. Its activities are supported by the UC Press Foundation and by philanthropic contributions from individuals and institutions. For more information, visit www.ucpress.edu.

University of California Press
Oakland, California

Library of Congress Cataloging-in-Publication Data

Names: Esch, Elizabeth D., author.
Title: The color line and the assembly line : managing race in the Ford empire / Elizabeth D. Esch.
Description: Oakland, California : University of California Press, [2018] | Series: American crossroads | Includes bibliographical references and index. |
Identifiers: LCCN 2017039784 (print) | LCCN 2017043314 (ebook) | ISBN 9780520960886 (e-edition) | ISBN 9780520285378 (cloth : alk. paper) | ISBN 9780520285385 (pbk : alk. paper)
Subjects: LCSH: Ford Motor Company. | Racism in the workplace—Michigan—20th century. | Racism in the workplace—Brazil—20th century. | Racism in the workplace—South Africa—Port Elizabeth—20th century. | Automobile industry and trade—Employees—Social conditions—20th century.
Classification: LCC HD9710.U54 (ebook) | LCC HD9710.U54 F27 2018 (print) | DDC 331.6/3—dc23
LC record available at http://lccn.loc.gov/2017039784

27 26 25 24 23 22 21 20 19 18
10 9 8 7 6 5 4 3 2 1

To my parents, Raymond Gates Esch, Junior,
and Janet Allen Esch

And to the millions of Ford workers across the world
yesterday, today, and tomorrow

THE GEORGE GUND FOUNDATION
IMPRINT IN AFRICAN AMERICAN STUDIES

The George Gund Foundation has endowed this imprint to advance understanding of the history, culture, and current issues of African Americans.

The publisher and the University of California Press Foundation gratefully acknowledge the generous support of the George Gund Foundation Imprint in African American Studies.

CONTENTS

ILLUSTRATIONS

PREFACE AND ACKNOWLEDGMENTS

Many years ago I became intrigued by the detail from Diego Rivera's *Detroit Industry* frescoes that appears on the cover of this book. Why, in the midst of an epic work celebrating human labor on one hand and technological innovation on the other had Rivera decided to insert the scowling figure of Ford production manager Charles Sorensen in such a literal way? Other named figures in the frescoes—arts patron Edsel Ford, Detroit Art Institute director William Valentiner, inventor Thomas Edison—appear largely as symbols, tribute to one or another accomplishment and in gratitude for offering this commission to Rivera. But Sorensen—popularly known among workers as the "slave-driver"—appears here doing just what he did in reality: pressing workers through fear and the threat of force to work faster on the assembly line. Dressed in a business suit and clutching the clipboard that—like the stopwatch—signified Ford's constant surveillance of workers' movements and attempts at self-expression Sorensen's fierce and hovering presence is a potent representation of how power was wielded and production was achieved on Ford's assembly lines.

This detail is also captivating in its depiction of who is being managed. The two workers who form a triangle with Sorensen are of different races, one with light skin and one with dark. In the Rouge that Rivera depicted these men could possibly both be European immigrant workers, one possibly Slavic, the other perhaps Italian. Representing such differences as highly visible between two people counted today in the United States as white would have been consistent with how people understood and saw racial difference marked by color and hierarchy in 1932. But we could also assume that here Rivera was intentionally situating a Black and a white worker side by side, co-managed by the same intensity, the same rules and in the same job in the plant. Not only would this be consistent with Rivera's own idealism about the harmonious potential of the factory, but surely Rivera would have known also that Henry Ford was famous for his unprecedented hiring of Black workers at the Rouge—this might even have been noted by the company itself as Rivera visited and studied the Rouge plant in preparation for his work.

It is nonetheless unlikely that Rivera would have actually encountered a Black worker next to a white worker on the production line in the early 1930s at the Rouge. While it is true that Ford boasted of his employment of Black workers in every department and had hired nearly 10,000 African Americans by 1930, the existing record and anecdotal evidence suggest that it is highly unlikely that a Black worker would have been employed in this aspect of production. It would be far more likely to see a Black and a white worker side-by-side in the enormous foundry at the Rouge where jobs that had been held at Ford's first assembly line by Eastern European workers were more and more frequently being filled by African American workers. Even this, though, was a department becoming segregated as Eastern Europeans refused to do jobs increasingly considered "Black."

That Ford hired such large numbers of African American workers led historians who studied Ford and the unionization of Detroit to accept the claim that the best way to describe Henry Ford was as a paternalist, a believer in uplift through work and wages. At a time when no other auto firms hired Black workers, surely, the thinking went, it would not be possible to view Henry Ford or his company as racist. Yet to not consider that racism may have structured Ford's decision to *hire* Black workers is to fall into a habit that has become far too easy in telling histories of race and segregation in the United States. After all, this was not the Jim Crow South, this was Detroit, soon to be named the Arsenal of Democracy, and because life conditions for African American workers may have been better there than in, say, Birmingham, Alabama, historians tend to thus describe it as "less racist." And certainly a firm that actually hired Black workers could not be "as racist" as those that refused to do so.

How then do we account for the subsequent history of racist segregation in work, housing, and education; the racist violence; the difference in life expectancy; and the denial of mobility that characterized the growth of Detroit and its suburbs? If the richest man in the world and one of the three most powerful employers in Detroit and in the United States as a whole was promoting non-racialism surely this should have given a different character to what used to be called "race relations" in Detroit. And how do we account for the fact that by 1965 Black rank and file auto workers at the Rouge plant were fighting against their segregation into production jobs they had once been excluded from? Access to job classifications had changed at the Rouge but the fact of racial segregation and differential treatment in the plant had not. Nor had deeply segregated patterns of housing or home ownership.

This project emerged out of an interest in reconciling those realities, in trying to come up with an historic understanding of how race in the United States continues to order, exclude, include, and categorize people in ways that might differ by region or workplace but that remained present across all regions of the United States through the twentieth century and that have hugely determinative impacts on what are now described as "life chances" and "outcomes." It also emerged from a lifelong fascination with the factoryscape, the built and social environments that factories both are and enable. Growing up in a deindustrializing city during the 1980s I listened as racist explanations took hold to explain factory closings, watched news reports of the bashing of Japanese "imports" and learned about Vincent Chin, a Chinese worker at an auto-parts shop beaten to death in Highland Park (site of Ford's first auto assembly line) by Chrysler superintendent Ronald Ebens and his stepson who wielded baseball bats and reportedly screamed at Chin that it was "because of you little motherfuckers that we're out of work!" My dear friend (and a lifelong community organizer) Elsa Barboza helped me understand the contours of that world as we encountered it together and worked to forge anti-racist possibilities for our lives. I am grateful for her friendship across all these years.

As a young activist in Ann Arbor and Detroit I was very lucky to come into contact with some of the smartest analysts of workplace power and the auto industry in the United States. Jane Slaughter, Mike Parker, and Kim Moody have consistently provided the most clear-minded and useful tools for understanding how managerial strategies change in response to both worker self-activity and crises of capital. That they have continued to research and write largely outside the context of the university and for workers underlines the depth of their commitments and the significance of their analyses. Indeed, this project emerges in part from conversations that started way back then with activist auto workers and their advocates in Detroit and beyond.

To paraphrase a novelist I admire: everyone we work with is smart. Thus the challenge is not to be smart, the challenge is to be kind. Like most of us who work in academic fields, I have experienced both kindness and unkindness at the hands of very smart people. Having the space here to thank those whose kindness, intellectual generosity, and devotion to using their energy and insights to change the world is the greatest pleasure and privilege. The actual research that led to this book began many years ago as a seminar paper under the direction of Robin D. G. Kelley. My first archive visit led me to the papers on Ford's rubber plantations, Fordlandia and BelTerra; on that trip I opened boxes that had been sealed since they were shipped from Brazil to the United States in the late 1940s. Bark samples and rubber tapping tools fell crumbling out of boxes and inspired me to follow their traces. While that trip was meant to lead to a paper on the history of the Ford Rouge plant it instead opened the door to studying the Rouge as the center of a global empire that itself centered on the labor of Black workers. My gratitude to Robin for his support before, during, and since that time knows no bounds; I have benefitted from his fine mind and big heart in ways too numerous to count and feel lucky to call him a friend.

Other scholars at NYU who likewise embraced my decision to pursue this work shaped my thinking in indelible ways. Tom Bender's invitations to participate in the La Pietra Conferences on Internationalizing the Study of American History gave me access to foundational conversations about the promise and peril of decentering U.S. power at a time when it appeared to be unlimited in its scope. Tom's support of my work in and out of his dissertation seminar, including for a research trip to South Africa, provided grounding I badly needed. Walter Johnson particularly helped me to understand the dangers inherent in syntheses that assigned capacities to elites for knowledge across space and time greater than they indeed possessed. His insistence that transnational studies of the U.S. past not do the "dreamwork" of contemporary neoliberal capital continues to focus my thinking. I thank him for many fun and challenging conversations and for a subsequent invitation to Harvard to think through my work with other scholars engaged in an array of transnational projects.

Long before I even met Marilyn Young and had the chance to work with her I read her work while living in the Israeli Occupied West Bank. I had learned about Marilyn from award-winning journalist Gloria Emerson who had inspired my decision to leave school and to try my hand at working as an itinerant journalist in the Middle East. Gloria was then at work finishing the research for her book *Gaza: A Personal Account from an Occupied Land* and introduced me to a generation of women journalists and scholars who tried to unmask the truth about the United States in the world. In preparing for the military buildup that would lead to the Gulf War then-president George H. W. Bush argued that the United States fought in Vietnam "with one hand tied behind its back" because of protest against it. In response to this claim Marilyn wrote that in Vietnam the United States fought "with both its hands and both its feet and all its teeth." This sentence characterized her continued determination to tell the truth about U.S. imperialism and its expansion and I will forever be grateful for the many hours I got to spend with Marilyn in New York and Italy. I hope some of the clarity of language and purpose she modeled is evident in these pages.

Molly Nolan likewise took me under her scholarly and political wing in more ways than I imagine she realizes. Her support for graduate student union organizing and commitment to activist expressions of disagreement with university and U.S. policies across a range of concerns provided a model for engaged professor-ing that we should all hope to match. I hope this work lives up to the example she set in her own early and excellent study of Ford in Germany.

Special thanks to Rick Halpern for providing multiple years of support through conferences and workshops at the University of Toronto and the Centre for the Study of the United States at the Munk Centre for Global Affairs. Rick's early and continued commitment to transnational and comparative studies that centered both race and labor have remained a model for decentering and reassessing the place of the nation state in histories from below.

George Lipsitz has inspired me to try to write the daily life of racism and resistance, culture and capitalism since I first read *Rainbow at Midnight* many years ago. I am eternally grateful for his support in making this book happen and for his continued generosity. George says that we don't write in isolation but in solitude; these words have sustained me through some lonely moments of questioning and helped me remember what writing is ultimately for.

Peter Rachleff provided assistance, close reading, and support at various stages of this project. His own work both in and out of the academy has taught me so much about internationalism, rank and file militancy, and solidarity.

In researching this book I benefitted from support from Mellon Sawyer Foundation–funded fellowships in transnational study at Stanford University and the University of Illinois. I wish to express special and heartfelt thanks to Joel Beinin, Monica Wheeler, and other members of the Stanford History Department Mellon Seminar, whose graciousness and kindness toward me at a difficult time provided a model of solidarity far too rare in academic contexts. At UIUC I am especially grateful to the transnational and critical interdisciplinary scholars who welcomed me: Faranak Miraftab, Zsuzsa Gille, Ken Salo, Kristin Hoganson, Antoinette Burton, and Michael Rothberg all provided space for feedback at the critical earliest moments of this work.

I want to thank Janet Jakobsen, Neferti Tadiar, Beck Jordan-Young, Dorothy Ko, Eric Foner, Severin Fowles, Paige West, Elizabeth Bernstein, and my talented American Studies students, especially Suzanne Walker and Anna Ziering at Barnard College/Columbia University. At the University of Kansas I finished this book while getting to know an inspiring community of colleagues, especially those in Faculty for a Safer Campus who continue to fight valiantly against the absurdity that is concealed carry on our campus. These include Maryemma Graham, Edgar Tidwell, Cécile Accilien, Darren Canady, Jennifer Hamer, Shawn Alexander, Ben Chappel, Cheryl Lester, Katie Batza, Henry Bial, Joo Ok Kim, Chris Perreira, Clarence Lang, Randal Jelks, and Ayesha Hardison.

I have benefitted from the opportunity to present this work over the years to audiences at Wayne State University, the University of Illinois, the University of Toronto, Oxford University, Goldsmith's University of London, the University of the Witswatersrand, the University of Mississippi, Queen Mary University, Harvard University, and at numerous scholarly conferences. In these and other rooms I have encountered scholars who have inspired me through their many contributions. These include Alan Wald, Salim Tamari, Nikhil Singh, Jordan Camp, Christina Heatherton, Manu Vimalassery, Zach Sell, Bashar Tarabieh, Robbie Shilliam, Gerard Hanlon, Sara Farris, Chris Newfield, Alberto Toscano, Brenna Bhandara, Moon Ho Jung, and Avery Gordon.

While it may be a little out of place in acknowledgments of this kind, it is important that I thank the surgeons, physical therapists, and their staffs with whom I have worked since this project started. Five spinal surgeries and countless hours of rehab made this book and the rest of my life possible and I am grateful to those talented medical professionals. Many friends sustained me through some very challenging years, and I will never be able to thank them enough. They include Kimberly Gilmore and Michael LaCombe, (both founding members of CANS, the Committee Against Nay-Saying who always hit the whole ball), Rachel Mattson, Catherine Sameh, Danny Widener, Fanon Wilkins, Steve Downs, David Levin, Pam Galpern, Simone Sagovac, Erin Small, Nico Pizzolato, Josh Fraidstern, Andrea Morrell, Sally

Cooper, and Blake Schwarzenbach. I used to say that I owed Blake especially for the adjectives but now I'd just like to thank him for, well, everything, maybe most for finding hope in hard times. All of us would be well served to remember Blake's lyric "it's not what you sell/it's what you make." Love and gratitude to my brothers Dan and Tom and to my sister Emily.

David Randall Roediger may be the only person happier than I am that this book is finally finished. He has shaped my life in immeasurable ways and because I can not find the words I will simply cite the refrigerator magnet: "Cancer (the Crab) June 22 to July 23. Tenacious. Intuitive. Perceptive. Supportive. Helpful. Encouraging. Caring and Kind. Devoted. Dependable. Imaginative. Sensitive. Self Reliant. Compassionate. Nicer than everyone else." For being all those things and more I am grateful to him.

Lastly I wish to thank my parents, to whom this book is dedicated. Shortly before my father died he reminded me of his conviction that the most important thing we can do is remain teachable. My parents have exemplified that commitment in lives filled with courage and openness to change even in the face of difficult odds. I hope this work goes a small way toward repaying all they have given me.

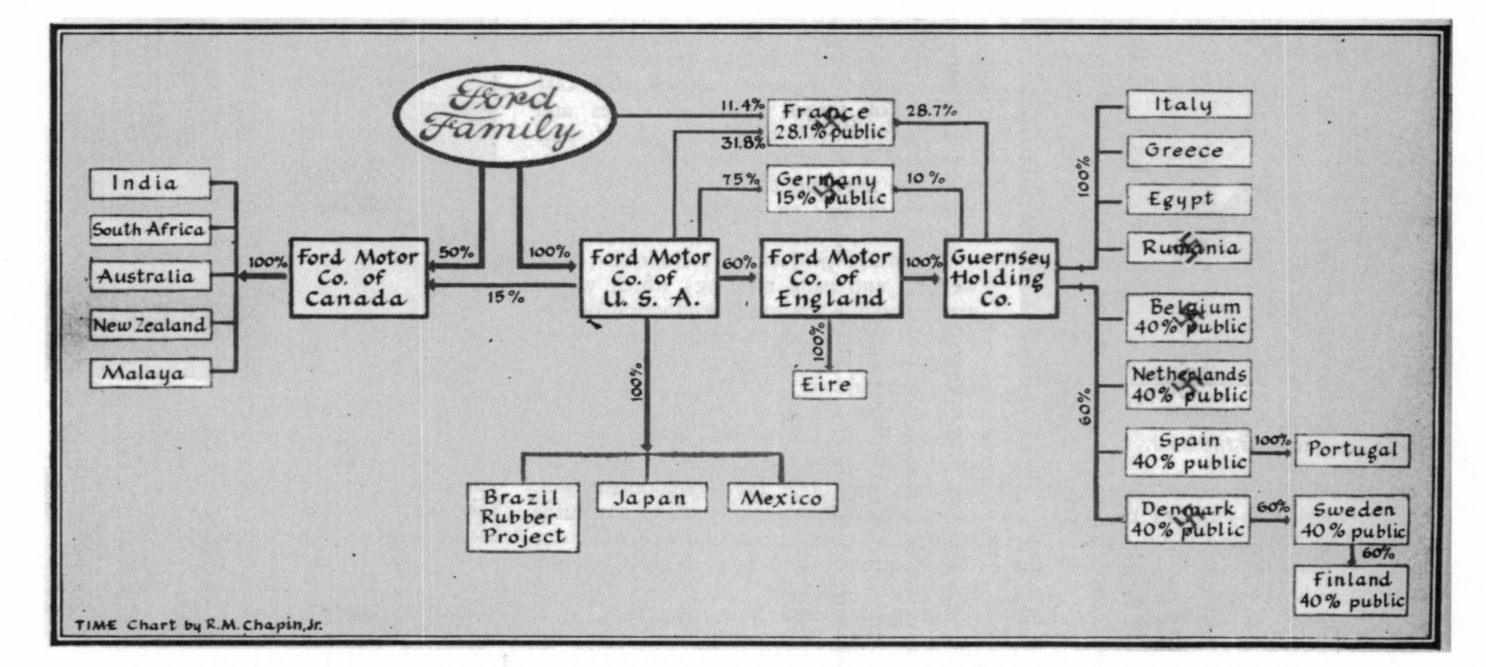

FIGURE 1. The Ford Family's holdings at the beginning of World War II. Courtesy R.M. Chapin, Jr., for *Time Magazine*, March 17, 1941.

INTRODUCTION

The Color Line and the Assembly Line

IN 1903 HENRY FORD INCORPORATED the Ford Motor Company. That same year the sociologist, historian, and activist W. E. B. Du Bois published this remarkably prescient claim: "The problem of the 20th century is the problem of the color line—the relation of the darker to the lighter races in Asia and Africa, in America and in the islands of the sea."[1] Within two decades Ford would expand to become one of the largest employers on earth, a global company with workplaces, dealerships, and customers in more than twenty countries. By 1927 its product, the Model T, would be far and away the top-selling car in the world, accounting for half of all cars on the planet. So, too, would the color line expand, to "belt the world" as Du Bois subsequently described it, bringing increasing rather than decreasing numbers of people into white supremacist–structured hierarchies. Despite this shared and simultaneous globality, however, both are conventionally treated as relating to far more nationally specific realities—Ford to narrowly American realities, and Du Bois to narrowly African American ones.[2]

This book is a study of how, and how unevenly, the Ford Motor Company promoted both the idea of and the application of the color line to structure mass production as it expanded globally. Simultaneously, it demonstrates how what I call the "ethos of the assembly line" was put to work in the service of white supremacist ideas and racial-segregationist practices at Ford and via Ford as the company built its self-described empire through the 1930s. In these years Ford relied on the color line and the assembly line as mutually reinforcing forces in the global production of not just cars but also "men," a goal Henry Ford himself bragged about regularly and often. Indeed, from 1914 through the Great Depression, Ford and his managers claimed to be as devoted to "making men" as they were to making cars in the United States and all over the world.[3] This book further argues that Ford's claim to do both—make cars and make men—accounted for broad transnational interest in and embrace of techniques in social engineering and mass production that by the early 1920s were coming to be known as "Fordist." Men-making was a core contribution of this early Fordism and led governments, social scientists, intellectuals, financiers, and nationalists globally to seek out the ideas associated with Ford as well as the actual investment of the company in their countries after World War I.

This study examines societies where Ford—the company as employer and Henry and his small coterie of managers as ideologues—was mobilized in the service of dynamics that I call "race development" and "white managerialism." It focuses explicitly on the white supremacist expressions and national developmentalist goals of Fordist men-making in Brazil, South Africa, and the United States. Relationships begun between transnational Ford managers and nationalizing elites in these years would prove to be hugely significant as Ford became one of the largest and most powerful industrial employers in each of these countries by the middle of the twentieth century. Specifically this work examines a set of sites where local elites and intellectuals accessed workers on the job and in their homes. Making common cause with Ford's ideas about men-making and the management of production meant thinking both dialectically and instrumentally about homeplace and workplace.

The fact that the assembly line affected ideas about and organization of work even in workplaces where no actual assembly line existed is an essential feature of the methodological approach of the book as well as of its findings. The massive changes that attended assembly line production in the emergent auto industry were felt largely in economic and social terms. But they were always imbricated in other systems of repression, dominance, protest, and struggle. As Ford management increased its capacity to standardize and control production via technology, it constantly needed to find ways to control the subjective expressions of workers. Thus "the assembly line" as a social problem entered the homes and lives of workers on multiple scales.

In each of these national contexts idealized notions of standardization and efficiency promoted by Ford influenced social scientific theory and became intertwined with beliefs in white supremacy as a mechanism of national improvement and progress. For the emergent class of liberal social scientists and managerial bureaucrats in Brazil, South Africa, and the United States in the 1920s, the "problem" of national development had been named a racial one. The case studies here demonstrate that this took very different shape because of different conditions in each of these societies. But they also show how elites in these societies shared in common an overarching belief in "white" as the racial designation of civility, progress, modernity, and order as well as a determination to use ideas and techniques associated with Ford in social reform projects.

Through the first four decades of the twentieth century, liberal elites across the globe who made arguments about the desirability and feasibility of racial segregation and national improvement increasingly did so in terms of efficiency and standardization. In South Africa and Brazil, like the United States industrializing countries with "mixed" European, African, Asian, and Indigenous populations, these debates reflected shared commitments to the idea that mass production, mass consumption, and white racial supremacy were parts of a twentieth-century modern whole. In each of these societies, as in the United States, ideas about work, consumption, and progress became inseparable from developmental concerns about the very bodies of those who worked and consumed. How such workers would be viewed, often through the prism of eugenic ideas—as citizens, potential citizens needing fixing, or those who needed to be excluded from citizenship—was framed in terms of racial "fitness."[4]

Looking at early evidence of Ford's presence in Brazil and South Africa shows that the company supported local and national efforts to name, draw, redraw, and harden the color line in the years between World Wars I and II. It also reveals that South African and Brazilian interest in Ford reflected the sense that the company was willing to accede to local political and social concerns that took the shape of exclusionary or segregationist practices. Elites believed that the practical and ideological application of Fordism served the interests of their own national and racial development dreams, seeing in Ford a source not just of jobs and capital but also of social and cultural direction in building "new" societies and "new" people. The company encouraged Brazilian and South African planners to borrow from Ford's modern industrial process, connecting Fordist ideas to white supremacist social initiatives that were local. This means that in each national case presented here, white managerialism was understood and promoted as progressive, civilizing, transformative, and efficient—all ideals associated with Ford's combined efforts in making cars and making men. Further, the case studies presented here show how these processes are much more aptly described as Fordist "Brazilianization" and Fordist "South Africanization" than they are as "Americanization."

It is perhaps ironic that through serious consideration of the range of historical *differences* in these societies, a *similar* transnational interest in racial development and improvement becomes discernable across the spectrum of liberal and corporatist ideologies in Brazil, South Africa, and the United States. In all of these places the word Ford—evoking both Henry Ford and his company—became associated with what one South African journalist described as a commitment to "saving human detritus from the scrap heap of history."[5] And as the historian Jerry Davila has shown in his meticulously researched *Diploma of Whiteness,* social scientists and planners in Brazil accessed Fordism not just as a source of economic modernization but for improvement of the so-called national racial stock via social scientific and educational reforms.[6]

DEARBORN AS CENTER OF THE FORD EMPIRE

The company's global expansion coincided with and depended on the growth of Ford in the United States itself. In 1927 Ford was the largest employer in the largest industry in the largest economy in the world. Throughout the late teens and twenties Ford's devotion to vertical integration was coming to fruition as the company sucked up coal mines, timber mines, gravel pits, raillines, ships, and land in its quest for total control of the terms of mass automobile production. By 1925 in Michigan the massive new River Rouge complex had eclipsed Ford's first belt-driven assembly plant in Highland Park. Plans for the new plant had begun even as Highland Park was being celebrated for its astonishing success in the use of moving assembly line technology and for productivity increases that date to the introduction of the five-dollar daily wage in 1914. But Ford was distinguished from its earliest years forward by management's attention to constant improvement in the search for what Henry Ford called "the one best way"; almost immediately the limits of production at the first assembly plant were seen as surmountable and would be resolved, or so management argued, both in and via the megafactory on the Rouge River.

More than a decade in the making, by the time the Rouge was fully on line (the period under study in this book) Ford's commitments to Americanizing immigrant workers that had famously attended the advent of the five-dollar day at its Highland Park plant were all but over. The timing of these developments is of significance to the argument of this book for several reasons.

Ford's reputation as a welfare capitalist interested in the well-being of his often immigrant employees was earned in an earlier political and economic era in the United States and in Detroit. As Stephen Meyer so brilliantly documented more than three decades ago, the "progressive" Sociological Department at Ford was replaced—by the end of World War I—with increasingly repressive techniques of surveillance and control of the workforce. Interest in the Americanization of European immigrants gave way to support for immigration restriction among Ford managers, culminating in their acquiescence to or outright support for the passage of the Johnson-Reed Act in 1924. Like many of their peers who supported immigration restriction, Ford managers increasingly saw themselves as Anglo-Saxons historically and Anglo-Americans politically, claiming the arguments for white Protestant racial purity that bolstered Johnson-Reed as their own.[7] Second, it was in these years that Ford began to hire African American workers overwhelmingly for work in the forge and foundry at the new Rouge plant and to attract Mexican migrants to Detroit. This hiring took place at the height of Ford's public support for racist political activism and anti-Semitism, which calls into question the oft-repeated idea that Henry Ford was unique among his peers for seeing African American workers as being "the same" as white workers. This study challenges the notion that hiring African American workers made Ford a more socially progressive firm than others in Detroit. Instead, by situating this history in the context of a transnational consideration of how Ford helped to strengthen belief in the color line, it asks us to rethink the terms in which we understand the history and dynamics of racism in the U.S. urban north. It argues that Ford thought of Black migrant workers to Detroit as more akin to colonized subjects and treated them as such. African American workers were to the company neither sufficiently American nor Americanizable, a fact that pushes us to find new language to describe Ford's relationship to Black Detroit in the context of overall arguments about the company's paternalism.

At home as well as globally Ford exploited unevenness, so much so that we ought to question whether debates over Fordism take sufficient account of questions of scale and therefore of race. From the Italian Marxist Antonio Gramsci's seminal "Americanism and Fordism" we gain a strong sense of Fordism as the product of uniquely U.S. conditions and innovations leading to an epochal bargain that offered workers relatively high wages in exchange for unprecedented high levels of sped-up exploitation. Gramsci inquired passionately (and with useful skepticism) about whether Fordism could revolutionize the sedimented production practices of Europe. Absent from his writing, however, is a consideration of Fordist expansion beyond Europe. Likewise lacking is the reality of the racialization of immigrants and African Americans in Ford's U.S. factories. Nor can Ford's initiatives in the global South be accounted for in "Americanism and Fordism." The result, which we inherit, is a lack of realization of the extent to which Fordism aligned itself with "productions of difference" in and out of the United States. Even David Harvey's provocative periodization of Fordism as applying to the world system only from the ascent of trade union power within the United States and the social power of organized labor in post–World War II Western Europe leaves us with a U.S.-European lens that flattens unevenness and distorts the process by which Fordism took hold in different locales.[8]

QUESTIONS AND METHODS

As the company most often credited with developing and improving assembly line production, Ford occupies a unique place in the history of mass production and the globalization of American investment and manufacturing. When the company created the "five-dollar day" in 1914, tying the alleged benefits of mass consumption to the promise of factory work and citizenship in the United States, it made necessary the continuous ideological and cultural reinforcement of the idea that consumer goods—things—were as beneficial to workers as time or skills or health or wages. Beyond the consumer market this effort included Ford's urging of belief in colonialism and empire, in racial hierarchy and white supremacy, in Christian civility and native savagery, and in U.S. exceptionalism. All were constantly evoked and deployed by the company for a variety of purposes both material and promotional. In thinking about what his workers needed, Henry Ford always expressed confidence in the ability of work to make or save the man. His extensive reliance on ideas developed by Frederick W. Taylor in *The Principles of Scientific Management* are well studied and often remarked upon.[9] However, for a time the company's concern with the lives of its racialized immigrant workers outside of the workplace was as insistent. For Ford, and for those reformers who leaned on Fordist ideas in social engineering schemes, controlling the realm of the home was an essential component of controlling workers on the job.

The above concepts are explored here through four related but distinct themes that form the backbone of my argument about why the social and cultural impact of Ford was so great and that structure its individual chapters. First is the relationship between life on the clock and life at home. These tend to be seen as separate spheres, one where production happened and the other where consumption happened. Here I show how dynamic the relationship between those spheres was and, from the viewpoint of Ford's management, had to be. The second theme concerns how Ford promoted and linked marriage, family, and gender-based behavior at home to the structure of work in its plants. Men-making, for Ford, ultimately necessitated family-making. This has been most thoroughly understood by scholars studying the earlier Americanization programs at Ford. Here I take those insights and apply them to Ford's efforts outside of the United States. The third theme that structures this inquiry is the centrality of managers to making cars and making men. I argue for an understanding of managerial power as being linked to ideologies that transgressed the factory walls but also lived within them. Finally, the fourth and overarching theme that links these chapters is the simultaneous promotion of white supremacy in varied registers in each of these societies.

One of the workplaces considered here, Ford Motor Company of South Africa's assembly plant in Port Elizabeth, was just beginning to bring moving assembly line production into being in the years under examination here. In two others, Fordlandia and Belterra, Ford's rubber plantations in northern Brazil, no assembly line would ever exist. Yet in each of these societies (and many others in the world) Ford's assembly line came to embody the idea of social improvement through efficiency, mass society, and progress. None of these concepts existed outside of belief in racial and national hierarchies.

The pairing in this work of the assembly line and the color line is not intended to be one of opposing forces. We tend to treat the assembly line as the epitome of the modern, scientific, productive, and standardized. The color line—the oppressive "worldview of race"—that Ralph Bunche, following Du Bois, strove to reduce to infamy, seemed on the other hand to have been drawn variously and arbitrarily, as the different racial systems of South Africa, the United States, and Brazil demonstrate.[10] Moreover, the brutalities associated with racial rule are retrospectively seen as unscientific and even atavistic. That the rationality of the assembly line must have challenged the irrationality of the color line thus becomes an easy assumption.

Such a mistaken view gains further traction if we focus narrowly on the most massive site of assembly line production in U.S. history, Ford's River Rouge plant, which was also its most celebrated site of the employment of

African American workers. Yet at the same time it pursued this multiracial hiring policy in this one Michigan factory, in South Africa Ford would work with the state to exclude from employment all but white workers for nearly three decades. In the two Brazil plantations studied here Ford deliberately sought out a labor force of men it understood as being "mixed-race."[11] Thus the energy that drives this book derives from the assertion that the assembly line's most advanced expressions proved compatible with a spectrum of white supremacist practice and ideology.

Indeed this work sees Ford as especially powerful but not especially innovative in this regard. In 1907, the labor historian John R. Commons argued that the decision to bring Black, immigrant, and so-called native (meaning Northern European–descended white American) workers together in industrial workplaces signaled a managerial interest in fostering racial conflict more than it did a commitment to racial equality. The Chicago meatpacking plants on which the assembly line in auto production was based are an early example of this practice, which featured the employment of Black workers. These plants housed the awe-inspiring assembly lines that Commons had just finished touring when he wrote that "almost the only device and symptom of originality displayed by American employers in disciplining their labor force has been that of playing one race against another." If we consider also, as this study emphasizes, Ford's frequent marketing of itself as a producer of "race development," the auto giant's practices were anything but a challenge to the ideologies that produced color lines.[12]

Though Ford was legendarily a transgressor of the color line in Detroit, such innovations unfolded within sharp and self-interested limits at the Rouge plant. Even there management overwhelmingly segregated Black workers into the most dangerous and dirty jobs. At the Highland Park plant, where the Model T was first produced in 1908 and the five-dollar-a-day wage introduced in 1914, Ford employed very few Black workers. There questions of race centered on the possible Americanization of variously racialized European immigrants, leading to experiments in social improvement that would first gain Ford its international reputation as a progressive reformer. Social interventions into the lives of these eastern and southern European newcomers to Detroit so overtly relied on attempts to "Americanize" them—herding workers into a literal melting pot at Ford English School graduation ceremonies—that the link between Ford and Americanism is almost assumed. In other Ford settings in the United States, however, exclusion remained the norm, as for example in continuing production at Chicago and

Dallas and in some sub-assembly and parts plants. The historian Howard Segal describes the small Ford plants—Christened "village industries" by the company—scattered in mostly rural areas: "Few of the village industries employed African Americans however and none employed Mexicans." Ford had come to be described as a progressive who was devoted to the uplift of Black workers and the possibility that "all men when given a job and a chance"—but only at certain times, in certain places, and, even at the Rouge, in certain departments. Ford management's devotion to the idea of "one best way," which the famous term "Fordism" tries to capture, did not lead to consistent racial practices, except in the most general sense that the racial knowledge its self-consciously white managers commanded could reorder the world.[13]

GROUNDINGS, CONTESTATIONS, AND CONTOURS OF THE STUDY

The most fascinating appreciations of Fordism, and the ones most attuned to Ford's attempted reduction of labor to a series of motions in which the race and nationality of the workers would seem to have mattered little, draw from rich traditions on the Marxist left. From the *Communist Manifesto* forward, historical materialist accounts have at times thought of capitalist production as imparting a "cosmopolitan character to production and consumption in every country." What Marxists have sometimes called "abstraction" describes capital as desirous of purchasing through wages a series of predictable motions and processes that exist independent of the history and personality of the workers who embodied the labor power. Indeed the historian Dipesh Chakrabarty has recently argued that Marx understood that such a desire on capital's part was necessary to a continuing and expanding process of accumulation, one which set for itself the task of vanquishing differences even at the level of motion. The acknowledgment, however, of such a universalizing quest has too often led, in Gramsci's writings as well as in the accounts of Fordism by later scholars who study the historical emergence of work processes, to the neglect of how thoroughly Ford managers believed the world was ordered by racial hierarchy.[14]

What the sociologist Grace Hong has called the "ruptures of capital"—strategies to make differences among workers meaningful—now seem in the context of recent scholarship to be as impressive, calculated, and productive as capital's universalism.[15] Over the past decades labor historians have begun to examine systematically the managerial use of race to divide workers, especially in Hawaii, in the deep and border South in the late nineteenth and early twentieth centuries, and within Asian American history.[16] "In the history of the United States," the literary scholar Lisa Lowe writes, "capital has maximized its profits not through rendering labor 'abstract' but precisely through the social productions of 'difference,' ... marked by race, nation, geographical origins, and gender." Indeed as Chakrabarty suggests regarding matters beyond the United States—his insight holds deep relevance for the study of Fordism transnationally—it may be that capital seeks not final universalizing victories that standardize all workers by eliminating differences but constant and varied new challenges in that regard.[17]

In a transnational economic context, growth often requires that development remain uneven. Such unevenness has produced not only opportunities to make races and nationalities compete but also to market Fordism to elites internationally as a mechanism for improving their own "national stock." Ford's direct impact on such heterogeneous international development leads us to take seriously not only the concept of combined and uneven development, as recent scholars have eloquently done, but of a combined and uneven Fordism. In political economic terms, but also in racial and national ones, Ford particularized as much as it universalized. It is for such reasons, and to underline the fact that Ford did not (and could not) evenly impact the entire world, that the critical engagement here is with particular transnational histories, rather than with a synthetic "global" history.[18]

In producing and selling the Model T as "the Universal Car" Ford promised to bring into being not just a universal product but also a universal method and thus a universal worker. In 1926 Henry Ford wrote: "An operation in our plant in Barcelona has to be carried through exactly as in Detroit ... a man on the assembly line in Detroit ought to be able to step into the assembly line in Oklahoma City or Sao Paulo, Brazil."[19] But the reality was quite different. Rather than dissolving historically rooted colonial categories, Ford in fact helped consolidate a modern racial reality in both Brazil and South Africa, as it did in the United States. Despite Ford's professed interest in a universal system, and despite convergences of interest in this idea across the political spectrum, the distance of history allows us to see that Ford made men by making race and gender. Given such specific national contexts and changing exigencies, any notion of a unified Fordist system becomes difficult to sustain.[20]

Questions about national differences, development, and the possible spread of Fordism have until recently been the concerns of those doing comparative history, an important source of ideas and inspirations for this study. The national contexts considered in this book—Brazil, the United States, and South Africa—have been among the nation-states whose histories have been most insistently compared. Legacies of slavery and colonial settlement and the subsequent place of racial categorization necessarily play a large role in these comparisons. Indeed the best of such comparative studies, including those of George Fredrickson, John Cell, Anthony Marx, and Stanley Greenberg, make the interplay between differing material circumstances and the production of race an organizing principle of their inquiries.[21]

Comparative history's basis in case studies, however, also potentially aggrandizes the nation-state as a unit of analysis and misses transnational processes that show how national histories are indiscrete, unplanned, and contradictory. Moreover, capital's role in the pursuit of empire can disappear in state-centered accounts, even comparative ones. This book has profited from recent works transcending what Ella Shohat and Robert Stam have called the "narcissism of national difference" by showing institutions and individuals operating in international networks within and across empires.[22] Other such supranational work has illuminated how white supremacy was created through international and imperial collaborations, as in the work of Marilyn Lake and Henry Reynolds. Likewise, the flowering of recent work on pan-Africanism shows how this form of Afro-internationalism made analysis of and opposition to the color line parts of a dialectical whole.[23] Andrew Zimmerman's and James Campbell's studies showing how ideas and practices regarding race moved between specific places in Africa and the United States have likewise informed my analysis. I draw special inspiration from Zimmerman's call for a scholarship attentive at once to a "geopolitical logic of white supremacy and a political economic logic of racial specificity." For him, such specificity unfolded within a "global division of labor."[24]

That division of labor occurred in much of the world's territory and in the lives of workers through the mechanisms of empires.[25] Ann Laura Stoler and Frederick Cooper have considered how such empires, like places of Ford investment, functioned as "differentiated spaces" in which "hierarchies of production, power and knowledge . . . emerged in tension with the extension of the domain of universal reason, of market economics, and of citizenship."[26] The labor historian David Montgomery recognized the complexity of this reality when he wrote: "Formal and informal empires have defined the realm of possibility for working people in both imperialist countries and the portions of the world that those countries dominated."[27] Ford, working to extract largesse from foreign governments and to control enclaves outside the United States, was a leading example of what Montgomery meant by informal empire, even as it also brazenly utilized, through its own creation of the wholly independent Ford of Canada, the established colonial networks of the British Empire.[28]

Keeping empire, transnational capital, and national specificity within the same frame is thus a hallmark of this study. The work is shaped by the sense that privileging the nation-state as the primary container of historical narrative can miss as much as it allows us to understand about the processes through which history is made and written. But it does not seek merely to replace the nation-state with another unit, such as the multinational corporation, as some scholars of contemporary capitalism have urged.[29] In Ford's case, especially in war production and immigration policy, the U.S. state was central to the company's expansion, its changing strategies of factory discipline, and its ability to go out into the world. Similarly, in Brazil and South Africa Ford helped spin the very webs that connected those states to U.S. capital, to various kinds of progressive professionals, to racial liberals, and to investors. The goal then is a history unbounded by nation-states but attuned to their specific histories. How Ford's vast privately owned enterprises in Detroit or the Amazon or Georgia sometimes acted like states is one historical reality that points toward the need for this kind of method.

Within the context of U.S. history a "transnational turn" has been especially salutary insofar as it can help make "America" a more foreign place to the historians who study, write, and teach about it. When that turn focuses on labor, race, and management, results have been especially promising. Few histories could benefit more from critical and de-nationalized treatment than that of Ford. Examining across borders the daily reality of how the Ford Motor Company built cars, sold tractors, mined timber, and tried to produce rubber, among other pursuits, enables a far more complex examination of this firm and of the handful of men who ran it in the years it expanded globally. Stepping outside the borders of the United States allows us to frame questions differently. In the case of the Ford Motor Company this means acknowledging that not only was Ford almost *always* a multinational corporation, but also that this necessitates seeing the company's actions as political and cultural, not just economic. Looking at Ford's practices inside and outside the formal borders of the United States provides a way to consider how racial ideologies enabled states and private capital to work together.[30]

ON METHOD: DAILY AND GLOBAL LIFE

Avoiding some of the pitfalls of comparative history and social theory while borrowing from their contributions has given *The Color Line and the Assembly Line* a particular structure. Within the three national contexts under examination, eight sites are highlighted, underlining the point that nations are not homogenous units to be plugged into comparisons. This also allows us to see how inequalities between nation-states did not preclude the existence of inequalities within them. In the United States the factories at Highland Park and River Rouge differ dramatically as managerial regimes and as racial projects. Each compares to and contrasts with the Fordist management of Black workers off the job in Inkster, Michigan, as well as management at Ford's plantation in Richmond Hill, Georgia. In the Rouge, Ford cemented a reputation as the nation's leading employer of Black workers; elsewhere in the United States it scarcely departed from the norms of Southern Jim Crow and Midwestern "sundown towns." In Brazil managers of mixed-race laborers on the rubber plantations that Ford created, first at Fordlandia and then at Belterra, sought to improve workers using strategies very different from one place and time to the next. Both Brazil sites contrasted sharply with the U. S. context, where mixed-race people were never a category constituting legitimate objects of management (or other forms of legitimacy or social control). In South Africa, Ford participated through its Port Elizabeth factory in national and transnational projects—the latter profoundly shaped by Ford's integration into the British Empire through its Canadian enterprise—to hire and thus redeem poor whites deemed to be failing in their racially assigned positions in a system of white supremacy. The African workers excluded by Ford meanwhile fashioned a community, Kwaford, from the company's discarded shipping crates.[31]

The book starts with a consideration of the first fifteen years of Ford during which the company gained its reputation as a social reformer for its work in attempting to Americanize European immigrants at its Highland Park plant. During those years Ford also became a transnational company, developing connections to world markets well before World War I would propel it and other American firms further into the world. However, the book's main focus is on the critical decades after World War I. Ford's Highland Park Americanization campaigns were over by this time but they nonetheless lay the basis for much of the embrace of Ford outside the United States. This work frames Ford's move into Brazil and South Africa through a discussion of the particular social goals of state-crafters in those countries who found in Ford a useful ally, and at times a guide. The company had garnered a reputation for linking social improvement to high wages and found adherents on all sides of the political spectrum—at home from socialists like Kate O'Hare to Ku Klux Klan members, and abroad from emerging fascists to V. I. Lenin and various Soviet planners.[32]

In focusing on the 1920s and early 1930s this study follows the lead of the Italian scholar of Fordism Ferruccio Gambino, who has eloquently urged attention to the heterogeneity of Fordist practices across time and space. Gambino has particularly called our attention to the importance of keeping the long period of "Fordism without unions"—and indeed against them—distinct from what some analysts regard as the "golden age of Fordism" after World War II. Even as innovative a book as political scientist Mark Rupert's *Producing Hegemony: The Politics of Mass Production and American Global Power,* which does devote considerable attention to pre-union labor relations, ends up seeing the global reach of Fordism as occurring after the U.S. entry into World War II, a development that coincided with industrial unionism's triumph at Ford. This overarching emphasis on international relations and on the project of incorporating unionized workers into support of U.S. empire allows Rupert to intervene interestingly in debates within his field of international political economy. But in missing the efforts of Fordism both earlier and beyond Europe and the United States, Rupert and others also pay only the most glancing attention to the role of race in Fordist management, within or outside the United States.[33]

THE ARGUMENTS AND THE CHAPTERS

This history of Ford focuses on uneven development and racial regimes that made Brazil and South Africa different from one another and from Detroit, which was in turn different from other U.S. sites. Implicit in its argument for a methodology that is at once transnational and comparative is that such multiple approaches help us to see how uneven development and varied mechanisms of white supremacy existed in the United States as well as outside of it. To examine in the same book such a variety of Fordist plans and practices with roughly half the study devoted to each—allows for appreciation of how the confidence and flexibility it gained domestically allowed Ford to penetrate not just new economic worlds but new social worlds. In those worlds it sought not to impose a system but instead to apply an approach inspired by a broad commitment to white supremacy, especially in the realm of management.

In the United States, Brazil, and South Africa, Ford jobs and wages were packaged in social engineering schemes that sought to distinguish, categorize, and segregate workers by deepening and naming national, racial, and bodily differences. Thus the role of mass consumption cannot be severed from the role of mass production, though historians of Americanization frequently do so.[34] Central to the book's arguments is acceptance of Gramsci's observation that being seen to possess the most rationalized labor process in the world enabled Ford to rule workers and reshape society in the interwar years. Gramsci's passing remark in "Americanism and Fordism" that "hegemony was born in the factory" is especially important.[35] As a literal truth, the provocation only gets us so far; its limits are clear for example in the case of Ford's rubber plantations. But as a point of departure it is fruitful. At its most basic level the linking of hegemony and factory enables a vital broadening of analytical possibilities, supplementing scholarship that places the United States in the world by stressing the spread of its culture and consumer products. Important as those matters were, it was the discipline of mass production at Ford, as well as its advertised ability to transform "backwards" workers through regimented labor, that first made Ford so attractive to foreign leaders and that slowed its spread to countries with stronger industrial unions.

Seeing Ford's managerial practices, labor processes, and claims to race development as commodities that it marketed alongside the Model T connects Ford to long processes that David Roediger and I have discussed under the heading "whiteness-as-management."[36] This book argues that an analysis of workplace management is essential to understanding both the daily life of a factory and the larger cultural and social development of capitalism as a system. In this regard, it is necessary to remember that it is managers themselves, not capital as an abstraction, whom workers confront on the job. Studying managers' actions and ideas helps us to understand not just the daily life of industrial production but the broader meaning of assembly line production in American and subsequently transnational, political economies. At least until the late 1920s "foreigners" were seen as racially, not just culturally, different, a phenomenon re-emerging starkly in the United States today. Indeed, as burgeoning numbers of immigrants from the poorest sections of Europe became the core of the U. S. working class, management increasingly compared the "races" from which these southern and eastern European "new immigrants" came with "old stock" Americans, with workers of color, and with each other. Racial knowledge was used directly by "supervisors, section heads, foremen and other minor functionaries" to establish not only workers' places but their own, "solidifying [their] own position[s] of belonging and Americanness."[37] Necessary precisely because of the alienating and backbreaking pace of work in Ford plants, managers played both supervisory and disciplinary roles in the daily lives of workers. However, such roles should not be seen as being without *political* impact or meaning. The political aspirations of managers and their self-conceptions are intimately linked to the jobs they did every day.

Thus within working-class studies this work seeks to shift the focus from "labor and capital" to the more daily and lived reality of "workers and managers." It recognizes the significance of Marx's observation that "capital is also necessarily always a capitalist" and calls us to study its human representatives. For Marx, capitalism itself creates the reality (and necessity) of managerial structure and ideology, even a "personality as against labor." Indeed as Marx later maintained, "An industrial army of workmen, under the command of a capitalist, requires, like a real army, officers [managers], and sergeants [foremen, overlookers], who, while the work is being done, command in the name of the capitalist. The work of supervision becomes their established and exclusive function."[38] To emphasize the centrality of management is made easier in Ford's case because the superb business history of the company, by Allan Nevins and Frank Ernest Hill; the best early biography of Henry Ford, by Keith Sward; the best fictional rendering of Ford, by Upton Sinclair, and the best labor histories of Ford, by Stephen Meyer and David Gartman, all take management as a point of departure.[39]

Recent biographical studies of Henry Ford have been less acute in this regard, preferring to focus on the personal roles, idiosyncrasies, and often genius of their subject in ways that offer little opportunity to understand managerial ideologies and structures. Most histories of the man and the company—however thorough in other ways—have not urged an analysis of the close connection between the company's vast international presence and the political convictions of Henry Ford and the managers who functioned as his lieutenants. Conflicts between Henry Ford's professed nineteenth-century cultural values and his modernizing impact are more dramatized than explained. Thus Ford is seen as the great modernizer who hated urban cultural life, supported Prohibition, and thought workers should learn to folk dance; as the paternalist who hired more African Americans than any other Detroit employer before WWII but who was also a vicious anti-Semite who authored *The International Jew: The World's Foremost Problem;* the richest man in the world who also despised banks; the high-wage payer who hated unions; and, perhaps at the heart of all of these, the enabler of mass consumption who believed that most workers were not civilized enough to responsibly organize their own relationships to time and money. But to call attention to such matters only as paradoxes is not to explain them, or even necessarily to connect them.[40]

Most of Ford's overseas production began as or after links among race, management, and colonialism were being made and national variations of white supremacy were maturing. The company's development and transnational expansion deepened these already-existing dynamics, but it did not challenge them. In Brazil and South Africa Henry Ford and his leading managers—Charles Sorensen, Ernest Liebold, and Harry Bennett—found contemporaries who shared an approach to industrial, political, and social life with them personally and with their company's approach to social engineering, mass consumption, and mass production. In the South African case, Ford managers abjured the opportunity to play race against race as they did in Detroit, working with the local state's legislation of whites-only hiring. In Brazil, it regarded mixed-race people as particularly improvable even as no such category was positively affirmed in the United States. Such diverging priorities clearly said as much about the significance of emerging racial systems in the countries hosting Ford as they did about the relevance of race to the Ford Motor Company where investment and production were concerned. In combination with its extraordinary wealth and power, it was confidence in the idea that Ford could apply racial knowledge across locality and nation—never insisting on a set configuration of such knowledge—that made Ford appealing to national elites interested in racial improvement. That a consistent belief in the supremacy of whites could transcend deeply contradictory applications of it in practice in different locales suggests that its power derived from something other than its veracity or internal consistency.

Ford's regime of production both necessitated and enabled the making of "new men," and the chapters that follow show that this uneven process was inseparable from both extant and emerging state-driven nationalizing practices around the globe. Ford apprehended specific racial and national subjects through mass production and mass consumption, engaged workers and their families in the physical spaces of work and home, and aligned itself with managers and others involved in nationalizing projects in Brazil, South Africa, and the United States.

The Color Line and the Assembly Line unfolds in five chapters. Chapter 1, "Ford Goes to the World; the World Comes to Ford," details how, from almost its founding moments, the Ford Motor Company was fully transnational. By the time Ford introduced the five-dollar wage the company already had sizable holdings and boundless ambitions outside of the United States. The chapter shows how this massive expansion was made possible by the changes in the labor regime and the patterns of social reproduction of immigrant workers in Ford's Highland Park plant. In the Highland Park years Ford managers bossed, and the "sociologists" Ford employed molded, those immigrant workers thought to be of multiple European "races." They were required to participate in Americanization programs that included learning to speak English and professing allegiance to new values on and off the job.

Chapter 2, "From the Melting Pot to the Boiling Pot: Fascism and the Factory-State at the River Rouge Plant in the 1920s," moves the investigation of Ford from Highland Park to the River Rouge plant, famously chosen in 1932 by Diego Rivera to be the subject of his *Detroit Industry* frescoes. Here we see how thoroughly the welfare activities that would earn Ford its reputation around the world had been replaced by brutality, surveillance, and arbitrariness in the control of workers. The Rouge came fully on line as the new home of Model T production while European immigration to the United States was being curtailed by war and then nearly stopped through the immigration restrictions of 1924. The chapter situates managerial changes in this new reality. It also considers the built environment and management of the Rouge plant in relation to Ford managers' political interests in fascism and fascist political interest in Ford. Indeed the Rouge functioned transnationally not as a model of racial integration but as an inspiration for Nazi factory management, a fascist-like factory-state run by managers who at times professed strong affinities for fascism.

Chapter 3, "Out of the Melting Pot and into the Fire: African Americans and the Uneven Ford Empire at Home," looks at the story of the Rouge plant, the only workplace where Ford hired significant numbers of Black workers, through the experiences there of African American workers. In the wake of immigration restriction Ford recruited Black and Mexicans workers by the thousands to work at the Rouge. Even as Ford was celebrated by local Black elites for hiring African American workers at the Rouge, those workers were increasingly concentrated in the hottest and worst jobs. One concern of this chapter is thus to shed light on the contradictory reality that the "best jobs" in Detroit for African Americans were in a factory that workers nevertheless described as "the house of murder."[41] In challenging the notion that paternalism is the framework through which to understand Ford's relationship to Black workers, this chapter also considers Ford's involvement in racial uplift projects in two contexts more aptly described as colonial than as paternal. In 1932, the company purchased the "Black town" of Inkster, Michigan, its segregation partly premised on Ford's failure to stand up for fair housing in and around Dearborn. Credited with saving the residents of Inkster from the crisis of the Depression, Ford's Inkster "experiment" was modeled on a plan of debt peonage and perhaps consciously constructed a colonial relation with African Americans in the United States. In 1936, Henry Ford bought one million acres near Savannah, Georgia, restarting a plantation he named Richmond Hill. There the company launched a series of Jim Crow social uplift projects designed to save the white residents from racial neglect and the Black residents from themselves.

Chapter 4, "Breeding Rubber, Breeding Workers: From Fordlandia to Belterra," continues the consideration of Ford as a colonial power in tracing its decision to buy and build two vast rubber plantations in the Amazon region of Brazil. From 1925 to 1945 the Ford Motor Company engaged in an experiment in social engineering at its new rubber plantations in the Amazon, Fordlandia, and Belterra. This chapter demonstrates how Ford's intervention was fully in sync with the aspirations of Brazilian politicians and modernizers. Further, the company's belief in the racial improvability of Amazonian people structured the very choice of location of the plantations. Specifically influenced by what it perceived as the racial potential of the people in the region, Ford first recruited single men and then whole families to the plantations. Social and biological reproduction of children replaced attempts to improve rubber tappers who resisted Ford's importation of its "one best way."

Chapter 5, "'Work in the Factory Itself': Fordism, South Africanism, and Poor White Reform," examines the earliest moments of Ford's arrival in Port Elizabeth, South Africa, where it would ultimately become one of the most powerful employers. This chapter examines how the Poor White Study of the

Carnegie Corporation provided a social scientific rationale for the racial segregation of industrial work with which Ford complied. Though in South Africa Ford's processes of mass production and mass consumption were both mobilized in projects of racial improvement, the Carnegie report specifically endorsed the idea of work in the factory as the most effective route to the racial improvement and discipline of so-called poor whites. While Ford would gain its reputation for investing in South Africa years later when the company was a supporter of apartheid, the roots of its relationship with this racist state are in the 1920s and 1930s, when Ford had a reputation for racial paternalism and even liberalism in the United States. In part because of challenges to the company's ties to the apartheid regime, specific records for Ford in South Africa are relatively scarce, but the existing record allows for reconstruction of the company as part of broader white managerialist efforts to address the "problem of poor whites."

A short Conclusion, "From the One Best Way to The Way Forward to One Ford—Still Uneven, Still Unequal," considers race, management, and uneven development in the so-called post-Fordist world of auto production.

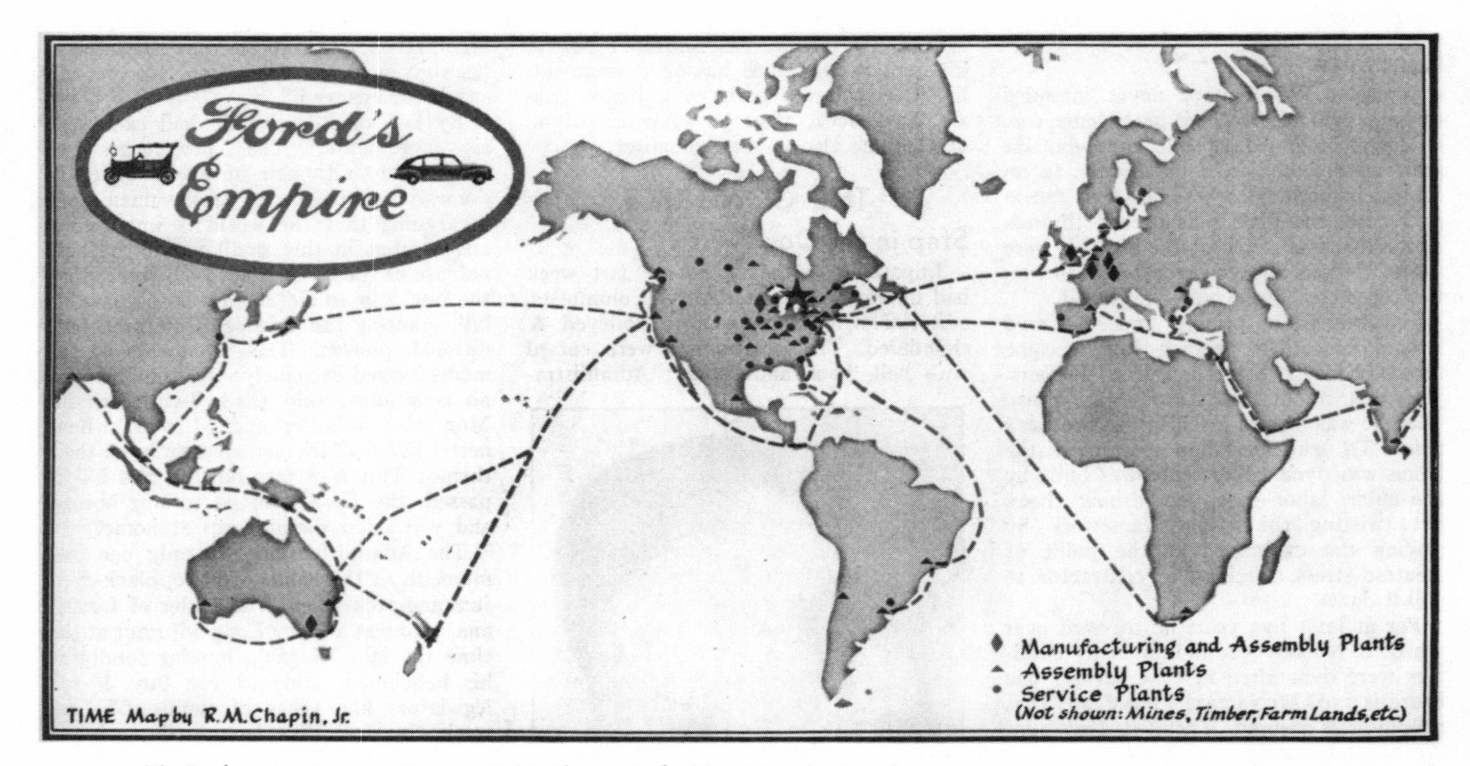

FIGURE 2. The Ford empire circa 1941. Courtesy R. M. Chapin, Jr., for *Time Magazine*, March 17, 1941.

ONE

Ford Goes to the World; the World Comes to Ford

> The worker who works for Ford is an individual who produces the means for a multiplication of the points of contact between individuals, but paradoxically he produces it precisely thanks to his own imprisonment for hours on end at the point of production, where he is deprived of the right of movement to an extent hitherto unheard of.
>
> FERRUCCIO GAMBINO

> All this was beginning there at Highland Park. He was building his own power-plant, his own steel plant, his own forges. Presently he would have his own iron-mines, coal-mines, ships, and railroads. It would be a gigantic empire, spreading over the whole earth.
>
> UPTON SINCLAIR[1]

NEAR THE NADIR OF THE Great Depression's misery, and at almost the same moment that Aldous Huxley and Antonio Gramsci published their classic accounts of life after Ford, the acerbic U.S. historian Charles Beard edited an anthology titled *America Faces the Future.* The collection featured an optimistic essay by William Trufant Foster and Waddill Catchings, which answered in the negative its title question, "Must We Reduce Our Standard of Living?" Foster and Catchings, whose prior collaborative work occupied the extensive gray area between economics and self-help, insisted that asking whether Americans could "maintain our standard of living against the rest of the world" was the wrong question. The United States did not prosper "against" the rest of the world but as a model for it. As they argued, "Every prolonged rise in our own standard of living has brought higher living standards in every other part of the world." The evidence that clinched the argument in support of this assertion was simple: "Nearly every nation has sent a commission to us to find out the secret of our prosperity; and we have sent abroad one of our citizens, by the name of Ford, to expose that secret in terms of scientific management, mass production, and high wages." From their point of view it was because of Ford that the United States had "rendered other nations the conspicuous service of a conspicuous example."[2]

The possibility that Ford's success would make the United States a world-conquering empire of good example also suffused the Italian Marxist Antonio Gramsci's work on Ford. However, Gramsci reckoned that national differences would shape the rejection of Fordism as well as its reception, leading to different patterns of partial transformation in Europe, which was the object of his concern during the rise of fascism. It was, ironically enough, the novelist Aldous Huxley who through his imagined, dystopian account of a "brave new world" expressed fuller confidence in the idea that the Fordist model would remake everything, everywhere. Despite differences, each of these intellectuals treated the Ford system as a model, a good or bad set of compelling ideas and practices being emulated, sought after by managers, and sometimes resisted outside of the United States. Concerns about how Ford's ideas were diffused and how the company was received locally are at the core of this book. Since Fordism was not only an idea to be discovered by the rest of the world, but also a kind of commodity aggressively marketed and relocated to every inhabited continent, Ford's own efforts to become a global power deserve the full accounting that they receive in the first half of this chapter.

Moreover, the Ford system was so appealing to foreign governments not only because of its technical improvements and promises of high wages. As the balance of the chapter shows, Ford became a world corporation in the United States as the workers of the world came to it and were forged into Americans. The Fordism of the pre-union period reached into homes to promote social innovations designed to reshape the habits, families, consumption, language, and values of racially suspect European immigrants. These practices—and the workplace discipline that attended them—contributed to Ford's cachet among the international elites it worked with in expanding its empire beyond U. S. borders. From the early twentieth century, this chapter shows, Ford defined the inside and the outside of the United States. Likewise the uneven, unequal larger world defined it.

THE WORLD AS A MARKET

When the handful of Ford shareholders met in 1903, just four months after the company's incorporation, acting secretary James Couzens reported the return of a clear profit. The small group agreed to reinvest their earnings toward the already-planned expansion of the firm from its Detroit-based Piquette Avenue workshop to the new Highland Park assembly plant that Albert Kahn had been designing with Henry Ford. Simultaneously, the board ratified a decision to "take all necessary steps to obtain foreign business."[3] These two early and simultaneous decisions—to transform the scale of its U.S. production and to seek out foreign markets for Ford cars and Fordson tractors—are critical to understanding the breadth and depth of Ford's dramatic growth.

The imagined scope of the foreign business was expressed by an early Ford lieutenant, William S. Knudsen, in terms as grandiose as they were specific. On the one hand, the reach of the company anticipated by its early plans revealed an almost absurd belief in U.S. diplomatic and political capacity. On the other hand, more than a decade before the United States entered World War I Ford was initiating a foreign-investment strategy that prefigured the massive postwar expansion of U.S. firms into world markets in material but also profoundly political ways. In 1919–20 Knudsen traveled across Europe. The map he followed both on his trip and in his description of Ford's emerging and future world-presence reveals the imperial structure the company relied on to further its own ambitions:

> The British Division would embrace the United Kingdom, Egypt and Malta, with headquarters in Manchester . . . The Northern Division would comprehend Scandinavia, Finland, the Baltic States, Poland and at first Germany and Holland . . . Obviously, Germany and Holland would in time demand separate facilities . . . The Central Division, with headquarters in Paris, would include France, Belgium, Switzerland and Algeria and would set up assembly plants as they were needed . . . The Southern Division would cover Italy, Spain, Portugal, Morocco, Tunis and Tripoli, with an assembly plant in a convenient Spanish city . . . The Adriatic Division would embrace Central Europe south of Germany, the Balkan lands, and Asia Minor, and would have headquarters and an assembly plant at Fiume [in present-day Croatia] . . . Finally the Black Sea Division would include the Ukraine, Central Russia, Turkey, Armenia and the Caucasus, a difficult region for which planning was shadowy.[4]

This strangely American sensibility—both confident and clueless—reflected in words such as "obviously," "convenient," and "shadowy" would continue to be echoed in Ford's private and public discourse about the world. Yet as its managers both imagined and encountered that world the company's convictions, however provincial or naïve sounding at first articulation, continued to find purchase in a wide range of political-economic contexts.

That Ford's leaders were so eager to reinvest their new wealth into global accumulation, production, and sales is not surprising—by 1903 dozens of other U.S. manufacturers were located on the European continent with still more in Canada and South America. U.S. corporations who sought raw materials like oil, diamonds, or copper had investments all over the globe. What is surprising is how little the international arena in which Ford operated from its very beginning is understood as having anything to do with the company's success, strategy, and self-image. Though historians tend to treat "domestic" and "foreign" policies and developments in isolation from one another, it is vital to bear in mind Sidney Lens's admonition that "modern imperialism is not a single act . . . It is a complex process that responds to the *internal* requirements of an industrial society."[5] Ford was a pivotal material and ideological agent of U.S. imperialism. As such the company was part of massive investment of corporate capital outside the United States. These investments and the export of machinery—not just consumer goods—played a central part in bringing the United States to the world in the first half of the twentieth century.

The company's plan for its global expansion reveals how thoroughly Ford relied upon, and thus maintained, long-standing colonial arrangements established by its political allies, who were also its industrial rivals, to gain access to markets, labor, and raw materials.[6] Nowhere was Ford's political and economic intervention into a national economy more important than in its early decision to incorporate in Canada. In 1904 Ford Motor Company of Canada opened as a fully independent firm, not a branch plant of Ford Detroit, outside Windsor, Ontario. The location was fewer than eight miles from Detroit and contributed to the growth of what came to be known as the Border Cities region, an area that included the newly minted town of Ford City.[7]

By incorporating within the British Empire Ford was able to avoid tariffs as it was now privy to "empire rights" in the Commonwealth countries. The company used extant colonial routes to establish its own worldwide presence. Without having to rely on its own nation-state to provide the military and economic intervention necessary to keep colonial relations intact, Ford benefited from the worldwide "dominion" created by Britain. More than a decade before the United States would enter World War I on the side of the British Empire, the company mapped its global investments by relying on Anglo-American goodwill. A report on sources of supply and territory outlined Ford of Canada's responsibilities for relations between markets and production in Rhodesia, British East Africa, Nyasaland, Tanganyika, Uganda, British Somaliland, Zanzibar, Mauritius, Madagascar, the Seychelles, Gambia, Sierra Leone, Gold Coast, British Togoland, Nigeria, British Cameroon, as well as the South Pacific, including Samoa and Fiji. Ford moved quickly to set up dealerships that could take delivery of "knocked-down" car kits for local assembly, or in some cases would simply sell cars imported from regional assembly shops.[8]

In 1904 Ford made the decision to establish what would become a century-long partnership with Firestone Tires. Owned by Henry Ford's good friend Harvey Firestone, whose company would provide first rubber and later tires used by Ford's cars, Firestone Tires introduced Ford to the world of direct American overseas investment beyond the Western Hemisphere, the "sphere of influence" already claimed by the United States.[9] The development for which Firestone would become notorious, its Liberian plantations, was funded by profits made in its massive Akron, Ohio operations.[10] There Firestone functioned with vicious anti-unionism, joining with its industrial competitors, especially Goodyear, to defeat unionism in their workplaces and at every political level in the state of Ohio. In 1913 the Industrial Workers of the World (IWW) supported striking rubber workers ("gummers") seeking affiliation with the United Rubber Workers of America (URWA). Goodyear's president Paul Lichfield said that his company would never sign an agreement with the URWA even if a majority of Goodyear workers voted to do so. Linking local struggles to the barbaric practices on rubber estates in the Belgian Congo, IWW leader Bill Haywood came to Akron that year and in a speech said, "The rubber manufacturers do not cut off the hands and feet of your children but they take the food from their mouths."[11]

In defeating the strike Goodyear and Firestone began to offer a modest form of the profit-sharing program and social "leadership" that Ford would get credit for inventing in 1914. Both companies built company housing, though rather than providing it to workers they sold them their own homes, and Firestone provided "a country club and golf course for employees, a savings bank, barber shop and a four-story clubhouse ... Harvey Firestone declared that his aim was to make 'every employee a stockholder'."[12] In his lifelong friendship with Firestone, characterized by frequent camping trips with their friend Thomas Edison, Henry Ford built a political and ideological comradeship that reflected interests that went beyond the material production of rubber and tires and beyond U.S. borders.

The unprecedented domestic achievements of Ford would set the stage for spiraling overseas expansion. In 1908 Ford introduced the Model T, produced in Detroit and designed to be a "universal" car. In 1909 the company announced the establishment of Ford Motor Company Limited, which would become Ford of Britain. Two years later, in 1911, the first Ford factory built outside of the United States was opened in Manchester, England, though a dealership had been in place previously there. In 1913, as Ford started its first auto assembly line in the Highland Park plant, thus revolutionizing production, the company also launched Ford Motor Argentina.

World War I, ironically for a time vigorously opposed by Henry Ford, accelerated such developments. The conflict proved good for corporate America in general and especially for Ford. The historian Daniel Rodgers wrote that the war "brought American capital, manufacturing techniques and consumer goods to Europe in unprecedented quantities."[13] Allied reliance on Ford cars, trucks, tractors, and ambulances brought the company staggering profits. From the time the United States entered the war until December 1918, the Ford Corporation's after-tax profits were $78 million. Henry Ford's personal share was close to $45 million in 1917 and 1918. These enormous profits were made almost entirely at Ford's Highland Park plant and, increasingly, at the Rouge plant that would soon replace Highland Park as the main site of Ford production. In the 1920s, the Rouge became the center of Ford's empire, both literally and representationally. As early as 1920 Ford manufactured most of the nearly 200,000 vehicles exported annually from the United States; by 1923 the company was making a yearly profit of $50 million from international sales.[14]

Ford's fears of disruptions of labor supplies and the flow of raw materials shaped his behavior at home and abroad in the postwar years. With the strong backing of a State Department eager to control the post-Versailles scramble for markets and armed with the confidence that came with expanded American political and economic dominance, Ford scoured the nation and the globe for strategic sites of production and distribution.[15] A commitment to controlling not just resources but also access to them meant that Ford's empire would need to include both sources of raw materials and the means of transporting them. In the early 1920s the company bought coal mines, sawmills, iron mines, farms, timber camps, sand quarries, forests, ports, railroads, land, shipping lines, docks, airplanes, and barges across the United States and around the world.[16] The idea of "vertical integration" was a direct outgrowth of Henry Ford's insistence on mastering as many aspects of production as possible. Following a particularly potent coal strike in 1922, Henry Ford wrote to James J. Davis, secretary of labor:

> We bought the mines not because we wanted to go into the coal mining business but because we had to be assured of an uninterrupted supply of coal at a fair price. That assurance we could not have without ownership. A large business cannot permit itself to be at the mercy of an industry with frequent strikes.[17]

The company's coal mines soon employed thousands of people. Henry Ford boasted that there was no industry that he could not make more efficient and productive, and he went to great lengths to sell this idea to the world. Though Ford never controlled even half of the resources his company required, the social and political impact of the idea of vertical integration and the efficiency it promised to bring nonetheless seems to have mesmerized progressives who fifteen years earlier had been fighting the juggernaut of industry. Ford came to be seen as a modernizer by foreign heads of state as well as domestic progressives. Since vertical integration meant that huge numbers of workers in and outside of the United States came under Ford's fiercely anti-union management, the restiveness of workers necessarily became part of the calculus about where the company would invest internationally.

Relying on its increasingly powerful place in the global marketplace, the United States in the 1920s sent trade commissioners to practically every country, especially intent on securing access to raw materials and creating markets in Africa and Latin America.[18] Ford was never far behind. The company committed itself to developing markets for its products long before local production would begin. In the first half of the decade this meant that the company established dealerships in more than two thousand locations worldwide, where delivery of Ford products would be taken from across an ocean if necessary.[19] Global production and sales, which had intensified during the war, were now clearly essential to the company's future. Ford's exports went from 152,000 units in 1923 to 303,000 in 1925 and the assembly of cars, trucks, and tractors was expanding in South Africa, Brazil, Ireland, Japan, England, and Mexico. Following the opening of the British and Irish plants, which had been producing for Ford during the war, the company opened shop in Port Elizabeth, Copenhagen, Cadiz, Stockholm, Antwerp, Asnieres, and Berlin.[20] Of 4,163,000 automotive vehicles manufactured in the world in 1927, the United States supplied more than 3,400,000. By this time, more than half of the cars on the planet were Model Ts.[21]

Like all empire-building enterprises Ford had to rely on a combination of tactics and confront an endless array of contradictions both within the borders of the United States and beyond them. Americanization is not the best way to describe this process. Always intently aware of its own interests, Ford was nonetheless a willing partner in the local imperatives of capitalist development in every country where it did business and often forwarded projects of race development as well. Though "Fordism" and "Americanism" are often treated as synonymous, the policies Ford pursued in its global operations always were at least tactically or pragmatically concerned with supporting local regimes' internal demands. Sometimes a willing collaborator, other times forced by workers' defiance, Ford confronted local and national dictates. In 1924 Detroit sent a directive to all managers of global operations announcing that Ford would increase the proportion of "home-supplied" materials like floorboards, wiring, and tires that went into the assembly of Ford cars. The company then turned this news into propaganda: the Manchester car was British, the car made in Antwerp was Belgian.[22]

Resistance to Ford's importation of the "one best way" as a managerial watchword came most conspicuously from Western Europe, where traditions of socialism and trade unionism continued to defeat Ford's insistence on its American model. In Germany workers insisted that the Ford plant be unionized. The violently anti-union company responded by saying that if workers insisted German custom be followed, then German wages would be paid: workers prevailed and kept their union.[23] Fascination with the rationalization of work provoked an enormous response from German managers, intellectuals, and social scientists, many of whom visited the Rouge plant in the 1920s. But the project of making new men, though broadly social, ultimately rested on the denial of any shop-floor worker control, which led to great ambivalence on the part of German unionists throughout the decade. Though industrialists and trade unionists alike registered great "technological optimism"—a belief in the liberatory prospects for the science of technology—this unity was not without limits. It initially led to improved potential for corporatist arrangements and, at times, to mutual perception of a positive, cooperative labor-management relationship even in economically unstable times. However, attempts to apply rationalization soon raised the questions of what exactly was to be rationalized (machinery and / or the motions of workers) and what the short-term ends were to be (increased productivity and / or an increased wage). In Germany, despite a huge Nazi influence anxious to identify with his anti-Semitism, Ford was at best a mixed success.[24]

But in the dream world that Ford believed in and advertised such realities disappeared. Ford remained determined to promote the global reach of the company and to sell to those living in the United States the idea that they were part of a process that would bring the whole world into the light of civilization. By 1920 Ford was the best publicized business firm in the United States, receiving more than twice the periodical press coverage of U. S. Steel, General Electric, DuPont, AT&T, and Standard Oil combined. Starting in 1920 the company began to publish its own newspaper, the *Dearborn Independent,* and required every dealer to promote and sell it.[25]

Coverage of the world, and of Ford's role in it, were constant features of Ford's publicity. In *The Ford Industries,* first published by Ford in 1924, the vast holdings of the by then completely global corporation were detailed. Its foreword begins:

> Its manufacturing activities are conducted on a colossal scale and the merchandising organization reaches to every corner of the civilized world . . . The Ford factories with their enormous production and unbelievable efficiency have become the Mecca of scientists and industrialists. They have also left a permanent imprint on the social system by reason of the industrial policies in effect.[26]

Ford was devoted to making sure Americans—and the world—knew that Ford was the "Universal Car." Promoting the significance of the car in the lives of people all over the world was a constant part of Ford's publicity throughout the 1920s and 1930s. Anecdotes from around the globe poured in and the company immediately packaged them as propaganda: the Methodist missionary in Korea who drove his Model T 4,000 miles in two months; an emergency evacuation of an injured man in a Model T 600 miles through the Australian outback; and the president of Mexico who drove his Model T to his farm where he plowed with his Fordson tractor.[27] Or consider this story:

> A driver from Jerusalem was bouncing, shortly after the war, over the stony face of Palestine, then British-ruled, following goat tracks from Jenin toward Haifa. Steering his Ford across an abrupt watercourse, he broke the drive-shaft pinion in the differential gear. He was in a quandary. The nearest town, Jenin, was ten miles back. He could trudge thither, pay ten Egyptian pounds for a horse-tow, and then wait several days for a pinion from Haifa or Jaffa. Indeed, that seemed the only course. Feeling hungry, he decided first to buy some food at a peasant village a half mile away. This turned out to be a collection of fifteen mud huts called Romani. An Arab there had no bread, but a bag of barley, some parched beans, and a pair of rude scales made of string

and two tin pans. In despair, the driver asked for beans. The peasant placed a handful in one scale, and from a box on which he was sitting produced a weight—a Ford pinion, worn but sound.[28]

Ford's *Dearborn Independent,* infamous for its castigations of the "International Jew," was itself relentlessly internationalist, offering articles on subjects ranging from the theories of Sigmund Freud, to the condition of England, to the romance of the South Seas, to Bolshevism in the Philippines, and to the perceptions of a French colonial administrator on "the weird and mysterious ethics of the darkest parts of the tropical jungle," among much else. Stories like these, repeated over and over again, became a kind of company trademark, simultaneously exoticizing and provincializing the world for American consumers and aggrandizing the masterful Ford brand.[29]

Ford's empire was both a vital material part of the American empire and a metaphor for its allure. Nowhere was this multinational allure better on display than to visitors to the Ford Exhibit at the "Century of Progress," the 1933 World's Fair in Chicago. Visitors were to be "amazed" by the enormity of the building that housed the Ford exhibit. Like the Rouge plant, it was meant to inspire by virtue of its vastness. The building featured a circular court 204 feet in diameter. In the center of this sat the "Court of the World": "the World's largest geographical globe, 20 feet in diameter, 12,000 pounds in weight, electrically driven and illuminated by concealed lighting which depicts the far flung outlines of the Ford industrial empire."[30]

Selling the idea that the future would be born out of the transformation of raw materials into cars and other commodities was a particular constant of the company's rhetoric. As in Chicago, Ford's exhibit at the 1939 New York World's Fair Ford boasted:

> Men in every part of the globe and in almost every land help build the new motor cars which today are rolling off assembly lines in Detroit. The Brazilian working on a vast rubber plantation in the Amazon valley, the nickel miner on Canada's "rand", the Alabama cotton planter, the Wyoming cow puncher, the Texas goatherd—all these play their vital part in the giant automobile industry. So, too, do the men who work in the metal industries, and in such varied trades and places as the tung orchards of China, the sugar cane plantations of Louisiana, the soybean fields of the middle west, the great oil fields in a dozen states, the silimanite mines in the high Sierras. These men and others in countless industries everywhere provide the materials which are transformed by the magic of chemistry and metallurgy into the gleaming cars America sends out over the highways of the world.[31]

In 1924, while the Rouge was still coming fully online, the company was already promoting it as the "greatest industrial marvel" in the world. Fifty thousand people visited the Rouge in 1926 and 1927, 121,000 in 1929. Thousands of these were "foreign" visitors, as the empire toured its new metropole. They learned that Ford's mission was a civilizing one. "Cars made roads and roads made civilization" was painted on the walls of the Rotunda where visitors touring the Rouge plant gathered. One writer, in a line that illuminates the pretensions underpinning Ford's project in rural Brazil, commented: "In the eyes of many a spectator this monument of Ford is more awesome that the mightiest sights of nature."[32]

Visitors would be treated to a celebration of American "progress in science, engineering and industrial management . . . Many of these wonders are distinctive Ford achievements. All of them represent the policy of never-ending progress." As visitors passed through the plant they watched workers bent over the line, virtually inseparable from their machines.[33] Each left the Rouge with a brochure, "A Visit to the Ford Rouge Plant," which detailed the enormity of the Rouge and its significance to people everywhere. "It is sometimes thought," read the brochure, "that all Ford V-8 cars are assembled at the Rouge Plant. Actually . . . in Ford branch plants throughout the United States, in several European countries, in China, Japan and Turkey, Canada and South America there are duplicates of this assembly line. From them Ford supplies the world with 'The Universal Car.'"[34] Detroit, center of such universalizing production, was meanwhile home to a huge immigrant population, which Ford sought to remake while the world watched.

THE WORLD COMES TO DETROIT: MAKING CARS AND HEGEMONY IN HIGHLAND PARK

Gramsci had what he called Fordism specifically in mind when he famously insisted that hegemony was "born in the factory" in the United States. The various ways in which the term hegemony has come to be used make Gramsci's provocation in this phrasing both compelling and problematic in thinking through the problems raised by this book. Gramsci himself took the term from Russian Marxists, and particularly V. I. Lenin, who had used it to name the dominant influence of the working class within insurgent movements that would be necessary to change society fundamentally. In Gramsci's theorization, the term applied to such influence gained by any class or fraction of a class able to lead "historical blocs" of varied social forces and to present its own class interests as the common sense of the allied groups capable of ruling. As such, hegemony transcended mere domination based on force—though coercion very much remained in play—by eliciting consent regarding which demands were viable and which could not be made, or even imagined. Politics, and especially culture, joined economic and military power in structuring such broad consent. Indeed at times Gramsci was most interested in dissecting how the capitalist class won broad assent to what the British critic Raymond Williams later called "certain dominant ideas which in fact express the needs of a dominant class."[35]

The scale of this process was for Gramsci mostly national—thus his "Americanism and Fordism" includes an extended meditation on the prospects for Fordism in different national settings outside the United States. Providing a useful complication, in the more recent past hegemony has come to be applied at the international and even global scales, describing how an imperial power gains dominance in a world-system of trade, production, currency, politics, force, and culture. A few theorists, mostly notably the late Giovanni Arrighi, have attempted to probe how Gramsci's insights themselves might specifically be applied on such a global scale.[36] Such a stew of issues raises a profound question: Was a kind of global hegemony also "born in a factory" run by Ford?[37] Clearly no hegemonic nation dominated the world in the 1920s. The British Empire had lost its sway and U.S. hegemony could not yet have been fully foreseen. However, Gramsci's brief speculations on whether a nation might somehow profit from "the ideological position [it] has in the world, in being representative of the progressive forces in history" might be asked about an ascendant corporation as well.[38] Ford certainly did benefit from, and cultivate, the image of Fordism's progressive stature, in the United States and the world.

But if a Ford factory simultaneously produced hegemony on the shop floor and hegemony on much larger scales, how did it do so? To answer such a question we need to understand how the two showplace Ford factories—the Highland Park and River Rouge plants—did so in very different ways, producing varied appeals to elites beyond the United States. By the time that Gramsci wrote, it was the giant Rouge plant that captivated the attention of elites abroad. Its setting in an era of immigration restriction, its appeals, and its terrors in brutally managing the mass "American" worker and the additionally exploited African American worker are described in chapters 2 and 3.

However, Fordist hegemony first came out of Highland Park, which opened in Detroit in 1910. Because that factory's heyday lay in the best-

FIGURE 3. Charles Sorensen sits with foundry workers at the Highland Park plant. At the Rouge plant Ford would replace most European immigrants with African American workers. Courtesy Collections of The Henry Ford.

studied part of Ford's labor and industrial history, the account of Highland Park below is brief and dependent on excellent existing work. However, the stage-setting qualities of that site do make it command attention as prehistory to subsequent chapters. At Highland Park Ford first showed itself and others that it could manage, and remake, the workers of the world. Ford's labor problem in the Highland Park factory was also a "race" problem, in the sense that managers, reformers, and scholars used the word race to describe European nationalities in the Progressive Era. Up to 70 percent of Ford workers were immigrants, often single men from eastern and southern Europe who were trying out Detroit as a source of work, often before moving on within the United States or moving back home. Ford was only one choice among Detroit employers of immigrants and before 1914 not at all a favored one. Indeed workers at that time referred to the Highland Park factory as the "House of Corrections."[39]

Company records from 1916–17 counted just 30 percent "American" workers, with the handfuls of African American and American Indian employees somehow not coming under that designation. No more than an additional 10 percent of workers were immigrants of the allegedly excellent British or north-western European "stock" that Ford would have heard extolled in the eugenics movement he followed and supported. Mass production required attracting "new immigrant" labor, and if improvement in the labor force were to occur, the obvious route involved "positive eugenics" stressing hygiene, language learning, family, and discipline as vehicles of what was called "race development" in the wider world and "Americanization" in the United States.[40]

Ford's initial faith in technological solutions to problems of labor productivity in his plants animated the very design of the Highland Park complex. In a factory in which up to 38 percent of workers could not really communicate in English, making as many jobs as possible repetitive and relatively simple solved communication and training problems even as it also served management by attacking the power of skilled workers. The moving assembly line that made the factory so celebrated identified bottlenecks in production without elaborate managerial consultations with workers. The line replicated in ultra-modern form the logic of plantation gang-labor in which it was supposed that workers with limited capacity to think, little reason to comply, and alarming potential to resist were best driven as a group.[41]

Drawing on their observations of assembly line production in meatpacking, but without the problems of dismembering irregularly shaped animals, Henry Ford and his managers and engineers were able to solve the problem of mechanization much more thoroughly that had been done previously. Through standardizing parts Ford was able to standardize processes to unprecedented levels. Still, productivity in Model T production was not immediately revolutionized in Highland Park. As Stephen Meyer's study of Ford brilliantly showed, even in the mass production framework of the auto industry, turning formerly skilled jobs into repetitive tasks took years. The unevenness of the process shaped the unevenness of the transition to full mass production at Ford. On the assembly line this did not just mean that inexperienced workers had to be taught factory discipline; it also meant breaking older workers of habits acquired as skilled craftspeople. Even as production at Ford was rapidly becoming deskilled and the company was furthering the idea that "intellectual activity should be separated from manual work," employees were not stripped overnight of the knowledge they possessed or their interest in self-defense. Auto production might have been new, but the metal workers who formed the first core of workers at Highland Park came from workplaces where they were the acknowledged experts. Between 1909 and 1913 the productivity of workers at Highland Park increased by 60 percent, an impressive figure but one limited by problems managing both skilled and unskilled workers.[42]

Spectacular but uneven technological advances quickly exacerbated the labor and "race" problem that Ford faced in getting out production. Highland Park exacted hard and routinized labor. Henry Ford's goal was to leave "not a single unnecessary second" in the worker's control. Every aspect of building an engine and auto body was broken into its smallest components, just as in meatpacking the job formerly done by one butcher had become the job of more than 150 line workers. Turnover skyrocketed as workers fled the new regime of efficiency. In December 1912 alone, 48 percent of the workers at Ford quit or were fired. In 1913, keeping a workforce of 13,600 workers required 52,000 hires. The 370 percent turnover rate reflected countless choices by individual workers who decided that there had to be a better place to work than Ford.[43]

The company, with John Lee as the key manager charged with addressing turnover, exercised control over firings. In 1913 Lee centralized termination decisions, removing them from the foreman's discretion. The working day went from ten hours to nine in that same year. However, even the shorter day and flexible management policies allowing interdepartmental transfers by underperforming and / or dissatisfied workers did not stem the tide of separations of employees from Ford. Since Detroit's population was only about half a million at the time, to run through 40,000 workers who quit or were terminated during a single year presented serious medium-term problems. More immediately, turnover had a major hand in generating 1,300–1,400 daily absences, which represented 10 percent of the labor force.[44] The fragile systems of communication between foreman and immigrant workers had to be constantly recreated in settings where miscommunication led to accidents that threatened lives and production.

In March 1913 the entrance of the militant Industrial Workers of the World (IWW) into Detroit threatened to add organized resistance to the existing pattern in which immigrants voted with their feet by walking away from Ford jobs. At a time when textile strikes in Lawrence, Massachusetts, and Paterson, New Jersey, demonstrated the IWW's formidable ability to weld together workers of various races and nationalities, organizing the auto industry seemed possible. At the least, in a city like Detroit, which was considered along with Los Angeles to be the most aggressively anti-union open-shop metropolis in the country, even a small union campaign galvanized fear and opposition among employers. Very quickly the "loyalty" of immigrants became a live issue. By 1915 the city was the center of on-the-job Americanization campaigns.[45] Facing particularly bitter repression at Ford, the IWW turned to organizing Studebaker, mounting a week-long strike there in May 1913. The failure of the strike did not lead to the union's withdrawal from Detroit and Ford remained a prime target of IWW initiatives. The union's appeals to workers there rested on overwork, the same issue that sparked the turnover crisis at Highland Park. Henry Ford became the "Speed-Up King" in IWW agitational materials. The labor historian Philip S. Foner wrote that it was "common knowledge" in Detroit that an IWW strike at Ford was planned for early 1914.[46]

The Ford Motor Company addressed its race and labor problems with startling decisiveness on January 4, 1914. In announcing a "five-dollar day" for its qualifying employees Ford roughly doubled the going rate even as it cut working time to an eight-hour day. Immigrant working-class Detroit, so eager to leave the Highland Park plant up until this point, was offered a bargain. The trade-off was that Ford would control line speed absolutely, requiring levels of exertion that would have been considered superhuman in previous workplaces. Talking, whistling, smoking, and lollygagging were outlawed in Ford's workplaces; a worker could not move from his workstation without the permission of a manager, which was infrequently granted; union organizing of any kind was cause for immediate firing. Workers received on the other hand spectacularly more free time and greater ability to consume. Ford's press release regarding the new plan emphasized that about half of the five-dollar payment was not a wage but a sharing of profits to be earned by being not only a good worker but also a good citizen and family man.[47] The five-dollar wage signified the most dramatic commitment on the part of the company to controlling production through controlling the lives of workers. The historian of management David Hounshell wrote, "the five-dollar day must be seen as the last step, or link, in the development of mass production . . . the five-dollar day assured the company that the essential human appendages to this machine would always be present."[48] Once securely present, they could be themselves worked on and improved. Ford managers accepted, but only provisionally, the limits on increases in productivity that resulted from the fact that "the 'human element' was not a mechanical automaton."[49]

So certain were managers that such a bargain solved the short-term turnover problem that only days after the new policy was announced Ford fired six percent of its labor force in a single stroke. Management terminated immigrants who celebrated Christmas on the Greek or Russian Orthodox calendar and thus skipped work on the wrong day.[50] This action by management bespoke confidence in recruiting and retaining workers. It also announced the insistence on coerced Americanization that would be Ford's hallmark for the next four years. If other capitalists regarded the five-dollar day with alarm and suspicion, Ford's Americanization initiatives became for some a model in Detroit and then in the United States more broadly. Calculation regarding how to attract and retain workers proved to be on the mark. Large crowds camped to apply for Ford jobs; when fire hoses were used to disperse 15,000 jobseekers, it was clear that workers now desired and even fought for Highland Park jobs. The turnover rate fell to under 46 percent annually by 1918, a massive difference from the 370 percent of the previous year and the lowest in Detroit.[51]

The company's overriding desire for labor that could be retained at Highland Park ought to make us hesitate before equating willingness to hire groups of workers with holding egalitarian views toward them. Still less was any simple "colorblind" employment policy at play. Certainly the company began to employ men it understood as being handicapped and later African Americans to a remarkable extent by 1920. However, such practices by themselves, as we shall see in chapter 3 regarding Black workers, did not necessarily predict fair treatment on the job. In the 1910s, the most revealing example of how hiring suspect nationalities could coexist with prejudice was that of Jewish workers. By the early 1920s the extreme anti-Semitism of Henry Ford and others in upper management was fully on display in the pages of the company's *Dearborn Independent.* Nevertheless Jews were in 1916–17 the sixth largest ethnic group in Ford's labor force. In July of 1916, Henry Ford pronounced to managers on the "weakness of the Jew . . . in commercial business" but trusted they might be "guided on the right path." In any case, in any "final judgment . . . the individual should be considered, not the whole race." Facing accusations of discrimination from a Jewish worker in 1919, the company called on an official from its Sociological Department to affirm that it had "never made any race distinction among its employees." When the case continued, the same official added, contradictorily enough, that "men of Mr. Goldman's nationality . . . are not always truthful."[52] In a 1920 letter responding to another discrimination complaint, this one from an African American worker, a Highland Park manager similarly verged on admitting to discrimination on the basis of race and nationality in the course of denying discrimination based on race and nationality:

> There are times when we have to pick certain kinds of men for certain kinds of jobs; for instance, our harder jobs call for a different caliber of men than do our so called easier and cleaner jobs, etc., and it is possible that at such times different classes of people, if they feel so inclined, can imagine that they are being discriminated against.[53]

Ability to glory in its own capacity for acting fairly and for transforming individuals while still trading in stereotypes similarly ran through the story of Mustafa, a Turkish practitioner of Islam who broke from his "race, who mostly wander in the mountains . . . robbing others." Racially benighted, Mustafa was—to the company—individually excellent. Being hired by the discerning Ford Motor Company allowed Mustafa's "natural intuition for honest living" to mature, if slowly at first. As he learned the value of time and money, Mustafa cut his prayer time from five times daily to three. He soon was Americanized in terms of dress and habits. Managers nevertheless recorded one final Orientalist trope, which had Mustafa, though miraculously Americanized and in the process of naturalization as a citizen, allegedly offering to sacrifice his child to Henry Ford.[54] A belief in racial development under expert tutelage thus did not necessarily temper continued racism, a key insight for understanding Ford's Highland Park plant, the Sociological Department, the treatment of African American workers, the policies of Ford in Brazil, and more.

Looking back from the 1930s and out from a fascist prison, Gramsci was not fully appreciative of such race-judging and race-making dimensions of early Fordism's relation to Americanization. He extolled the "rational demographic composition" of the United States, by this meaning the absence of holdovers of class forces derived from feudalism. Gramsci understood the biggest obstacles to Fordist expansion in Europe as coming from what he called the "parasitic" layers, those possessors of wealth, status, and influence whom he imagined as representing decaying and obsolete social orders. In this sense he saw the growth and expansion of a managerial class as being a modernizing development, viewing it and the regime of production it represented as creating the potential for true freedom from the past.[55] Therefore, Gramsci reasoned, just after his famous provocation regarding hegemony beginning in the factory in the United States, Fordism in its U. S. country of its origin "require[d] for its exercise only a minute quantity of professional political and ideological intermediaries."[56] However, for the managers originating Fordism at Highland Park, the demographics of the United States appeared anything but rational where race and immigration were concerned.

Though brief in historical terms the intervention of professional intermediaries schooling and policing eastern and southern European immigrants' introduction into the ways of the American race was intense. Such intervention was important in connecting the company and race development in its own mind and that of world leaders.

GETTING INVESTIGATED AND BEING WATCHED: THE APPEALS OF MAKING NEW MEN

John R. Lee, the same Ford manager who addressed problems of turnover before the announcement of the five-dollar day, then headed the Sociological Department. That innovation became fully operational three months after the spectacular raises instituted by Ford in 1914. Lee's earlier focus on making reforms inside the factory and his new role in supervising the Sociological Department in both helping and harassing employees outside of work were only seemingly at odds. Supervision of the working-class immigrant family, suffused by reformist impulses, found justification also as an industrial process designed to solve race and labor problems that interfered with production. The English language, U. S. standards of consumption, and "good manhood" served to racially develop a highly suspect population of southern and eastern European immigrants into an American working class. The Sociological Department, following an earlier such venture at Rockefeller's Colorado Fuel and Iron, did not in fact seek to employ trained sociologists. Ford reckoned college-trained investigators would have too much to "unlearn." Instead 50–80 active investigators were quickly identified as the most able among 200 white-collar Ford workers internally transferred to Lee's new department.[57] Overwhelmingly U. S.-born, relatively well educated, and middle class, such investigators defined the norm of the racially uplifted worker. All Ford workers came under the Sociological Department's gaze, but investigators generally confined intrusive questions on private lives to immigrant workers and their families. They often decided to forego even ascertaining whether other white-collar workers had proof of marriage, a requirement in most cases for profit sharing and therefore for the five-dollar day. As a Bureau of Labor Statistics report said of the Sociological Department's practices, "employees of the commercial and clerical occupations who are mostly native[-born] Americans" seem to "need not to be told how to live decently."[58]

Immigrants meanwhile required scrutiny on every front. In a categorization scheme calling to mind David Roediger's description of immigrant workers from eastern and southern Europe as racially "on trial," the Sociological Department implemented a three-tiered rubric of evaluation. A top group was qualified for profit sharing, having assimilated American speech, "manner of living," and values. The bottom, unqualified group awaited something like a religious conversion—the Episcopal minister Samuel Marquis had succeeded Lee as director of the Sociological Department in 1915—to a "realization of the fact" of their own need for redemption. Between these extremes, a third category "qualified by a very small measure and would need a tremendous amount of supervision to stay so."[59]

The investigator's visits to workers' homes brought factory discipline into private immigrant lives. Ford believed that "every family working for him" had to earn the five-dollar wage, not simply individual male workers. Home visits at times aimed to directly address absenteeism, lateness, and lack of productivity at work. Not only did this follow from the belief that "wrong family relations" sapped efficiency, but also the back and forth from factory to home presented fresh opportunities for surveillance and coercion. Company doctors, who worked closely with the Sociological Department, were said to occupy excellent positions from which to "exercise a watchfulness" over those missing work or working poorly. As one Highland Park observer wrote of Sociological Department practices, if "a man is late to work once or twice—this throws a monkey wrench into the [factory's] machinery—and he is threatened at once with a loss of 'profits.'"[60] Although Alan McKinlay and James Wilson are correct that Ford generally did not mine data generated in the Sociological Department for broader managerial studies, the links of sociology and the factory floor were sometimes impressive. Certainly Lee had the Sociological Department firmly in mind when he credited the cutting of absences from work to one-twentieth of former levels by 1916.[61]

The Ford English School, which operated with great fanfare and success between 1914 and 1922, commanded the strongest measures of coercion in the service of mixing factory discipline and after-work behavior. Management connected the immigrant labor problem and the school in several ways. Ford believed that lack of language learning left workers likely to engage in an especially threatening form of quitting—returning to Europe. English speakers, it was thought, would not leave, or would find their homelands alienating if they did go back and therefore would ultimately return to the

United States. Moreover, the reduction of on-the-job accidents depended on communication in English and the classes themselves imparted vital lessons in "industry and efficiency." As Marquis insisted, instruction had to be all-but-mandatory for the system to succeed. Workers who balked were apt to be offered a chance to reflect full-time on their poor choices by being laid off. The Ford motion picture department meanwhile churned out films of non-English-speaking workers being turned away from factory jobs.[62] But as critically important as these directly utilitarian cross-fertilizations between Ford's factory production and extra-factory programs were, the Sociological Department and the English School also had broadly pitched missions bound to make them attractive to progressive reformers, to socialists, to some feminists, and to political leaders in the United States and abroad.

The theatricality of the Ford English School graduation exercises underlined and symbolized its infectious confidence that the company was remaking the world's workers in Detroit. When Lefty, the grandfather of the narrator of Jeffrey Eugenides's novel *Middlesex,* literally climbed out of a "melting pot" constructed for his graduation ceremony and managers at the English School handed him his diploma, he had become an American. He had climbed into the pot wearing an "embroidered *palikari* vest, puffy-sleeved *poukamiso,* and pleated *foustanella* skirt," the clothes of his native Greece. He emerged from it in a suit and tie. Never mind that Lefty would spend most of his waking hours wearing the clothes of a working man; on graduation day the suit and tie signified America. So too did the training he had received in table manners, hygiene, Protestantism, gendered etiquette, proper domestic values, and the English language. Arranged alphabetically by nation of origin, the graduates shed the attributes of those nations. In a further tribute to Fordism, another graduate told Lefty to hurry up through the ceremony. The reminder came from a German graduate, in German, suggesting that the school was not so much about learning English as learning a new pace of activity. John Lee's account of the Fordist reforms at Highland Park similarly underlined the point that productive energy, and not language, was the central issue. Writing in 1916, Lee remembered, "three years ago we . . . used to be able to use the phrase 'hurry up in forty or fifty languages and dialects.' At present," he continued, "this expression is rarely if ever heard." Even if we allow for hyperbole in the latter boast, fantastic human transformations could be claimed.[63]

While working people in other industrial societies were confronting the pressures of conforming to middle-class norms, it was in the United States

FIGURE 4. At the Highland Park plant workers climbed in and out of the melting pot in order to receive their diplomas from Ford's English School. They went into the melting pot as Italian-Americans or German-Americans but emerged as Americans, "having learned to view the hyphen as a minus sign." Courtesy Collections of The Henry Ford.

where such a practice was elevated to the level of patriotic identification with something called Americanism. The melting pot was embraced by Ford as the place where Americans and workers were to be made, actually forged as steel was forged, the new whole greater than the sum of its parts. A similar claim was made by the Mexican muralist Diego Rivera when describing his frescoes of the Ford Rouge plant and Detroit industry.[64]

Ford's campaigns to Americanize workers managed to convey grandeur even as they started from the assumption that immigrants *lacked* some characteristics that they must acquire in order to become American and *possessed* others that they must try to overcome. Workers who climbed into the pot as Irish-American, or Italian-American or German-American; when they emerged they were just Americans, "having learned to view the hyphen as a minus sign."[65] In a story called "The Making of New Americans," the *Ford Times,* which prefigured the *Dearborn Independent,* described the scene as immigrants climbed into and out of the melting pot. "Any spectator . . . saw the pride which shone on the former aliens' faces as they waved little flags on their way down the steps from the huge cauldron, symbolic of *the fusing process which makes raw immigrants into loyal Americans.*" Graduation from the English School was accepted by naturalization authorities as a qualification for first papers in the process of acquiring citizenship. Peter Roberts, the originator of the English School, tellingly held that "good citizenship means . . . keeping busy." Federal authorities perhaps agreed.[66]

Such Fordist experiments had tremendous appeal, which particularly colored the responses of radical journalists accustomed to being around the ravages caused by class exploitation and anti-immigrant racism in the lives of southern and eastern European newcomers. The socialist writer Kate O'Hare specifically praised the English School and the "melting pot." Very differently from Gramsci's later account, O'Hare, having specifically investigated the Highland Park plant, placed racial and national difference at the center of her account. She contrasted Fordist race development to the words of a welfare director whom she had met in St. Louis. The director had pronounced, "We can't apply the same rules to these ignorant foreigner workers as to our higher class of American labor." For O'Hare, Ford was the salvation of " 'Wops,' 'Dagoes,' and 'Bohunks.' " Glorying in the uplift of the "most amazing aggregation of human beings ever gathered under one roof," O'Hare noted with pleasure that she witnessed the addition of workers from many Indian tribes, sent by the Carlisle School.[67] The left-wing reporter John Reed so hated Marquis as a moralizing busybody who spied on immigrant workers that he was led to temper his initial praise of Henry Ford as a "revolutionist." Nonetheless, Reed settled for a mixture of condescension and admiration of Ford as a "simple-minded saint" even on second thought.[68]

The coercion and surveillance that troubled Reed did not necessarily clash with progressive impulses (or as it soon tragically turned out, with Stalinist practices) where the uplift of people regarded as backwards was concerned. In any case, for a time Ford seemed responsive to criticism that it went too far in its sociological investigations. In 1915, as Marquis took over leadership the unit at least briefly changed its name to the less clinical "Educational Department" and "investigators" were rechristened as "advisors." That same year, an investigator assigned to report on what workers thought of the process briefly admitted that in the recent past "private affairs were needlessly pried into, confidences violated, and ungentlemanly acts perpetrated" in workers' houses.[69]

Whether care regarding privacy was exercised or not, the Ford system won support from reformers by promising paternalist interventions that produced results, especially in making men and not just cars. In 1915, when the muckraking journalist Ida Tarbell visited Ford, she intended to write an expose. As it turned out, however, her audiences with Henry Ford made her into one of his most determined supporters. It was with Tarbell that Ford emphasized men-making for one of the first times. Although she was also a champion of Frederick Winslow Taylor and of scientific management generally, it was almost certainly Ford's family-centered appeals that brought her around to imagining that he looked like a young Abraham Lincoln and that his schemes were similarly emancipatory.[70] Indeed Fordist coercion could so earnestly claim to be remaking immigrant masculinity, family, and community that it could hardly be denounced.

Much of the appeal of reformers rested on the company's declaration of war against traditions and social forces perceived as holding back the immigrant communities that were on trial racially. Management at Ford interestingly regarded itself as in combat against "petty empires" ensnaring workers from southern and eastern Europe. Not surprisingly, the labor contractor, typically referred to as a *padrone* no matter what nationality was involved, drew specific opposition. But the saloon keeper, the landlord, and the inner-city immigrant community itself also seemed threatening. The boardinghouse represented all that kept immigrant men from learning English and from desiring to rise socially. Henry Ford doubted that any progress could be made so long as workers boarded, and therefore the Sociological Department prohibited profit sharing among boarders. Ford's commandment to the single man became "do not occupy a room in which another person sleeps."[71]

More broadly the immigrant neighborhood was associated in the minds of Ford and of other reformers with substandard housing, with exploitative rents, and with institutions catering to specific nationalities, all of which could be cast as inimical to advancement. Sociological Department investigators took it as their task to "bodily remove" immigrants from such sites, relocating them near to the Highland Park factory and then near to the Rouge. "Plans" for making those not fully qualified for the five-dollar day acceptable sometimes involved loans being made so that investigators could rent properties for workers, deciding not only on neighborhoods but also on furnishings and even on the kind and amount of soap to be kept in the home. Lee bragged that 13,000 families were relocated to better lodgings in the first year of profit sharing, with only tiny increases in outlays for housing. Having workers live near a Ford factory, and not near other enterprises, further combatted turnover, especially as plans came to include workers buying their own homes. In trying to make immigrants Americans, the resulting new communities did not so much mix nationalities—city neighborhoods already did that—as break older institutional ties. English became a *lingua franca* in the new mixed communities near factories.[72] Two decades before New Deal agencies instituted "redlining" practices that victimized immigrant and Black communities seeking home loans, the Ford Motor Company produced a mapping of city neighborhoods that outlined where it was impermissible to live if you worked for Ford. According to Lee, "One of the greatest crimes a man of the Ford organization can commit is not to keep us posted as to change of address."[73]

Ford particularly intervened in marriage and family relations, seeing the family as the bulwark of productivity and anti-unionism. Sociological Department investigators diligently pried into questions of marital status among immigrants, who were seen as prone to bigamy (adding a wife in the United States to one at home), to cohabitation without marriage, and to "fake marriages" designed to take advantage of preferences for married workers in profit sharing. Beyond the documentation of immigrant marriages, continuing scrutiny of working-class families was required. In the valuable recent work of Andrew Zimmerman, which argues that racial consciousness derives in part from the remaking of the "logics of kinship," such coerced marriage and movement to a new community might be thought of as encouraging marriage into the American "race."[74]

Close investigation of immigrant workers both reinscribed male supremacy and produced interesting challenges to it. At the most basic level Ford management explained that just as Henry Ford shared profits with his overwhelmingly male workers, those workers were expected to share with their dependents. In that sense, the men became junior partners in Fordist patriarchy or, as it has been more typically called, paternalism.[75] On the other hand, investigators listened closely to wives' complaints regarding drinking and abuse by husbands. As Lee insisted, the "rights" of male workers did not extend to "getting drunk and beating up one's wife [and] abusing one's family." Such concerns, at a time when the sexual predations of supervisors against working-class women were very much a problem in U.S. industry at large, switched the script by making the company a defender against the allegedly uncivilized behavior of new immigrant men. Standard inquiries by investigators included questions regarding "domestic troubles." As part of the very complex mechanisms of disciplining male workers not through layoffs but instead by withholding profit-sharing payments, the Sociological

Department occasionally gave the pay of a male worker to his wife until he reformed. The presence of a wife whose smile "won't come off" became a stated goal of Ford management.[76]

Similarly Ford both denied employment to women workers and managed to appeal to a maternalist reform tradition. Only handfuls of women received the five-dollar day as workers. Ford overwhelmingly barred women from production jobs, with the few exceptions being widows of Ford workers and of those men whose disabilities prevented their return to work. Ford manager and future U. S. senator James Couzens explained why almost all highly paid jobs went to men after the introduction of the five-dollar day by holding that women "are not considered such economic factors as men."[77] Even after feminist-generated 1916 reforms enabled a few more women to earn the five-dollar day at Ford, the larger reality was that Ford did not hire women workers. On the other hand, the Fordist insistence that labor at home undergirded the efficiency of the factory recognized the importance of the unpaid labor of women as the policies of few other firms did. Ford grounded the payment of the "family wage" in economics as much as in ideology. This sometimes gave women plausible claims to the shared profits, if not the wages, earned by their husbands.[78] Moreover, the growing friction on what Meyer has called the "dense masculine space" of the auto factory floor, the exalting of the male as breadwinner, and the ways that the Ford factory ran on a combination of exhaustion, aggression, and nervous energy produced new and troubled forms of manliness that further kept women out of production jobs and in relationships featuring new problems.[79]

The highly contradictory reforms at Highland Park proved to be very short-lived. They lasted so briefly that they cannot be said to typify Fordism in the United States. The English School continued for just eight years. By the time it was disappearing in 1921 the Sociological Department was likewise on its last legs. Ford downsized the Sociological Department nearly out of existence during the postwar cost-cutting crunch around company refinancing in order to buy out early stockholders. Sociological investigators fell under the axe due to the theory that they did no productive work, suggesting that Ford had not fully believed its earlier-stated claims about the investigators' roles in producing efficiency. Perhaps, as Meyer suggests, the fact that even those workers who were certified as Americanized found ways to resist speed-ups sapped Ford management's faith in the system. The naked spying on potentially "disloyal" opponents of World War I—*The Ford Man,* a fascinatingly named house organ begun in 1917, went so far as to regard wartime turnover among workers as organized sabotage of the U. S. war effort—had by then tarnished the department's reputation. Moreover, as Ford's competitive advantages declined and as wages in the rest of the industry generally increased, the bounty of profit sharing became less grand. Half of total compensation in 1914, the "profit" had fallen to just a fifth of the total by 1918, making acquiescence to an investigator's whim perhaps seem less of an imperative.[80]

But there was a rosier possible narrative as well. As Ford reported, and as academic journals and popular writers held, the company could be said to be putting its reform enterprises to rest because they had succeeded in making men of the world's workers who had come to work for Ford. The English School bragged between 1915 and 1920 it graduated 16,000 workers. In 1914 over 35 percent of the labor force did not speak English. By 1917 that figure dipped below 12 percent. Spectacular gains in homeownership, quality of lodgings, bank account balances, and even the value of workers' life insurance coverage were similarly said to have occurred in a burst.[81]

Ford's Rouge management, to which we will turn in the next chapter, proceeded more terroristically than sociologically. "Hurry up," and more vivid phrases, were prominent in its managerial vocabulary. However, in managing Black workers living in Inkster and Richmond Hill, poor white workers living in South Africa, and mixed-race workers living in the Brazilian Amazon, elements of the swagger, the appeals to modernizing elites, the close attention to race, and the marketing of alleged miracles in assimilation—that is, characteristics of the Fordism of Highland Park—would reappear.

FIGURE 5. Ford's various publications regularly offered Americans glimpses into worlds where the car was meant to draw attention to the savage or exotic nature of those who consumed. Here people in Gold Coast, Africa, are pictured with a Model T. The original caption reads, "These blacks down in Gold Coast, West Africa, find considerable more of interest in the Ford car than in the head-hunting and flesh-eating sports that amused their fathers." Courtesy Collections of The Henry Ford.

TWO

From the Melting Pot to the Boiling Pot

FASCISM AND THE FACTORY-STATE AT THE RIVER ROUGE PLANT IN THE 1920S

The Ford Empire is the Hitler Nazi Empire on a small scale.

GEORGE SELDES (1943)[1]

FOR A TIME, THE WORLD CENTER of the production of anti-Semitic hate literature was the Ford tractor plant in what would become the engineering department at the River Rouge plant. There, the new home of the recently acquired *Dearborn Independent,* Henry Ford and his close confidantes Charles Sorensen, Ernest Liebold, and William Cameron churned out endless early 1920s columns connecting Jewish plots to everything from the control of finance, to the fixing of baseball games, to world revolution, and to jazz. When Ford published this propaganda as the multivolume *The International Jew: The World's Foremost Problem,* the columns gave weight and the luster of Ford's celebrity and success to anti-Semitism. In late 1922, while printing speculations that Henry Ford secretly financed Germany's emerging Nazi movement, the *New York Times* noted that the then obscure Adolf Hitler's office featured a large portrait of Henry Ford. Books translating Ford filled the table in his office. Hitler later counted Ford his "inspiration" during Nazism's rise to power.[2]

The advantages of examining how Ford operated in multiple geographical and political scales are perhaps nowhere more evident than consideration of his anti-Jewish writings and his flirtations with fascism. In taking over the *Dearborn Independent,* Ford kept its very specific local name. However, its early issues also featured the subheading *The Ford International Weekly.* The paper's contents placed it squarely within anti-Semitic internationalism even as the subtitle also resonated with desires for a Ford empire of automobile production and sales. The *Independent* combatted the "International Jew" with its own global reach. That reach had its origins in the Rouge plant. Both

Ford's international concerns and his international appeals were grounded in the plant itself as the center of his world. Thus this chapter departs from the many useful existing accounts of Ford, Nazism, and fascism that simply chart the extent and nature of Ford's cooperation with the racist far right.[3]

The emphasis here is on the role of the spectacular factory as a repressive state in miniature and on its affinities with fascism, most of which would not ultimately be expressed in enduring political alliances. The transition from managing and improving immigrant races to managing the mass worker in a factory regime that deliberately drove managers and workers to the brink of breakdown coincided with the move of the leading edge of production from Highland Park to the Rouge by the mid-1920s. Ford's relation to fascism was due more to his implementation of the kind of discipline demanded by Hitler and Mussolini than to wistful lamentations of its absence. In creating such discipline Ford become an inspiration and later a practical model for management-as-social-control among fascists. This chapter therefore moves from a consideration of the production of new differences, new uniformities, and new terrors at the Rouge to a reconsideration of the relation of Ford to fascism. Ford's affinities with fascism, to paraphrase Gramsci, began in the factory.[4]

Such a factory-centered approach to Ford's anti-Semitic internationalism was not unknown among those who watched it unfold. The bold epigraph that begins this chapter came, during the heat of an anti-Nazi war, from a leading U.S. radical journalist. While Seldes could not claim that Ford and his managers formally adopted far-right politics wholesale, he could and did assert that this model plant pioneered new levels of surveillance, segregation, repression, and fraternalism, all under the umbrella of the exaltation of managerial leadership. The Fordist system approximated that of the Nazi ideal of *Betriebsgemeinschaft* or "factory community" in important ways and was consciously regarded by Nazis as a worthy model. However, a factory built on alienated labor is not the same thing as a nation built on genocide.[5] In making history at such different scales Ford was linked to Italy's Mussolini and Germany's Hitler far more by sensibilities and affinities and far less by actual common projects. However, those affinities are critical. They help us to see how thoroughly Ford's command approach combined with race-thinking made his place in the world and why, if Ford could not quite stay the fascist internationalist course, he did not depart from it completely.[6]

A revealing point of entry to Fordism and fascism lies in a postcard from a trip abroad. In 1925 a vacationing friend sent Ford production manager

Charles Sorensen a card from Italy. On the front was a picture of Benito Mussolini. On the back the friend had written, "M. is to Italy what you are to the Ford Motor Company. Best regards to you and the secretary."[7] The postcard's author was not alone in how he imagined the role of managers at Ford. In 1928 a *New York Times* writer extended the same comparison to a globally present Henry Ford. "He is an industrial fascist—the Mussolini of Highland Park, Fordson and Dearborn—not to mention works in Europe and in every part of the world."[8]

Such comparisons would have been received by Sorensen, Ford, and the secretary mentioned above, Ernest Liebold, as praise. In 1922 the *Dearborn Independent* had already begun extolling the virtues of fascism to its readers:

> Fascism, briefly, represents the awakening of the youthful element of Italy . . . fascism is sponsored by that element of the male population that believe in having something to do . . . it is as yet rather mixed but it is undeniable that its aims are modern and progressive . . . What the fascists are trying to do in Italy today is just about what Americans in the United States are trying to bring about.[9]

Ford, Sorensen, Liebold, and a fourth Ford manager, Harry Bennett, shared with Mussolini several tenets: modernization equals progress; racial hierarchy orders civilization; imperial expansion is a necessary complement to local power; and workers are necessary but must be socially, sometimes violently, controlled. Such tenets animated the management of the Ford Rouge plant and propelled the company's rapidly growing global operations.[10]

The comparison to Mussolini also urges us to view the management of the Ford Rouge plant, a vast conglomeration of processes that at its height employed up to 100,000 workers, as a *political* endeavor. Such was not often or mostly the case in the partisan political sense that sometimes leads us to reduce politics to mere elections. Ford's 1924 possibilities as a presidential candidate—pursued in as desultory a manner as his earlier initiative in the 1916 primaries—saw him positioned first mainly as a Democrat, at times mentioned as a third party's possible nominee, and eventually throwing support to the Republican candidate Calvin Coolidge.[11] For Ford, Sorensen, Liebold, and Bennett, casting themselves as the rulers of the Rouge workers was instead their key political goal. They embraced the role of ruler every bit as much as they did the role of manager. Operating as a factory-state, the Rouge generated a managerial regime whose commitment to constant production speed-ups of the assembly line required rule by stress, intimidation, and force. For nearly two decades, Henry Ford and his cohort of managers at the Rouge opposed attempts by workers to control any aspect of their lives in the plant. They outlawed talking, laughing, smiling, or any expression of what management considered to be unnecessary movement. The sheer speed of production and the coercive nature of the built environment where they worked made it practically impossible for workers to openly organize, let alone talk to each other on the job. The interwar Rouge isolated workers from others outside the plant, and isolated workers from one another inside the plant through work rules and production standards, and as this book argues, through race.[12]

When considered by historians, each of these aspects of life in the Rouge has been treated separately. Ford's anti-Semitism is taken seriously, but not seen as having anything to do with his treatment of workers or the running of the plant. Because Ford actually hired African Americans, he is not seen to incarnate white supremacy. Yet his anti-Semitism and the record of how Black workers were treated at the Rouge point to another conclusion. All of this must be apprehended in connection to the staggering profits wrung from Rouge workers through unprecedented speed-ups in production, even through the opening years of the Depression. Moreover, the men whom Henry Ford hired to run his empire were active supporters of reactionary political organizations. Their efforts in and outside of the plant were linked and some contemporary observers saw as much. Writing within the context of Ford's brutal anti-union campaigns in the Great Depression, the Irish, Jewish, and U.S.-based poet and journalist Michael Sayers reported, "The Kingdom of Henry Ford is a fascist state within the United States. All the characteristics of Fascism—Jew-baiting, corruption, gangsterism—exist today wherever King Henry Ford reigns over American workers."[13] Treating Ford's politics outside of the plant as being connected to what Ford was doing inside the plant reveals yet again that more was being produced in the Rouge than cars.

Thus this chapter treats together the appeals of and affinities to fascism at Ford, the authoritarian factory-state, and the development of a system for managing European-born workers less as immigrant races than as highly imperfect individuals needing to be driven by surveillance, fear, consumption, and debt. The seemingly gently percolating melting pot that effected the racial development of new immigrants into Americans gave way to the boiling pot of management-by-stress. In it the typical worker was cast as white;

African Americans and Mexicans became the other to be improved but not transformed—but were ruled by stress as well.

THE ROUGE: AN IDEAL IN STEEL AND STONE

As the center of the Ford empire, the very design of the Rouge was essential to the social and ideological impact the company had on those who worked in it and on the world that was meant to be awed by it. In the Rouge, products and ideas that would be shipped around the globe were made, vast quantities of the planet's resources were consumed, and thousands upon thousands of workers from around the United States and the world experienced work in *the* plant that was meant to represent the future.

As early as 1915, when he purchased 2,000 acres of land on the Detroit River, Henry Ford had "envisaged a super plant—an industrial complex rising from flat land to serve a new Ford empire and alter the work habits of the world."[14] Certain it would take ten years to realize the project, even then Ford's dream was driven by a desire for total control over all aspects of the natural and built worlds necessary to making his product cheaper and faster. He was unwilling to let natural limitations interfere, and imagined he would "make the Rouge [River] a harbor for craft that will . . . carry the Rouge cargoes of motors direct to England, France, Germany, South America, Australia and the Orient."[15] Though the Rouge was far removed from residential or commercial areas, it was ideally situated for the movement of materials and products; the site lay at the center of a network of railroads and roads that would soon come to surround a man-made deepwater port.

The pressing interest of Ford, and the massive improvement over Highland Park that the Rouge represented, lay in "flow." At Highland Park, Ford and his managers had proved to themselves that the moving assembly line was essential to the flow of production. However, it was now also possible to imagine that "without the flow of materials *to* the point of manufacture the flow *at* that point might be impeded or stopped" (emphasis added).[16] Thus what happened outside the plant was vitally connected to—and sometimes determinative of—what happened inside. Structuring the flow of materials to the plant rested on the vast network of rails, ships, trucks, and roads that Ford was already beginning to control. By mid-1923 the Rouge River had been deepened and widened by the company (with the support of the U.S. government) and the inaugural cargo of ore arrived from northern Michigan.

Two years later the port became international when its first supply of rails arrived from Belgium aboard the Polish steamer *Anders.* In 1923 565,000 tons of materials had come into the Rouge by water; in 1924 it was 800,000 tons, a number that would continue to rise.[17]

When the industrial architect Albert Kahn designed the Rouge plant he, like Ford, meant to expand on and perfect his design of Highland Park, home to Ford's first assembly line. As he had at Highland Park, Kahn relied on poured concrete, glass, and steel components that set his industrial designs apart from those of virtually all his peers. Kahn's use of poured concrete and steel reinforced beams allowed for the wide-open, high-ceilinged space in which assembly lines could function from below and be surveilled from above. Working hand-in-glove with Ford, Kahn linked each individual building in the complex by rail to the original assembly line that itself covered nearly half a mile. The Rouge, which was designed to maximize "*moving* rather than *making*" (emphasis added), required huge amounts of space and would have been impossible in the urban areas that had housed auto factories until then. More importantly, it reflected Kahn's commitment to "[making] the organization of space assume the fundamental role in affirming the principles of scientific management."[18]

The proportions of the plant were themselves staggering. Imagine working eight or ten hours every day in what an admiring history of Ford describes as

> The mature Rouge—it was still to change and grow—now occupied 1115.12 acres . . . a total of 93 different structures stood on the site . . . railroad trackage covered 93 miles, conveyors 27. It contains the world's largest foundry, covering 30 acres. Its power comes from the largest industrial steam generating plant in the world. It uses in a single day more than 538,000,000 gallons of water—more than the cities of Detroit, Cincinnati and Washington combined. It has a mile and one-third of docks. The Rouge was an industrial city, immense, concentrated, and packed with power.

In realizing his dream of continuous, integrated manufacture Ford engineered "a conversion of raw material into cash in approximately 33 hours."[19] This celebration of commodification was common in the Ford propaganda that popularized the awesome quality of what was being accomplished technologically at the Rouge. Few such celebratory features focused on the human labor that made these incredible leaps in productivity possible. Indeed, references to the way iron and coal and sand entered one end of the factory and a car came out of the other became commonplace, minimizing the presence of the tens of thousands of workers who labored in the middle.

As the transition from the Highland Park plant to the Rouge continued, the numbers of people working for Ford grew. In 1924, 42,000 people worked in the Rouge. At this time there were still more than 68,000 working at Highland Park, making the combined Detroit-area Ford manufacturing and production workforce total more than 110,000. Over the course of the next year most production would be moved from Highland Park to the Rouge where soon nearly 100,000 workers would keep the vast plant operating 24 hours a day. In 1910, 60 percent of Ford's workers were classified as skilled. By 1917 that number had dropped to just 8.6 percent. This deskilling was essential to, and enabled by, the practice of uninterrupted flow.[20] An early observer of Ford's propaganda reported that the company's tour guides boasted about the simple and repetitive nature of work at Ford. They claimed that "most of the workers have had little or no schooling . . . they have never been taught to think; and they do not care to think . . . all of which means they get to like their monotonous jobs." Henry Ford's 1922 autobiographical writings endorsed this view.[21]

BEHIND THE FACTORY-STATE: RESTRICTION OF IMMIGRATION AND NEW PRODUCTIONS OF DIFFERENCE AND UNIFORMITY

Management at the Rouge responded to changed conditions by finding new ways to make men. As the River Rouge complex moved toward leadership in Ford's auto production, Congress virtually eliminated the traditional source of supply of unskilled Ford workers. The Johnson-Reed Act of that year initially promised to tie immigration quotas to formulae that took the ethnic mixture of immigrants in the United States in 1890 as a point of departure for quotas determining future immigration, eventually settling on the ethnic composition of the U. S. population in 1910 as the benchmark. Both calculations ignored the actual contributions made by southern and eastern Europeans to the United States for the previous thirty years. Policy makers set out to invent a bygone United States as the real core of the nation. Only small numbers of those poorer European immigrants who were now considered racially inferior—the same groups who initially had been targeted for Americanization at Ford and who manned the assembly line—would be allowed into the country.[22]

In this shifting political environment Anglo-Saxonism was revived through appeals to elite and "old stock" working-class Americans. Such an environment allowed South Carolina senator Ellison DuRant Smith to attack, in his celebrated "Shutting the Door" speech, the "melting pot" ideal even as he championed certain types of immigrants. Smith argued for immigration preferences to go to Anglo-Saxon groups whom he claimed were the descendants of those who "cleared the forests [and] conquered the savage." He warned, "We have been called the melting pot of the world. We had an experience just a few years ago, during the great World War, when it looked as though we had allowed influences to enter our borders that were about to melt the pot in place of us being the melting pot."[23]

There were logical reasons for the acquiescence of the business elite to the 1924 immigration restriction law. Neither progressive reformers nor industrial capitalists in general rallied to defend the optimistic, albeit coercive, assimilationism that had undergirded the Ford English School and the Sociological Department. Ford, though he needed tens of thousands of new workers at the Rouge and elsewhere, was no exception. The pages of the *Dearborn Independent* reflected the embrace of eugenic sentiments that had made headway among old elites and many industrialists. Washington legislator Albert Johnson appointed Harry Laughlin, founder and head of the American Eugenics Society, to appear in front of congressmen as an "expert eugenics agent." Also a member of the Eugenic Record Office of the Carnegie Institution (a body of great importance to understanding the Ford managerial project in South Africa—see chapter 5), Laughlin ran in intellectual circles that were much the same as Ford's. Both men had connections to the Race Betterment Foundation in Battle Creek, Michigan, run by John Harvey Kellogg, Ford's physician. Laughlin endorsed both negative and positive eugenics, championing racial hierarchy, racial purity, and race development. He used Census Bureau data and a survey of the number of foreign-born persons in jails, prisons, and reformatories to present an argument that the "American" gene pool was being polluted by intellectually and morally defective immigrants—primarily from eastern and southern Europe. His research culminated in his 1924 testimony to Congress in support of a eugenically crafted immigration restriction bill. Ford's own anti-immigrant propaganda deepened with the winding down of the Ford English School and Sociological Department, in each case coinciding with immigration restriction.[24]

The fact that so many recent immigrants had been seen as leaders in opposition to World War I and in the strike waves that followed strengthened the case against them among employers. A long pattern of prewar legislation and policies directed against people with disabilities and those deemed sexual minorities buttressed the case that restrictions were proper; eugenics itself blurred the line between attacks on alleged "social inadequates" and putatively inferior European races. Moreover, even as immigration had slowed since the war in Europe began and since 1921 restrictions had ushered in sweeping federal limitations on migration, production continued to rise in many industries. By 1924 Ford and others had long experience with reduced flows of immigration and no deleterious consequences seemed to be at hand. Indeed most of the Ford policies responding to changes in the labor supply were in place well before Coolidge signed the Johnson-Reed Act into law. The Sociological Department, for example, was gradually transformed during the war into an agency intent on sniffing out disloyalty instead of addressing immigrant cultural habits, and after the war it was allowed to fade into insignificance.[25]

Indeed, Ford management credited the five-dollar day's inauguration of a high wage policy as key to solving recruitment and retention issues. The policy made finding labor less pressing, as mechanization likewise did. More often overlooked is the extent to which Ford boasted of increasing the labor supply from the existing pool of the nation's workers. This was true of course of the recruitment of Black and Mexican workers discussed in chapter 3. But it also applied to his recruitment of the "disabled"—Ford sometimes included "Negroes" in this list—the sick, and those whose size, intelligence, or vigor made them unlikely to be hired elsewhere. Those convicted of crimes were another growing cohort of Ford workers by the 1920s. In 1922, in *My Life and Work* Henry Ford could already reflect back on almost a decade of professedly hiring workers under the rule that "no one applying for work is refused on account of physical condition." In addition, he wrote, "no one should be discharged on account of physical condition, except, of course, in the case of contagious disease." These employees were to do work as fully as other employees on jobs for which they fitted. There were to be no differentials in minimum wages according to ability. As Ford put it, "The blind man or cripple can, in the particular place to which he is assigned, perform just as much work and receive exactly the same pay as a wholly able-bodied man would. We do not prefer cripples—but we have demonstrated that they can earn full wages."[26]

Much that could seem visionary and much that was chilling went into Ford's disability policies, in factories that also themselves massively produced disabilities from accidents and overwork. As early as 1920, when the eminent labor economist and founder of labor history as an academic field, John R. Commons, toured Ford's plants, his glowing tribute to Henry Ford as the "miracle maker" in charge included "2000 men go around with the labels, 'For Light Work Only'. A blind man does the work of 3 men. [Ford] is positively too democratic for this world. One is just as good as another, he thinks."[27] At the Rouge, egalitarianism and obsession with marking difference coexisted—universalism was always attended by particularism. Management identified 7,882 separate jobs at Ford in the early 1920s, of which only one in eight required "strong, able-bodied, and practically physically perfect men." Almost half fit the abilities of "the slightest, weakest sort of men. In fact, most of them could be satisfactorily filled by women or older children." Almost as many job categories could be filled by the "legless" as those that required near-perfect bodies. A third of the classifications were open to those with one leg. Reckoning production in terms of lost body parts, as the cultural historian Mark Seltzer has observed, both naturalized the factory's tendency to produce "violent dismemberment" and offered hopes of transcendence of bodily limits via technology. Ford concluded that "out of 7,882 kinds of jobs, 4,034 . . . did not require full physical capacity." They could be done by those not "ordinarily included in any normal community." Similarly Ford believed—at a time when the uses in industry of "morons," as measured by highly culturally biased I. Q. tests, were much under discussion by industrial psychologists—that only "idiots" could not be profitably employed. A 1925 Ford study of 44,500 workers at the Rouge enumerated about 7,000 with conditions marking them as "physically substandard" and that number almost doubled if those with hernias and hearing loss were included. These figures did not include disabilities mismeasured by intelligence test results.[28]

Ford had reported similar numbers of what he called "sub-standard men"—this despite the fact that many were, according to the company, more productive than the "able" workers—as early as 1922.[29] Attention to them unfolded in the context of the company's commitment to using "scrap" and "salvaging" materials in the factories; the turn to using the labor of disabled men came explicitly under the heading of a "salvage" operation. Ford attempted, according to a lavish company publication of 1927, to place men found to be "sub-standard" in jobs involving recycling of scrap materials. At the Highland Park Salvage Plant "nearly every one" of the large number of workers suffered from "nervous and mental complaints" or were without a limb, without hearing, or without sight.[30]

Like the buttons worn by workers marked as disabled indicated, in no sense was Ford management seeking to transcend normativity. As Gregory Wood's important work shows, any implication that workers easily moved from heavy work categories to light work as they aged and their bodies wore out is misplaced. Auto work, as observers at the time knew, remained a "young man's game." Ford was a hard place for older workers to hire on in the 1920s and one in which those with jobs reported closer and closer scrutiny as they aged. Workers joked that sales of hair color went up when rehires following layoffs were announced, acknowledging what everyone knew: younger workers were rehired first. And despite what all workers knew about the backbreaking character of speed-up at Ford, men sometimes treated one's ability to meet production standards as a marker of masculinity, berating themselves when unable to do so and goading others who failed to keep up as fit only for women's work such as cutting ribbons.[31]

Likewise added to the mix of the labor force in the 1920s, and very much part of the building of a repressive, ultra-masculinized factory state, were thousands of ex-convicts. In 1926 there were 2,600 such ex-convicts employed, and Ford was promising to hire 5,000 more young men he reckoned to be on the verge of getting into trouble.[32] The turn in this direction had seemed modest and laudable when Commons praised Ford's miraculous goodness and efficacy in 1920. "Even men with a prison record have done big things at Ford's," Commons wrote. "There are 400 of them and the majority making good."[33]

While Ford held to sweeping critiques of prisons and the firm belief that work cures all, the sevenfold increase in the ex-convict labor force for which he took credit reflected less of a "salvage project" than an attempt to use these vulnerable men to police the plant, to spy for him, and to create a workforce out of workers with very few options. Ex-convicts were integrated into the police power of the Service Department, and therefore best discussed in the section below. But it is worth noting here that gang activity in the plant and the recruitment of a stratum of workers exempt from the production-is-everything logic of the Rouge—paid, that is, to be "the eyes and ears" of Ford, sometimes not even reporting for work—meant that the most rationalized factory in the United States was also run by an unpredictable lawlessness.[34]

Two other additions to the workforce at Ford each came in a relative trickle but emphasized trends toward new axes of division within a factory state. The Service School, designed to "prepare foreign-born students for work in our branches abroad, but more largely to spread the idea of our methods of production," enrolled 450 students when Ford published *Today and Tomorrow* in 1926. Since students circulated through factory departments doing regular work, it was part technical education and part guest-worker program. Its students came overwhelmingly from nations not seen by the United States as having white residents and thus not eligible for naturalized citizenship, or from ones whose whiteness and rights had been under scrutiny in the courts. Also vulnerable were the few women in the plants. As a Labor Department report asserted in 1928, "In no industry studied was there found such violent prejudice against employment of women [by employers] because of the mere fact that they were women." Ford was no dissenter on this matter. Always less than two percent of the Ford workforce in the 1920s, women's numbers approached zero in the Rouge by the start of World War II. Those who were employed were forbidden from having other means of support. Ford himself reported that in 1919, the last year for which statistics on discharges were tabulated by the company, "Eighty-two women were discharged because their husbands were working—we do not employ married women whose husbands have jobs." The ideal woman worker was a widow of a Ford worker, or wife or daughter of a severely disabled male Ford worker. Her presence thus ratified rather than challenged the gender system of "fraternalism" that pervaded the factory.[35]

At the same time differences ripened among men in the style and pitch through which masculinity was to be expressed. Wayne Lewchuk's seminal account of men-making at Ford sees a transition from appeals by management to masculine "pride" in the teens to mobilizations of "fear" by the late 1920s boiling pot. Fighting became, for example, a big problem in the factory. But Henry Ford professed to regard it with equanimity, adding that managers were encouraged to find disciplinary mechanisms that did not penalize the family by loss of a breadwinner and did not involve time away from work. Said to be set by scientific criteria, such rules nonetheless allowed for and sometimes encouraged the physical "letting off of steam," another instance of an industrial metaphor being used to endorse behavior that might have seemed, by company standards, uncivilized.[36]

It is sometimes argued that the restriction of immigration, combined with mass consumption of popular culture in the 1920s and '30s, changed the U.S. working class and laid the basis for new unity. Reading back from the successes of the Congress of Industrial Organizations in the late 1930s and early 1940s, this is not an implausible case to make. However, in the Ford empire in the 1920s and '30s it seemed that the power of the factory-state's rulers went from strength to strength. While race development was abandoned as a strategy for ruling European American workers, management did not jettison racial competition as a tool. As David Moore, an African American foundry worker at Ford, put it regarding those years, the bosses could first say: "N***** if you don't want to get that production we got some honkies out here . . . who'll do it." Then they could "go back to the Southern white guy [and say] If you crackers can't get this production, we got some Dagoes [Italians] and some n****** gonna do it."[37] In the unionizing drives of the late Depression years, organizers still complained about how adeptly Ford played on Black-white mistrust and even worked to keep European national rivalries alive long after immigration restriction.[38]

As such older forms of management continued and as new divisions and differences regarding age, ability, criminal record, and especially gender accompanied management-by-stress, Henry Ford emerged as the necessary leader unifying his men. He seemed, after all, to care about a whole community of workers, if in different ways. In ways akin to fascism, the workers at Ford were aggrandized even as they were cast as perpetually in need of a leader to discipline and realize their potential. In part Ford's centrality was produced by his astoundingly good press. The poet T. S. Eliot noted in 1929, "Fascism is the doctrine of success. The feeling towards a dictator is quite other than that towards a king; it is merely the consummation of the feeling which the newspapers teach us to have towards Mr. Henry Ford or any other big business man." Ford commanded just such "success," in 1920, when he ranked third in a popularity poll among college students, trailing only Jesus and Napoleon. They were privileged to work, Ford workers learned in the company's press and beyond it, for someone like a god.[39]

Beyond propaganda that exalted the great leader, the very technique of work at Ford also diminished the worker. Though management saw workers as capable of exhibiting a "Ford spirit" in support of the company and each other, managers overwhelmingly treated the mass of workers as incapable of thought. Ford's development of his ideas on disabled workers came next to his assessment of all workers. He wrote, "I think that if an industrial institution is to fill its whole role, it ought to be possible for a cross-section of its employees to show about the same proportions as a cross-section of a society in general. We have always with us the maimed and the halt." The workers represented a society that included some who, like Ford, wanted to advance, to break from monotony, and to think. But in the great majority the Ford worker was estimated by Ford to embrace monotony and to want "to be led." When Abner Shutt, Upton Sinclair's duped worker in his *The Flivver King: A Story of Ford-America,* expressed a contentment with letting Ford do his thinking for him, he conformed not only to Ford's prescription for how workers should behave but also to Ford's view of what they desired. Of course when challenged by the labor movement such ideology proved eventually to be extremely brittle, but through most of the interwar years it had seemed plausible that an (over)working class tied to the deadening rhythm of machines might be in search of a great leader to structure its dreams. Perhaps more than it was plausible this was viewed as desirable by elites, as the frequent enthusiastic comparisons of Ford to Mussolini suggest.

FEAR AND FORDITIS

In his wonderful 1932 collection *The American Jitters,* the social critic and historian Edmund Wilson captured the unpredictability and rancor on the shop floor at Ford, quoting at length the testimony of a British immigrant worker. Sorensen in particular and management generally stood at the center of the terror:

> It's worse than the army, I tell ye—we're badgered and victimized all the time. You get wise to the army after a while, but at Ford's ye never know where ye're at... The bosses are thick as treacle and they're always on your neck, because the man above is on their neck and Sorensen's on the neck of the whole lot—he's the man that pours the boiling oil down that old Henry makes. There's a man born a hundred years too late, a regular slave driver—the men tremble when they see Sorensen comin'. He used to be very brutal—he'd come through and slug the men. One day when they were movin' the plant he came through and found a man sittin' workin' on a box. "Get up!" says Sorensen. "Don't ye know ye can't sit down in here?" The man never moved and Sorensen kicked the box out from under 'im—and the man got up and bashed Sorensen one in the jaw. "Go to hell!" he says. "I don't work here—I'm workin' for the Edison Company!" Yes: I can't understand a man committin' suicide and not takin' Sorensen with 'im![40]

Ford himself emphasized the need to pressure salaried managers for constant improvement, writing in 1926 that "the slack worker is a product of slack management." Such extreme productivity demands reflected, as the management historians Alan McKinlay and James Wilson argue, how mythical the elaborate rationalisms of the Highland Park and Rouge factory regimes actually were, and how fully Ford's top management ruled by force and fear.[41]

There was not much slack for workers or for managers in what the rollicking history of Detroit by the Old Left activist B. J. Widick called the "terror regime of the Service Department" at Ford.[42] According to *Indignant Heart,* Charles Denby's journal of Black working-class life in Detroit, Ford workers could be identified—Denby avoided working for Ford—because they always fell asleep on the streetcar coming from work. Jokes held that wives of Ford workers were asked for their phone numbers as Ford employees were too "worked down" for sex.[43]

Like most first-generation Ford managers Sorensen started in the skilled trades, in his case as a pattern maker in 1904, just one year after the company was founded. He soon became head of the shop in which he worked; from there he began to assist P. E. Martin, director of production in the Highland Park plant. Together, Sorensen and Martin worked with Henry Ford to bring mass production into being. As early as 1914, "legends of [Sorensen's] fury . . . and harsh whip-cracking on the factory floor were already forming." From the mid-1920s until the early 1940s Sorensen was the production manager of the Rouge, second only to Henry Ford, and responsible for the oversight of the global operations of the company. In the eyes of one writer, Sorensen "is seen within the gates of the Rouge, felt outside it wherever Fordmen are—and they dot the globe . . . for every man who has met him face to face there are ten thousand to whom his name is familiar."[44]

Around the time that the five-dollar day was introduced, Henry Ford said that men work for only two reasons—wages and fear of losing their jobs.[45] Having already created the wage incentive, Ford's reliance on Sorensen reflected his endorsement of what Sorensen's colleagues described as the "boiling pot" theory of management. The elevation of Sorensen and his management technique signaled the permanence of the shift toward rule through fear and repression started in the late 1910s and early 1920s at the Highland Park plant. In the mid-1910s, management at Highland Park had been about both a process of visionary social uplift of immigrants, typified by the "melting pot" pageant at the Ford English School graduation ceremony, and a commitment to making citizens, as well as subjects. The Rouge plant unabashedly functioned as a boiling pot, where the concern had become not to make citizens but to make workers and tie them to their jobs. Preventing those workers from exercising any control over their working conditions or work process was vital to the constant flow of production.[46]

Anxiety and fear were central weapons in Sorensen's arsenal; arbitrary firings were "calculated to spur the firm's surviving executives," a tactic the company relied on to keep workers in line as well.[47] The liquidation and reorganization of whole departments was not an infrequent occurrence. Samuel Marquis, former head of the Sociological Department, remembered in his writings on Ford a group of salaried workers who arrived at work to discover that their desks had been chopped to pieces with an axe.[48] Indeed, Sorensen routinely removed the desks and chairs that belonged to managers, insisting that they always be moving about the plant. The manager of Ford's steel operation in the early 1920s said, "You really were on your toes from the time you got there until the time you left. You couldn't afford not to be. If you started to show any evidence of weakening you were replaced."[49] He described accompanying Sorensen on "department raids" that were designed to "teach" the "men." Even when supervisors of departments were not "fired or hurt . . . their feelings were hurt very often."[50] Managers complained of a condition they called "Forditis: A nervous stomach and all parts of your body breaking down. Maybe a week or two of rest would build you up, and you'd come in fighting again."[51]

Not only did Sorensen bring a ruthless new management style to the Rouge, he also presided over the purge of the previous generation of Ford's managers from Highland Park. Described by Keith Sward as the "Alumni Association," these were men who had helped build the company, and who were then either forced out or left. Their departures represented the consolidation of Sorensen's power. Sward cast Ford as an "empire builder who . . . often lacked what it took to put his mandates into actual operation." He wrote: "As Ford was consolidating his reputation as a model employer . . . his production chief was, at the same time, making a name for himself as the most despised factory boss in the industry."[52]

Though the very real distinctions between the material realities of life as a worker and life as a lower-level manager cannot be overlooked—workers could never take "a week or two [of] rest," for instance—Sorensen, "aggressive and unrelenting," was lower management's boss, too.[53] Lower-level managers and supervisors were caught between that handful at the top and the workers, a place in which an ideological commitment to one's role acquired a greater salience. Facing insecurity and exhaustion as workers did, supervisors and foremen had, in many ways, material experiences on the job that were not so far removed from workers. Still, though their life conditions at work might be similar to workers, managers would not identify with workers' struggles to change those conditions. The stories that they told themselves to mediate their situation and make clear their difference from workers were political and ideological. The idea that racial hierarchies were real surely bolstered their sense of belonging to Ford's self-identified Anglo-Saxon leadership and confirmed their sense of difference from the workers whom they managed.

How the managerial class in the Rouge was treated reflected the overall political economy of the enterprise before it was unionized in 1941. The culture these practices created made it much more likely that managers would be willing to treat workers as they themselves were being treated. While this was a strategic choice on the part of Ford it was also necessitated by the very scale of mass production there. Ford maintained that "The work and the work alone controls us," so that hierarchies and titles mattered little. At the same time, he held that "We expect the men to do what they are told." The tension between these two ideals proved palpable. At first it seemed that the moving line itself would eliminate the need for massive numbers of lower management personnel, whom Ford suspected were unproductive and lacking in an appreciation of system. Even bathroom breaks, a source of much friction between foremen and workers, might be magically made to conform to the rhythm of the assembly line. One manager told a worker "We don't regulate the line by your bowels; you regulate your bowels by the line." Of course, in very real ways, as the worker-sociologist Al Nash was told by a worker, the line acted as a second foreman, one being the "regular foreman" and the other "the damn line itself." For a short time at Highland Park just after the introduction of the assembly line, Ford boasted of having only one foreman for every fifty-eight workers. Yet within six years the company had to introduce the five-dollar day, and due to the levels of exploitation required in the boiling pot of the Rouge, close supervision remained necessary. As the labor historian Nelson Lichtenstein has written, "Since the technical process of production was incapable of maintaining labor discipline and productivity, this burden fell upon the foremen and building superintendents within the various units at the Rouge." Not only did the elimination of the lower levels of management stall but a vast proliferation of company security forces supplemented foremen. By the Depression there lurked one "Serviceman," as a security employee was called, for every thirty production workers at Ford. At one major Kansas City plant the ratio was one to fourteen.[54]

If a characteristic of fascist rule is the desire for the annihilation of opposition and the attempt to produce awe at, rather than just obedience to, authority, Ford and Sorensen ran a fascist factory-state. Resistance among managers was punished swiftly and severely, and for workers it was simply forbidden. Ford himself captured both the authoritarian spirit—he wrote of it as a necessity—and the totalitarian presumption of factory rule in 1922. "Discipline throughout the plant is rigid," he boasted, adding that there are "no rules the justice of which can be reasonably disputed." Workers were disciplined not only by the pace of work, which required they be constantly physically attached to their workstations, but also by the arbitrariness of punishment. What constituted a punishable crime was determined entirely by Sorensen and the lieutenants he empowered.[55]

The physical capacity of the plant to insure uninterrupted flow and a cohort of managers who ruled by fear led to astounding successes in speeding up production. Ford's output—and profit—was phenomenal. A worker on tire production who collected statistics on his job and how it changed noted the following:

1925:	3,000 units produced with 160 men
1926:	3,400 units produced with 50 men
1927:	4,095 units produced with 39 men
1928:	4,950 units produced with 25 men
1930:	6,650 units produced with 19 men
1931:	6,970 units produced with 16 men

Another worker reported that in the fall of 1929 the production quota on his job was raised from fifteen pans of stock to twenty-two, with the result that an entire shift was laid off.[56]

Such a transformation was made possible in part by the physical layout of the plant, which did not waste a single inch of space. Each worker had room to perform his assigned task but not more. This meant that any worker who was falling behind in his tasks was immediately visible to his supervisor because his stock piled up. The room to maneuver or to control one's work time was contained on every front. Sorensen and Ford masterfully created new avenues for increasing productivity, constantly tinkering with the subjective, human arrangements in the plant.

This subjective and brutal nature of Ford's management was never more apparent than when the company announced mass hirings. These spectacles were designed not just to raise productivity but to demonstrate Ford's absolute power both to those seeking work and to those already in its grip. Mass hirings were exacting affairs. At the end of 1928 Ford announced that it would be hiring 30,000 new production workers. The plan, announced by Henry Ford personally, was to hire 400 new men each day for three months. On the day that hiring was meant to begin more than 30,000 people lined up outside the plant gates. They had begun arriving at midnight the night before, waiting in subzero temperatures. When people began to push to get close to the employment office they were dispersed with fire hoses. One *New York Times* reporter described the hiring method as being "like a lottery"—a perception reinforced by Ford's disavowal of the idea that strength or past record guided hiring. Ten men were allowed in, the next ten told to leave. Those who had waited all night to get a position close to the gate were rejected for no apparent reason. For two weeks, thousands of workers continued to gather outside the plant gates. And in the end it was reported that the entire hiring scheme had been put in place in order to lower wages: longtime workers were fired and offered their jobs back at lower wages. If they refused, new hires replaced them. In the end, of the 30,000 hires promised, only 8,000 were actually new Ford employees.[57]

On another occasion, Paul Boatin was one of those who waited outside the Ford plant. He described shivering in a freezing cold parking lot with his father and uncle. Though it was cold and wet he said, "You felt like you were part of humanity on the move." For five months, day and night he and others waited for the employment office to open. Boatin was hired into the foundry machine shop on the midnight shift. He remembers:

> all the long conversations that had taken place in that parking lot as you waited night after night and day after day. All of a sudden it came to a standstill. No talk. No walk. Don't leave your job without permission not even to go to the toilet. Not one step away from your operation. All you heard was your own heart beating. You asked yourself: I waited five months on that goddamn parking lot to wind up with this?

Occasionally Black workers subjected themselves to these shape-ups, but as discussed in chapter 3, separate recruiting networks generated nearly all African American hires.[58]

Sorensen regularly fired people whom he saw standing idly whether he knew the reason that they did so or not. One manager said, "They would lay off men and when they started to hire again there was no hiring back according to seniority or anything. He might get the job back if he knew the right people or if he had letters from some of the judges or police downtown. There was no seniority at all, just a political type."[59] As Allan Nevins and Frank Hill write, "The tension was the important factor. As Ford reduced prices on cars there was inevitable pressure from Sorensen on down to weed out men, to keep the vast plant moving at its maximum pace ... The pace was never too fast for accomplishment, but it was enough to make the job relentless, harassing and, to many, hateful." Workers developed a technique they called "fordization of the face," which allowed them to talk without moving their mouths where talking on the job was forbidden.[60]

A popular song among Ford workers, sung to the tune of "The Battle Hymn of the Republic," also known as "Glory, Glory, Hallelujah," went:

> Mine eyes have seen the glory of the making of a Ford
> It is made under conditions that would offend even the Lord
> With a most ungodly hurry and amidst a wild uproar
> Production marches on.
> Hurry, hurry hurry hurry,
> Hurry, hurry hurry hurry ...[61]

For every gain in wages or time, workers paid in exhaustion. In 1926 the company publicly announced that it was going to pay workers for six days of work in a five-day week. What did not get reported, though workers surely knew it, was that six days' worth of productivity were to happen in those five days—a fact a *Life* cartoonist brilliantly skewered when he imagined the workers as well as the machines at the Rouge being retooled. In the fall of 1929, when Ford announced the minimum wage of seven dollars, productivity demands skyrocketed. The entire plant was sped up, resulting in the layoffs of 30,000 Ford employees in 1929. For those lucky enough to keep their jobs a wage of six or seven dollars a day was high in 1929 even as the company was still wildly profitable. That was Ford's genius. What the company never admitted was that many Ford workers were only working one or two days per week after the Depression hit. Not only did this allow the company to say it was keeping large numbers of men employed while other firms were closing, it also enabled greater speed-up. Managers could expect more physically from a worker who was working two days a week than one who was working five or six. Reliance on "directly coercive methods but no standard rules other than to get the work out" described management policy at the Rouge, according to the classic biography of Ford, which continued, "[Foremen] under pressure from their own superiors in turn used a series of intermediaries—straw bosses, leading men and pushers—to force the pace of production in their departments."[62] The more workers came to understand—individually and in groups—how management at the Rouge worked, the more reliant on the hierarchy of authority the company became and the more viciously it ruled life in the plant. The rule-bound and the arbitrary coexisted uneasily.[63]

Notorious Ford manager and thug Harry Bennett had come to Henry Ford's attention in World War I, when Ford got the former boxer and sailor out of jail. According to the *Monitor,* a publication of the Ford Service Managers Association, Ford's sole job interview question to Bennett asked, "Can you shoot?" From early in his working relationship with Ford, Bennett was given total access to the plants, carrying out whatever assignment the boss had for him. For Bennett, the Rouge factory was also a site of target practice and at times a place where he walked his pet lions and tigers. Bennett aided Sorensen in the "slaughter" of the "hundreds" of managers who were kicked out in the transition from Highland Park to the Rouge. In the 1920s, Bennett took over, without title, the management of the Service Department at the Rouge and from there slowly built his own internal police force.[64]

Published as a popularly styled tell-all after he was on the losing end of a bitter power struggle within management, Bennett's memoirs are rightly suspected by historians as self-serving and self-aggrandizing in the extreme. However, in its early sections that recount the several years in which Bennett's career at Ford struggled to gain traction, *I Never Called Him Henry* is of considerable interest. It capably punctures, for example, the Ford-created ideology that the centralized system of authority overrode the petty daily power of foremen. Bennett noted that while one day a worker's job might be saved by Henry Ford's miraculous intervention in a conflict with a foreman, the latter had ample time and opportunity to effect the worker's removal later. Bennett realized that from the start Ford saw in him a person to police the "tough brawling place" of the Rouge. Fights and forgery marked his advances in authority but so too did his role in putting the final nail in the coffin of the old racial, gender, and managerial project that the Highland Park plant had typified. Bennett remembered winning Ford's ear by arguing that the Sociological Department represented "a stupid waste of time and money for the company and petty tyranny over the employees." Ford reportedly responded with "well go ahead and stop it," and Sorensen agreed.[65]

This change did not immediately result in Bennett coordinating the more directly repressive factory regime that replaced the Sociological Department's work, and for a time Bennett angled against the leaders of the Service Department by holding that a leaner mode of policing workers with less employees was possible. But soon Bennett was at the helm and the police forces at the Rouge became the unquestionable source of authority, functioning as a sometimes secret and sometimes hypervisible arm of the factory-state. Bennett hired ex-boxers, former policemen, notorious gangsters, football players, and anyone who owed him a personal debt. Bennett's vigilante organization ruled the Rouge and was critical to making Ford the last major auto company organized by the United Automobile Workers (UAW). In the service of Ford's profits there was no tactic that he did not use if it helped to keep the union out and patronage in. Bennett employed more than 2,000 people whose job was to prevent shirking and union activity. These "spotters" were spies whose job was to report people for "stealing time," one of the most insidious crimes invented by industrial capitalism. As the Service Department became more and more integrated into the life of the plant, workers were recruited to spy while they worked. These and others were paid or promoted for filing reports naming workers who were participating in labor organizing meetings or cultural events. The seminal history of Ford notes, one "Ford veteran . . . relates that it came to be a question, in 1933, whether Bennett or Hitler had first thought of the Gestapo idea." Bennett, for his part, maintained in his 1951 memoir that Henry Ford's "profound, morbid fascination with criminals" and admiration for their uses in industrial intelligence and control of plants exceeded his own. Rehabilitation of ex-convicts was, in Bennett's view, rare and incidental. Ford was, on Bennett's account, particularly eager to hear ex-convicts endorse the view that women caused all of their troubles.[66]

Bennett was everywhere. One observer noted that he "made and unmade the mayors and chiefs of police of Dearborn."[67] Tasks that we would now consider to fall under the purview of Industrial Relations were controlled by Harry Bennett. "The [vestigial] Sociological Department was part of employment. The payroll was under Mr. Bennett; the entire payroll was under his control," H. S. Ablewhite recalled. "The Service Department, as they called it then, was also under his control. Those were the major things *directly* under his control, although indirectly he controlled everything because everybody was afraid of him."[68]

As director of personnel, Bennett launched a program to expand hiring prisoners and ex-prisoners at the Rouge. In 1928 the *New York Times* reported that Ford was employing 2,600 ex-convicts. By 1934, after Bennett's consolidation of the Service Department, that number had risen to 8,000. In 1935 Bennett was appointed to the Michigan Prison Commission. While serving his two-year term Bennett got a resolution passed that inmates could be released on "extra good time" and paroled to the Ford Motor Company at the rate of five per week.[69] From 1937 to 1939 Harry Jackson, the former warden of the notorious Jackson Prison in Michigan, worked for Bennett.[70] Though the *Times* coverage of Ford's unique hiring practice was meant to evoke an image of the rough characters in Ford's employ, in reality these were men who would simply never get jobs during the Depression. Vulnerability made for loyalty.

DEPRESSION AND HUNGER IN THE FACTORY-STATE

To prevent worker organization, Ford service men routinely relied on fear and intimidation. But on March 7, 1932, they used real bullets against Ford workers. Since late 1929 plant layoffs and speed-up had been constant, keeping the company's assembly lines profitable through the first two years of the Depression. In 1930 Henry Ford's personal income was $30 million. But by 1931 the company was losing money. By 1932, 80,000 of Detroit's unemployed were former Ford workers.[71] Thousands of other former Ford workers received paid passage to the border to facilitate their "repatriation" to Mexico. Detroit's government could not afford to feed or house unemployed workers and their families and Ford did very little to ease the city of its welfare burden. He *loaned* the city $15 million in 1932. As unemployed councils organized in Detroit—twelve emerging from existing ethnic organizations—Ford became an important symbol of everything that was wrong. Henry Ford had publicly said that "the depression is a wholesome thing in general . . . otherwise people wouldn't profit from the illness . . . the average man won't do a day's work if he can get out of it."[72] Henry Ford's interest in improving immigrant workers through Americanization and social engineering had devolved into a commitment to crushing any links such workers had to radicalism and to each other. His constant references to the need to force men to work through wages, desperation, and fear speak to Antonio Gramsci's neglected insistence that the moments in which workers consent to participate in repressive systems are structured by the moments in which they are coerced.[73]

Workers often withheld their consent. In early 1932, Detroit-area Unemployed Councils, led by the Communist Party, decided to hold a march against hunger, joblessness, and evictions. They chose Ford as their target and secured a permit to march from the west side of Detroit to the Rouge plant in Dearborn. By this time 30–50 percent of Detroit's workers were unemployed; in nearby Toledo, whose economy was dependent on the auto industry, the number was 80 percent.[74] The workers who marched to the Rouge plant demanded jobs, the right to organize, and changes in work rules. When they reached the Dearborn / Detroit border they were stopped by Dearborn police. But the marchers refused to be deterred and continued on the next mile to the gates of the Rouge. They were immediately fired upon with tear gas as Ford service men turned Ford-owned fire hoses on them. At one of the Rouge gates fierce fighting started; at this very moment Harry Bennett decided to enter the fray. He drove out of Gate 3 of the Rouge plant and stepped out of his car. When he did he was hit on the head with a rock. As he was being rushed to the hospital a *Detroit News* photographer reported hearing him say, "Get your gats out and let them have it." At this point not only the Dearborn police but also Ford's private police—service men—opened fire on the crowd.[75]

Foundry worker David Moore was there that day and said it all seemed to happen within minutes. Moore saw Joe DeBlasio, Coleman Leny, and Curtis Williams hit by gunfire. When all was over, twenty-five people had been shot and four killed on that day. More than 15,000 people turned out for the funeral services of the four murdered protesters. At the funeral red wreaths shaped like stars bore the slogans "An injury to one is an injury to all" and "Ford's bullets killed 'em," underlining how thoroughly old forms of brutality coexisted with modern ones. According to journalist George Seldes, Ford had the march filmed so that individuals could be identified and fired. The process of the factory "seeing like a state," to borrow James Scott's phrase, found full expression in such acts.[76]

The actions of Bennett and his service men reveal the factory-state in operation in its plainest form. Relying on fear, spying, and intimidation to control workers paved the way for the use of real bullets, as the goal of total control over workers' bodies made any means acceptable. In his classic work, *Fascism and Big Business,* Daniel Guerin described the nature of the police under fascism, calling the Italian Ovra and the German Gestapo "states within the state." The comparison should not be overdrawn, but a legitimate parallel exists with Bennett's private police force, which functioned with impunity inside—and on occasion outside—the walls of the plant where tens of thousands of people spent more than a third of their day.[77]

THE FACTORY-STATE, THE KU KLUX KLAN, AND ANTI-SEMITIC INTERNATIONALISM: AFFINITIES AND PROBLEMS OF SCALE

Beyond the workplace but always in its shadow Ford's direct links to the main organizations of the far right in the United States remained vexed, though his visibility as an international spokesperson for anti-Semitism for a time admitted no doubts and his desire for business in Nazi Germany was profound. On the one hand there were strong and persistent suggestions that Ford secretly funded the Ku Klux Klan, the incredibly popular "Invisible Empire" then growing to three million members, and other main organizations of the racist right in the United States. The Independent Order of B'rith Abraham had raised the charge at its 1923 convention, amidst Ford's anti-Semitic campaigns and just after the *New York Times* had relayed reports that he bankrolled Hitler's movement under the table. Given how thoroughly Ford's records have now been combed for evidence of company use of slave labor in its Cologne plant during the war, it seems unlikely that evidence of either charge against Ford exists. But the affinities detailed above, and the tremendous global publicity of his anti-Jewish screeds, lent plausibility to them. The world would later learn of the uninterrupted production of Ford Cologne during the war and in an era when the Nazi regime took 30–40 percent of earnings in taxes.[78]

In 1922 the leading Black newspaper, the *Chicago Defender,* thought that Ford would enjoy solid support of the "Krazy Klansmen" in running for the 1924 Democratic presidential nomination because he reportedly controlled the purse strings of the organization. The *Pittsburgh Courier* editorialized that he would be a fit president only for the "Kleagles, Goblins, and Wizards" of the Klan. In Michigan itself there were some places in which Ford's anti-Jewish writings, his friendships, and the sale of cars brought him close to the Klan. The Ford dealership in Fremont, for example, was run by Ford's friends who were Klan activists and who distributed his *Dearborn Independent.* In 1924, when the *Detroit Free Press* quoted local Methodist minister Dr. William Stidger endorsing the Klan as "one of the great moral movements of the world," the story was big news because Stidger acted at times as an official spokesperson for Ford. That year, the *Montreal Star* quoted Henry Ford:

> It [the Klan] is the victim of a mass of lying propaganda and is thereupon looked upon with disfavor in many quarters. But if the truth about it were

known it would be looked up to as a body of patriots concerned with nothing but the future of the country in which it was born and the preservation of the supremacy of the true American in his own land.[79]

Detroit newspapers featured rumors of Ford as a Klan funder as late as 1925.[80] Ford's local superintendent in Dallas—a site of especially vicious repression of Ford workers—served on the Klan's steering committee there.[81]

Nevertheless Ford, a creator of industrial enclaves and of a world that he sought to dominate not just economically but politically, often wanted to be left alone. He was thus mostly unattuned to national and even state politics and mercurial at the local level. He made a poor Klan ally electorally. The factory was Ford's first concern and the global market second. Ultimately there was only one organization Ford believed in and that was his own. For the Klan to seek to be present as a force independent of management inside Ford's own factories raised especially troubling prospects. In the pivotal 1925 Detroit mayoral election Henry Ford endorsed the candidate opposing the Klan's choice in a contest so close that controversial spoiled ballots led to victory for Ford's candidate. Stidger's reported endorsements of the Klan, and specifically of its anti-Catholic slanders, were retracted by the time afternoon papers came out. If, as Bennett wrote, Ford opposed Catholics about as much as he did Jews, such sentiments largely stayed out of the public record. Moreover, as Ford expanded Black employment, *Ford News* began to issue ringing denunciations of "race hatred in America," promising in 1923 to work to "remove every injustice that gives soil for prejudice." As the Black press observed at the time, Ford fell quite short of acting on those words and some of the article's professed racial liberalism encouraged African Americans and whites to "identify the common enemy that is trying to stir hatred between them"—that is, for Ford in 1923, the Jews.[82] Nevertheless Ford insufficiently signed on to the full Klan program to create a basis for alliance.

Ford's backing for an anti-Semitic international proved also to be episodic but it was far more consequential and considered. Beginning in 1920 with "The International Jew: The World's Problem," the *Dearborn Independent* launched its series of anti-Semitic articles. The organ's location in the Rouge's engineering department underlined the fact that the anti-Semitism of Ford and his managers needs to be viewed not as a throwback to a provincial, rural past but rather as a proposed solution to a pressing modern set of concerns. The articles, which would later be compiled as *The International Jew* distributed by the Ford Motor Company, earned Ford its place as a worldwide leader in the production of anti-Semitic ideas and in supporting anti-Semitic, fascist, and racist organizations.[83] Operating behind the scenes but very much at the center of these campaigns were two men, *Dearborn Independent* editor William Cameron, the manager most active in Anglo-Saxon supremacist politics, and Ford's personal secretary, Ernest Liebold, the manager most susceptible to Nazi blandishments.[84]

The Protocols of the Elders of Zion, a now-notorious classic of anti-Semitic vitriol that had first appeared in Russia in 1905, lay one basis for the series of columns the *Independent* published under Henry Ford's name. The *Protocols* were allegedly written by a group of rabbis whose plot to take over the "Aryan" world was exposed when the book fell into the wrong hands. Liebold was offered an opportunity to purchase, for $25,000, what were marketed as the originals of the *Protocols*; he turned the offer down because, he reasoned, if he claimed to have the originals he would be under pressure to verify that they were real. Liebold said, "A copy serves our purpose just as well because we don't have to prove anything," adding, "of course, if the *Protocols* were a forgery a forgery is merely a reproduction of the original."[85]

Liebold passively defended the decision to publish the *Protocols* alongside what he considered confirming evidence of Jewish perfidy within the United States. He agreed with "what Mr. Ford said: here we have the *Protocols,* and this is what happened. It is absolutely identical with the procedure outlined in the *Protocols.* If the *Protocols* hadn't been authentic we never would have published them . . . In the various activities they performed we could show a definite trend or definite instance of the actual things as set forth in the *Protocols* and where they took place."[86]

To this day the spurious *Protocols* stand as the basis of much popular and organized anti-Semitism. Equally potent were the *Dearborn Independent* columns that crafted a uniquely U.S. anti-Semitism. Building on the same themes that the Klan promoted, the paper claimed Jews were responsible for chorus girls, cabarets, liquor, disease, and jazz. Baseball was said to have been corrupted by the "vile" and "criminal" Jewish presence invading every aspect of American life. In ninety-one consecutive columns Ford alleged that "the Jews are the conscious enemy of all that Anglo-Saxons mean by civilization," and offered a eugenicist calculation of the distinction between Jews and "white men." These columns ultimately had a powerful impact inside the United States and were frequently reprinted beyond it. They targeted white Protestant workers who were trying to make sense of just what was happening to their lives. Ford's invocation of Jews as the source of the destruction of baseball and other things "American" and their introduction of barbarity and excess was precisely designed to offer "Americans" a place to direct their frustration and sense of anxiety about the new world in which they found themselves. The core of the anti-Semitic critique led straight back to the factory and to Ford management's view of itself: No other race, it was charged, exhibited such a "decided aversion to industrial employment. The Gentile boy works his way up taking employment in the productive . . . departments but the Jewish boy prefers to begin as a messenger, salesman, or clerk."[87]

Following a libel suit Ford issued a public apology for the anti-Semitic publications and claimed the company would see to it that all copies would be removed from circulation. Ford denied all knowledge of their publication and disingenuously declared that *Dearborn Independent* editor William Cameron was no longer in the company's employ. This came as a shock to Cameron, who had been willing to take full responsibility for the publications in court. While Ford denied knowing about the anti-Semitic writing appearing under his auspices, the process also rendered his apology suspect. Harry Bennett handled the details and wrote later of forging Ford's name to the document. Gerald L. K. Smith, the Detroit-based populist and then fascist preacher who befriended Ford around their shared anti-Semitism and anti-unionism in the late 1930s, recalled learning of this forgery from Ford in 1940. Smith, who had many reasons to misremember or distort the conversation, further reported that Ford relayed the story to signal that he maintained his anti-Semitic views and might still republish *The International Jew.*[88]

Reading Ford's own autobiography makes it impossible to accept that he was not involved in the political and moral direction of his publication's articles. About the series he wrote

> The work which we describe as Studies in the Jewish Question . . . needs no explanation to those who have followed it. Its motives and purposes must be judged by the work itself . . . Readers of our articles will see at once that we are not actuated by any kind of prejudice, except it may be a prejudice in favor of the principles which have made our civilization . . . There had been observed in this country certain streams of influence . . . The fact that these influences are all traceable to one racial source is a fact to be reckoned with, not by us only, but by the intelligent people of the race in question. It is entirely creditable to them that steps have been taken to remove their protection from the more flagrant violators of American hospitality, but there is still room to discard outworn ideas of racial superiority maintained by economic or intellectually subversive warfare upon Christian society.[89]

Long after the company claimed to be removing the books from circulation, requests for copies of *The International Jew* came into Liebold's office. To Mr. J.A. Bower, vice president of the Liberty National Bank in New York, Liebold wrote, "At Mr. Ford's request I am sending you three copies of leather bound booklet, *The International Jew,* in which you will undoubtedly be interested." Duncan Bradby, a Washington, DC–based lawyer and former justice department employee, wrote to ask for "six more copies of your pamphlet the *International Jew.*" H.H. Timken of the Timken Roller Bearing Co. forwarded to Liebold a violently anti-Semitic letter written by his brother-in-law, which was received with thanks. The middle class and managerial backgrounds each of these men share typify those who wrote to the company seeking out the wretched little book.[90]

By 1927, the company claimed that it had done what it could to remove the book from circulation. Rabbi Leo Franklin, a longtime acquaintance of Ford's and tireless in his efforts to counsel Ford against circulating the articles, became a kind of global watchdog of the continued publication of *The International Jew.* He drew Liebold's attention to instances where the book was still being promoted under Ford's name: in Vienna and Brazil in 1933; at a Chicago Nazi meeting in 1934; by a Wichita-based organization called Defenders of the Faith in 1934; in Germany, Argentina, and Uruguay in 1935, for example.[91]

In response to a request for a Portuguese translation Liebold replied, "We have granted no permission for translation and publication, which apparently is unnecessary in view of the fact that the book has not been copyrighted in this country." While not quite the same as endorsing publication of the book, Liebold signaled effectively to the would-be publisher that they ran no legal risks. In reply to Franklin's concerns he wrote, "The books, when published, were not copyrighted and we, therefore, will no doubt find it impossible to prevent their publication."[92] Of course, in order to claim the copyright violation Ford would have to admit to having authored the essays. The company would not do so and to this day copies of these articles circulate under Henry Ford's name.

Ford associations with Nazi Germany were more durable and reciprocal than any association with the Klan. Ford's management technique modernized social life, but Ford himself sought to reinvent the so-called "traditions" of family, small towns, and folk dancing he claimed were disappearing, providing another source of affinity to Nazism. More significant was Ford's and Hitler's hatred of the left and desire for the suppression of "Bolshevism," which the company consistently identified with Jews, from the *Dearborn Independent* forward.[93]

Both Ford and Liebold received the German Award of the Grand Cross of the High Eagle from the Chancellor of the Third Reich in 1938. Liebold embraced the award and Ford refused to return it. Hitler praised Ford in the American edition of *Mein Kampf*, published in 1939, calling him the "one great man" who had defied the power of Jewish money in the United States. The neutrality Ford professed until the war began tilted to Nazi interests consistently. When a reporter asked Ford what he thought of Hitler he replied, "I don't know Hitler. But at least Germany keeps its people at work."[94]

Nevertheless such an emphasis on work reminds us that Ford's role as the dictator of a factory-state structured and limited his relationship to fascist ideas as much as a shared anti-Semitism had. Henry Ford's consistent stance that humans were perfectible through work and that work methods were themselves perfectible resonated with Italian and German fascist practice and ideology. One recent account of Ford and fascism suggests that the homilies in Ford's autobiographical and inspirational writings of the 1920s made them read like "thrillers" to the European far right at the time. In power, Nazis sought Ford's aid and expertise in factory management, especially on the ill-fated Volkswagen project, an incredible testament to Ford's international presence. German overtures to Ford were brokered by a Prussian prince, grandson of the deposed Kaiser. The prince had become a Ford worker in Michigan and in Argentina and a protégé of Henry Ford. The resulting factory used the Rouge as its direct model with Fritz Kunte, chief engineer of the power plant at the Dearborn complex, sketching the layout for the German works.[95] Enduring business relations with the German conglomerate I. G. Farben, on whose board Edsel Ford sat along with other U. S. industrial leaders, gave Ford a presence in the German economy even during the war. If Ford's lavish funding of the Nazis is unproven and improbable, that provided by I. G. Farben was significant and indisputable after 1933. As we shall see in the chapter below in the case of the U. S. Ford plantation Richmond Hill, Ford experimented on residents with an untested I. G. Farben anti-malarial drug.[96]

Ford's accelerated contacts with the U. S. pro-fascist far right in the United States in the late 1930s also came in the context of the factory-state, as figures such as Elizabeth Dilling and Gerald L. K. Smith received funds and in-kind services to spy on radicals—they conceived the category very broadly—who were seen as spearheading union organizing efforts in Detroit industries. Smith referred to the collection of index cards on alleged Communists that he compiled as the Ford Company Red File.[97]

The twinned concerns with the narrower horizon of the factory and with calculating geopolitical advantage for the Ford empire meant that Ford's ideological reliability as an associate of the Nazis waxed and waned. In the mid-1920s he not only recanted his public anti-Semitism in the face of possible financial losses in a lawsuit but also became soft on Communism at times when trade with the Soviets was at issue. One 1926 *Dearborn Independent* editorial predicted that "Under Stalin [the U. S. S. R.] is inclining toward sanity and rationalism."[98] And in 1935 Ford infuriated Mussolini's Italy by cancelling a delivery of 800 vehicles through the company's Egyptian dealer that had been ordered for the planned invasion of Ethiopia.[99] Thus operating on different scales, the Ford empire and Nazi expansion saw something appealing in each other, if only at times. Ford's factory-state sought to parlay endless divisions into a need for ersatz unity under a great leader. Similarly his high-profile anti-Semitism made Ford heroic and "inspiring" to Hitler, if not a reliable ally. The peculiar ways in which racial paternalism and the super-exploitation of Black workers coexisted at the Rouge, explored in the next chapter, further complicated Ford's factory-state, its commitment to exploiting difference, and its place in the nation and world.

FIGURE 6. African American workers were overwhelmingly employed in the hottest and most dangerous jobs in the Rouge plant such as the forge and the foundry. When the Rouge plant opened, it housed the largest foundry in the world. African American activists referred to the Rouge as "the house of murder." Courtesy Collections of The Henry Ford.

THREE

Out of the Melting Pot and into the Fire

AFRICAN AMERICANS AND THE UNEVEN FORD EMPIRE AT HOME

ONE OF HENRY FORD'S HABITS was to scribble notes on scraps of paper as he went through his day. Perhaps not quite as legendary as many of his other quirks, Ford has nonetheless been celebrated for the constancy of his personal productivity, his nonstop brain, his ability to generate ideas and then jot them down in seemingly random ways that might yield remarkable results when found later in a pocket or on the back of an envelope. Ford claimed that in his own life as in the life of his company he was always looking for what he famously called "the one best way." He was an early proponent of the principle that would not be truly named and articulated until the late twentieth century in the auto industry, when it came to be known as "constant improvement."[1]

One such handwritten note found among Henry Ford's office papers asks, "What is the best way to handle the Negro?" On the reverse side of the same scrap Ford wrote, "Colonize the Negro."[2] While it is certainly possible that Ford could have become aware of demands for colonizing African Americans from Detroit's powerful Ku Klux Klan or from local followers of the Black nationalist Marcus Garvey, there is no evidence that Ford was a supporter of any actual colonization projects. But his note is suggestive in important ways: Henry Ford was thinking about colonization at a point in time when the practice clearly shaped the international economic, political, and racial context in which he did business. Even as colonialism and empire were absolutely rejected as mainstream frameworks for describing the global political-economic practices of U. S. firms, the language of colony and empire consistently appears in Henry Ford's and his company's discourse. As an industrialist who described his company as an empire, and as an Anglo-Saxonist and eugenicist, Ford's musings about the "Negro problem" urge us again to heed

W. E. B. Du Bois's call to study the "problem of the color line" as an international development.[3]

We cannot know what motivated Henry Ford to scribble this particularly enigmatic note, nor what he was thinking when he did. But his Depression-era experiments in running first the African American village of Inkster, just eight miles from the Rouge plant, and later in redeveloping the former rice plantations in Georgia that he named Richmond Hill suggest that Ford might not have been thinking of Africa when he wrote "colonize the Negro." Indeed, Ford may not have been thinking deeply at all but rather describing a reflexive position that helps explain Ford's insistence, for example, on maintaining Dearborn as an all-white city, even as the company's giant Rouge plant there hired unprecedented numbers of African American workers in the 1920s. Most importantly for the purposes of this chapter, the pairing of "Negro" and "colonize" underlines that the Black worker, despite liberal hiring policies at the Rouge, was thought of as different from other workers. He remained outside of the melting pot, to be brought into employment and left out of it for different reasons and in different places more than even the immigrant white worker. Connected to the colonized and underdeveloped world such workers needed to be managed differently. To appreciate this drama and tragedy requires that we apprehend the story of African American breakthroughs at the Rouge thoroughly, but as an exception, premised on specific company needs rather than on any commitment to equal opportunity. Seeing how partial the gains made even at the Rouge remained leavens a narrative of progress with the harsh realities of labor better described as man-killing than man-making. As importantly the chapter's emphases on other Ford workplaces and initiatives in the United States, particularly those in Inkster, Michigan, and Richmond Hill, Georgia, underscore how Fordism was invested in unevenness of social conditions, and how it adapted itself to varying forms of white supremacy at home as well as abroad. At home with the real and really limited reforms on African American hiring and wage equality it fostered at the Rouge, it was equally comfortable with Jim Crow, North and South, and with the mostly Midwestern exclusionary practices of "sundown towns."

BEFORE AND BEYOND THE ROUGE

In the post–World War I years at the Rouge Henry Ford's company did something remarkable where race was concerned. In her excellent recent study of African Americans in Detroit in the "Age of Henry Ford" Beth Bates observes, "Ford challenged the idea of the black man as servant when he put out the welcome mat for African Americans two decades before General Motors and Chrysler hired blacks."[4] However, the very enormity of this change, the real possibilities it opened up for the Black community, and the iconic nature of the Rouge factory have sometimes left historians debating the motivations of Ford—was it a commitment to paternalism, to racial liberalism, or to capitalism?—as if practices at the Rouge typified his company's practices where race and employment were concerned. To miss the broader universe of discriminatory practices to which hiring at the Rouge constituted an exception occasions misapprehension of the Rouge's history, the U. S. practices of the company, and the ways in which an ease with uneven conditions regarding race applied domestically and globally.

Just fifty African Americans worked in 1916 at Ford's flagship Highland Park plant. As late as 1917, the 100–200 African American employees held largely menial positions at Ford, where Polish Americans outnumbered them by almost 75 to 1.[5] Twenty-five hundred African Americans would be hired by 1920 first in the context of wartime labor shortages occasioned by the drafting of workers into the army and then by the steep wartime declines in immigration, both of which shaped a context in which southern Black migrants began coming in greater numbers to Detroit. There could be no assurance that such trends would continue. By 1939 at the Highland Park plant, by then much smaller and less important to Ford's overall enterprises, the number of Black workers had dwindled to sixteen, less than two percent of those employed.[6] Reformers understandably pointed to the example of Ford at the Rouge rather than to the drift toward exclusion at Highland Park. In late spring of 1932, the *Pittsburgh Courier* tellingly formulated its praise for "the great significance" of Ford's intervention at Inkster. "The fact that he is the leading American industrialist and has been generally praised by social workers as being fair to Negroes in giving employment opportunities in his automobile works may prove beneficial to Negroes in other centers where they have been the last to receive unemployment aid."[7]

Such understandable attempts to use Ford's example to leverage change nationally tended to soft-pedal the company's own poor record of Black hiring outside of the Rouge plant. Beyond the Rouge Ford's inclusionary practices regarding Black workers seemed to matter very little, even at other Ford enterprises. Despite its close relationship with the Ford Motor Company management and members of the Ford family itself, the Detroit Urban

League was unable to assist African American leaders in other major cities, North and South, in breaking color lines at Ford. Richard Thomas cites correspondence from the Atlanta Urban League Secretary to the Detroit leadership that concludes, "The Branch of the Ford Company in Atlanta not only refuses to employ Negroes but is not desirous of Negro patronage." A similar concern was raised by Urban League activists in Milwaukee in 1926 who described "little success" in getting Ford to hire African Americans there. As late as 1957 a President's Committee on Government Contracts report stated that "Ford assembly plants in Atlanta, Dallas, Memphis, Kansas City, Missouri, Norfolk-Portsmouth, Virginia and Long Beach, California documented discriminatory patterns" and noted that there was a "wide regional divergency in the implementation of Ford's stated policy of non-discrimination in employment." And in 1961, "In Atlanta the two automobile companies contacted employed no Negroes in assembly operations ... all Negro employees observed were engaged in janitorial work."[8]

Equally revealing of the impact of Ford on the region and on questions of employment and social uplift in general are the company's practices in the branch plants and "village industries" it promoted and built on various points along the Rouge River and across the state of Michigan. As the chart below shows, the numbers of Black workers hired were miniscule outside of the Rouge plant before World War II, with Highland Park being the norm rather than the exception.

Black Workers in Ford Michigan Plants, 1939–1940

	Total	Black
River Rouge	84,096	9,825
Lincoln	2,332	31
Highland Park	992	16
Ypsilanti	805	9
Flat Rock	548	1

In addition to the branch plants, which tended to be in areas already urbanizing, Henry Ford developed what he called village industries as further supplements to these larger regional factories. From the mid-1910s Ford had been playing with the idea of helping to bring industrial jobs to rural areas without undermining the fundamentally agricultural economic and cultural basis of these communities. Ford believed that it was quite possible for much of the work of industrial production to be accomplished in a decentralized way that would bring small plants to towns that would otherwise remain farm towns. Ford sought to provide an economic basis for these farming communities to not just survive but to prosper during what could be very brutal winters. He further believed that through the creation of these jobs his company could provide an incentive for young men in particular to remain in these towns rather than leaving for the higher paying industrial jobs in urban and urbanizing areas. In addition, Ford developed an early worry about preserving the "heritage" of these towns. Because Henry Ford had himself castigated farming as tedious and dreadful work and had fled his family's farm as soon as he possibly could at age 17, we can imagine that a certain amount of guilt shaped Ford's desire to see the village industries work.[9]

But it is also clear that the so-called "heritage" that Ford wished to support included a belief in not just racial segregation but racial hierarchy, one in which "old stock" white Americans were particularly deserving. In the first years of the development of village industries this meant keeping immigrants in the city and maintaining the countryside's alleged tradition of Anglo-Saxon independence. As life in Michigan changed following World War I and then immigration restriction in 1924, Ford and the leaders of these villages themselves shared an interest in keeping these towns white. Sociologist James Loewen's remarkable and troubling book, *Sundown Towns: A Hidden Dimension of American Racism*, lists the Michigan towns that we know to be sundown towns—so called because African Americans working in such towns had to leave by sundown—and those which might have been (and were according to oral testimony and lore). The list for Michigan includes towns where Ford had village industries, branch plants, and, of course, where he and his top coterie of managers made homes. Many of these, such as Grosse Point, the wealthy eastern suburb of Detroit where Henry Ford lived, were known for anti-Semitic and racist restrictive covenants, as of course was Dearborn where the Rouge plant was located. But many of the other towns, several of which are today included in historic registries because of their village industries, are rural working-class communities that long excluded African Americans.[10]

As the historian Howard Segal writes of small plants scattered in mostly rural areas, "Few of the village industries employed African Americans however and none employed Mexicans." A 1937 survey found no African Americans in ten of the twelve sites and, at the larger Flat Rock and Ypsilanti plants, only one and nine respectively or .18 and 1.12 percent of the workforce.[11]

Such exclusions were not accidental or based on some kind of historical inertia. They were the direct result of Ford's plan for village industries and for arguments about retaining local heritage. Juxtaposed to the confinement of Black workers to the Rouge plant and the radically different method of "improving" life in an African American town, the village industries explode the narrative through which Henry Ford and his company were said to be interested in creating equality. Ford had come to be described as a progressive who was devoted to the uplift of Black workers, but only at certain times, for practical reasons, in certain places, and, even at the Rouge, in certain departments.

BLACK WORKERS AT THE ROUGE: CONTEXTUALIZING THE MAKING OF AN EXCEPTION

In her pathbreaking study of Black autoworkers Joyce Shaw Peterson wrote, "In Detroit economic opportunity meant the jobs of the automobile industry."[12] For African Americans, it more specifically meant the Ford River Rouge factory. In 1923, before the plant was fully operational, 5,000 Black workers were employed at the Rouge. By 1926 more than 10,000 African Americans held jobs there. Those workers accounted for "ten percent of its entire workforce, over half of all Black auto workers in the country, and about three-fourths of those in Detroit."[13] The story of how they arrived had much to do with timing and the efforts of reformers well outside of Ford's employ.

This opening had been facilitated by the Detroit Urban League. As an organization of uplift the Urban League had a leadership whose ideals melded with many of the managerial and behavioral controls Ford promoted. As early as 1916 the group operated as a hiring hall for the anti-union Employers' Association of Detroit to which all the auto companies belonged. The Urban League sent recruiters to the South and an agent to Cincinnati whose job was to send recent migrants to Detroit. The organization brought a missionary-like zeal to teaching Black workers "appropriate" behavior, such as how to dress, worship, or work. Leadership of the Detroit Urban League strenuously opposed trade unionism, even as the national organization moved toward efforts to secure union jobs for Black workers. The Detroit chapter, supported directly by the Employers' Association, warned recent Black migrants to the city of the dangers of becoming involved in union activities.[14]

In a paradoxical way, the success of the Urban League hinged on the politically reactionary character of Detroit where hostility to trade unions and the immigrant population was concerned. By the early 1920s Detroit had earned its reputation as the most employer-friendly, anti-union northern industrial city. The city was a Ku Klux Klan stronghold in a state filled with them. Recently reorganized under the banner "One Hundred Percent Americanism," the Klan enjoyed enormous popularity in the region, making Detroit one of its bases.[15] Henry Ford and his cohort of managers contributed to this culture in which the politics of Pure Americanism thrived and a fierce racial segregation defined the norm. Despite such truths, Ford's decision in this period to begin opening industrial jobs to African Americans in its Rouge plant, something no other auto employers would do until World War II, earned Ford respect among reformers of various kinds. Following the history of the five-dollar day and the Sociological Department welfare schemes of the previous decade, this practice deepened the sense among many that Henry Ford was a progressive, despite the concomitant brutal repression of the mass American worker, discussed in the previous chapter, and the increasingly reactionary politics Henry Ford and his managers shared.

Notwithstanding Ford's reputation for creating oppressive and exhausting working conditions, African American migrants to Detroit took jobs at Ford in expanding numbers from 1918 on. The tens of thousands of white immigrant workers who had frantically sought work at Ford in pursuit of the five-dollar day in 1914 at least had other choices of industrial jobs elsewhere in auto, increasingly with the same remuneration as at Ford. Black workers at Ford had far narrower choices. Although they suddenly had the best-paying so-called unskilled jobs in the United States these workers were seen as objects of control and uplift, first by the local African American leaders who recruited them on Ford's behalf and then by the company upon hiring them. Black workers stayed in these jobs, some of the most dangerous in Detroit, because Detroit's industrial horizon offered them few others.

The range of jobs open to Afro-Detroiters at the Rouge was for a short time as remarkable as the sheer number of jobs. In the early 1920s African American individuals could be found in small numbers in many Ford departments, in manufacturing and production and occasionally in the skilled trades as well. William Perry was hired by Henry Ford himself in 1914, having worked with Ford cutting timber on his family farm. James Price, who had been Henry Ford's personal dietician, became the first Black salaried employee in 1924 when he was hired as a purchaser of industrial diamonds.

According to the historians August Meier and Elliot Rudwick there were at least two African American foremen in the opening years of the Rouge plant.[16]

The placement of Black workers in departments throughout the Rouge plant was a Ford practice that burnished its reputation for fair employment, but the practice was neither unique nor without self-interested motivations. At Ford and beyond, such hiring was justified as a strategy to increase management's control over labor. With the strike wave and immigrant rebellion of 1919–22 in mind, some employers doubted that the threat of importing faraway Black strikebreakers unused to the struck workplace sufficed to provide what was called at the time "strike insurance." The African American historians Lorenzo J. Greene and Carter G. Woodson wrote in 1930 of employers who had "fortified themselves against strikes by intermixing Negro workers among their white laborers." "Every large foundry in St. Louis," according to one report, "employs enough Negroes to offset the likelihood of a damaging strike." St. Louis's Scullin Steel factory adopted, also with Urban League assistance, the broad placement of African Americans in jobs across the plant, including many tasks operating machinery and seen as skilled, far more than Ford did even at the Rouge.[17] The benefits to management of such policies came from day-to-day production, as well as in weathering labor disputes. While Ford had earlier tended to segregate work gangs hoping to foster competition among races and nationalities, by the 1920s it began to experiment with a strategy to encourage competition based on race within gangs. As one foreman put it, "It was a good thing to hook up white workers with Negroes for the Negro often tries to outdo the white man, who may be teamed with him. This also reacts on the white man, with a tendency to greater effort."[18]

Procuring enough Black workers required multiple and shifting strategies of recruitment, all of them quite distinct from white hiring. African American recruits were far more thoroughly vetted. In 1918 Ford shifted from its concentrated reliance on the Urban League and began a relationship that would lead to a fundamental reorganization of, and increase in, its Black labor recruitment. After a meeting with Henry Ford and Charles Sorensen, Reverend R.L. Bradby, pastor of the Second Baptist Church, became an informal labor recruiter for Ford, promising to bring in "very high-type fellows." Just as the patronage system was coming to an end for immigrant workers, Black workers found themselves needing a "pass" from Bradby, who strikingly functioned like a rural labor contractor. The Bradby pass was a letter signed by him verifying the worthiness of the candidate. It almost goes without saying that Bradby would find good candidates among churchgoers; from 1910 to 1926 the congregation of his church swelled from 200 to 4,000, the largest in the city and including many Ford employees. From 1918 until unionization in 1941 Bradby played an essential part in Ford's relations with Black Detroit; until 1925 he was a daily presence in the Highland Park and Rouge plants, patrolling the shops, monitoring for conflict not just between white and Black workers but, and perhaps more significantly, among Black workers whose behavior was particularly surveilled.[19] Though not on Ford's managerial payroll, the Reverend tasked himself with teaching Black workers "the responsibilities of employment." He sought to promote race consciousness by appealing to Black workers to see themselves as models for future employees, proving the worthiness of all by being "steady" themselves. Bradby's congregants were thus promised benefits via his relationship to Ford and the well-paid jobs the company provided. The great historian of race and class in Detroit, Richard W. Thomas, has held that Bradby's Second Baptist Church functioned as "the gates to the kingdom of Ford."[20]

By 1923, when more than 5,000 African Americans already worked at the Rouge, Sorensen decided it was time to supplement the work that Bradby was doing and to expand Ford's formal relationship with Detroit's Black clergy. He sought out Father Everard Daniel, pastor of Detroit's leading African American Episcopal Church and home of the city's Black elite, a parish avowedly seeking to separate itself from the "masses of the laboring classes." Daniel had conflicts with the Baptist minister Bradby over just about everything, some of which would have been linked to the history of the two churches. Second Baptist had been the first and leading African American church in Detroit and its Episcopal rival came into being from a split among that organization's leaders.[21] But despite their differences, the ministers agreed on the need to challenge the increasing participation of Black Detroiters in the "storefront churches" whose popularity far outpaced either large congregation. Black community leaders especially deplored such outlets, and "attacked the predominantly southern-born pastors for their lack of education" and lamented that "they [did] more to retard the progress of Negroes than anything else." Detroit's Black elites were panicked that Southern worker migrants sought out religious services in which "shouting, dancing hither and thither, groaning, howling, crying, protracted prayers, frantic embracing, the waving of handkerchiefs, groveling on the floor, the throwing up of arms and similar 'hysterical' outbursts" were common practices. At times elite commentary on what Black workers needed echoed Ford's techniques of Americanization training given to immigrant workers a decade earlier.[22] Bradby may have had the largest congregation, but Daniel was clearly preferred by the white Detroit elite as the leading spokesman for Black Detroit and was promoted as such. Trained at New York University and the Union Theological Seminary, Daniel was immediately embraced by Sorensen. Unlike Bradby, Daniel spent little time in the plants, preferring to build more private relationships with Black workers by visiting them in their homes.[23]

At the same time that Daniel and Bradby were recruiting and helping to discipline Black workers, Ford's enforcer Harry Bennett hired Donald Marshall, a Detroit police officer and the first African American to work directly for the Ford personnel sector. Marshall, who reported directly to Sorensen and Bennett, interviewed prospective Black workers and was responsible for keeping order among them on the job. Through the Depression Marshall became known as the "unofficial Mayor of Detroit's Harlem." H. E. Ablewhite, a Ford service department operative, recognized the essential political role Marshall played for Ford. In his words, "Marshall was [Bennett's] political contact man for the colored vote in Detroit. I think he wielded a tremendous influence with the colored votes in Detroit. There were no colored votes in Dearborn." Marshall, Ablewhite continued, "was just the same type of man as Harry Bennett . . . If a colored man would give any back talk in his employment office . . . Marshall would take him out in the back room somewhere and give him a working over, just the regular old police method, and beat the very last daylights out of him."[24]

THE LIMITS OF LIBERALITY AND THE PERILS OF "NEGRO WORK"

Given Ford's outreach to Black clergy and the company's opening of jobs to African Americans in an industrial city in which virtually no Black workers thrived, some historians have come to the conclusion that Henry Ford was a liberal reformer where crossing the color line was concerned. In their pathbreaking 1979 book *Black Detroit and the Rise of the UAW,* August Meier and Elliott Rudwick characterized this reform impulse as reflecting a liberal paternalistic commitment to racial uplift. Meier and Rudwick captured one side of the Ford record profoundly.[25]

The African American press also reflected an appreciation for new opportunities, especially given the bleakness of the overall job picture for African American workers in Detroit. Despite the very small number of Black workers employed at the Highland Park plant when the five-dollar day was announced the *Chicago Defender* nonetheless published a glowing story in 1915 under the headline, "All Races Get Slice of Ford Motor Co. Melon." The subhead read, "Credit to Henry Ford." By the time the Rouge plant was coming online in 1923 even a critical article in the *Defender* still allowed that Ford's "Detroit shops give men of color a chance." When Ford died in 1947, the *Los Angeles Sentinel*'s obituary credited him with providing "equal job opportunities" in his factories, claiming that Black workers wore "I work for Henry Ford" badges as a "boastful expression." Ford himself gave the African American press much to quote; even at the height of his anti-Semitic publishing campaign he said, "There is no need of race-hatred in America. Our modern industrialism, changed to motives of public service, will provide means to remove every injustice that gives soil for prejudice."[26]

The whole of this chapter means to complicate such assertions. It considers Henry Ford and his company as developing a range of uneven relationships with African Americans from the Rouge plant to the plantation South. In 1928, in an article titled "Henry Ford—Fictionist" the *Pittsburgh Courier* offered a reminder that paternalism has as often been associated with violence as with reform. The paper insisted that there were bread lines in the United States much as in Puerto Rico, Santo Domingo, and Cuba. "The plantation owners [in those places] have been forced to establish free kitchens on their estates to prevent large numbers of workers from starving." Here, the *Courier*'s coverage of Ford reminds us that "paternalism" is an historical practice fraught with complexity and limitations and is redolent of colonial relationships.[27] Such colonial dynamics mattered especially in the industrial suburb of Inkster and on Ford's Southern plantation Richmond Hill.

Even if confined to the Rouge itself, any judgment that Ford practiced liberal paternalism requires significant qualification. In the massive new plant, the fact of having been hired and the absence of wage discrimination did not lead directly or even necessarily to expanded social and political opportunities for Black workers. Indeed, even though African American wages were largely the same as those of their white and immigrant co-workers, this did not translate into the kind of mobility that white workers were beginning to experience inside the plant and, more significantly, in living in and around Detroit.[28]

In the plant, the earlier practice of spreading African Americans across the range of jobs, skilled and unskilled, quickly gave way to segregating workers in hard, hot, and dangerous workplaces, especially the foundry. A militant United Auto Workers organizer at Ford, the Black communist Christopher Columbus Alston's story has been told by many scholars. In his 1937 pamphlet *Henry Ford and the Negro People* Alston wrote:

> We contend, and can prove, that the Ford Motor Company pursues a conscious policy of relegating the Negro to the hardest jobs in the factory; that Ford hires Negroes on a Jim-Crow basis and he maintains that status regardless of how many men are employed in his factory . . . In 1937 the Ford Motor Company employed 9,825 Negroes. Of these, 6,457 worked in the worst and hardest jobs in the company—namely: the foundry, rolling mill and open hearth.[29]

One Ford manager picked just those jobs as the "hard and body-killing" ones at the Rouge.[30]

Such segregation reveals the magical thinking that shaped racial practices and national development schemes, even those describing themselves as scientific. White plant managers across Detroit were known to express the opinion that Black workers had superior abilities to withstand extreme heat and exhaustion. It was, of course, the presence of Black workers in these jobs that led white managers and workers to believe the racist notion that Black workers were better suited to withstand the hazard. Such circular thinking has proved to be a hallmark of racist ideology and a reason for the continued existence of "racecraft" in the face of mountains of evidence that race is a biological fiction.[31]

The clearest answers to the question of the extent of the racial liberalism of Ford come from the work of economic historians. Starting from a desire to examine the documented record that confirmed or challenged such narratives about race and work in Detroit, Christopher Foote, Warren Whatley, and Gavin Wright were among the first scholars to gain access, later withdrawn, to Ford Motor Company records dealing with racial difference in Ford's workplaces. Their studies have allowed us to see the broadest contours of the hiring and working conditions of Ford's African American workers and draw on raw data on hiring and job classifications in the Ford plants from 1918 to 1947. Foote, Whatley, and Wright confirm existing historical perspectives about African American work at Ford. But in deepening and sharpening our focus their studies help us understand Ford's internal logics and assumptions; in turn this allows us to think more expansively about the meaning of African American work at Ford.[32]

The detailed records of its employees that Ford collected included age, sex, language, nationality, education, performance, termination, birthplace, previous employment, and wage. From these records Foote, Whatley, and Wright observed no real differences in the hire-in wages of whites and African Americans. This is consistent with the company's own narrative of what it did and how it did it. But what the records do show is another kind of inequality between African American and white workers. Across the board African American workers were far more likely to be married than their white peers. The records also show that African American workers had at least as much education as whites and, in 1928, more.[33] Though there was no measurable wage discrimination upon hiring, "attributes which warranted higher pay for whites (age, marriage, and education) received little or no weight when Blacks were involved."[34] Indeed, those criteria were virtually necessary for African Americans to be hired at all.

The small numbers of Black workers employed before the Rouge, especially as a result of World War I, had never been seen as candidates for Ford's Americanization programs. Because Black workers were typically older and married, two of the criteria Ford's sociologists had looked for in granting access to the five-dollar profit sharing plan, they were not seen as being "in need" of the kind of Americanization schooling that was required of presumably less stable, unmarried, and younger immigrant workers. At the same time, Black workers were not considered fully American. By any of the various criteria social scientists, nationalists, ideologues, and politicians have used to describe what makes a person a part of a nation, Black workers logically fit as Americans far more fully than any of the first-generation or immigrant workers in the plant. Nevertheless they were seen as neither American nor Americanizable.[35] In *Souls of Black Folk* W. E. B. Du Bois had written that the Black male "wishes to make it possible for a man to be both a Negro and an American without being cursed and spit upon by his fellows, without having the doors of opportunity closed roughly in his face." Ford's man-making schemes were never extended to such workers or embraced such a dream.[36]

Although the Rouge plant as a whole became famous for many of its revolutionary innovations in production, its steel making and foundry processes were its most awe-inspiring features. From across the region, local people would see the night sky light up as great ladles of molten steel poured the compound into railcars that would be carried into the center of the plant itself. Fiery representations of this process fill the background of Diego Rivera's *Detroit Industry* frescoes, bathing Rivera's workers in a golden light. By 1924 the Rouge plant processed all the coke its own foundry required for its own production and for that of the Highland Park plant. Though the percentage would come close to 50 percent, the majority of the steel needed in Model T production was never produced at the Rouge alone. Nonetheless, that an automobile factory was making this much steel was staggering and the plant's capacity to forge and press its own steel was perhaps the most extraordinary aspect of Ford's vertical integration of raw materials into production and manufacturing.[37] "The foundry was the most impressive single unit of the Rouge," wrote Ford historians Allan Nevins and Frank Ernest Hill in 1955. The largest foundry in the world, its productivity increased from 7,700 Model T and Fordson motor blocks in 1922 to 9,000 in 1923 and by 1924 more than 10,000 motor blocks were emerging from the foundry. In order to generate such enormous productivity it required up to 12,000 workers.[38]

Ford did not collect qualitative data on working conditions, but there is little doubt that the foundry was far less inspiring when viewed from within than from outside. Though Foote, Whatley, and Wright can show through company records how thoroughly segregated into foundry jobs Black workers remained after being hired, conditions of work in the foundry were not part of the official record. The authors fully accept the accounts of Black and other Ford workers who maintained that jobs in the foundry were the worst in the plant. Such was certainly the image of the place even when it was overwhelmingly a department of white immigrants. An *Iron Age* reporter described it in 1915 as the "dirtiest, meanest job" at Highland Park and associated a worker's presence in the foundry with being scorned. Placement in the foundry had already become "the probable lot of the man who had been too lazy to do a day's work at an easier task." A stint in the foundry was often "punitive." *Auto Workers' News* wrote of it in 1920, as the place where "recalcitrant" workers ended up, describing them as "sentenced to hard labor" in a job that "occupies the same place in the Ford scheme as the 'hole' does in the penitentiary." The authorized history of Ford put the matter more gently, observing that "new hands suspected of idling might be sent to the stern toil of the foundry," being fired the only other option.[39]

Even before African Americans made up the literal majority of foundry workers such work was becoming understood as more "suited" to them, not just at the Rouge but in the array of foundry and metal pressing workplaces in and around Detroit. A Packard spokesperson described this phenomenon to an interviewer: "White and colored get along all right in the foundry because the average white worker doesn't want a foundry job anyway. White foundry workers are foreigners." A Ford official said, "Many of the Negroes are employed in the foundry and do work that nobody else would do."[40] As with the myth, specifically subscribed to at times by auto management, that Black workers had higher tolerance for hot and exhausting work, such a statement brings into being the truth it claims to describe—it is a perfect example of how racism becomes race-lore, an a priori assertion claiming to be based in observed and material reality.[41]

The full concentration of Black men in foundry work happened in two waves, with the 1930s exceeding even the patterns developed in the 1920s. The war and then the 1924 Immigration Restriction Act solidly closed the gates on those European immigrants who had until then been foundry workers, helping to generate a dramatic shift over the following decades that consolidated the foundry as a site for Black labor. Additionally, though specifically excluded from the provisions of immigration restriction, during the Depression more than 75 percent of the Mexican residents of Detroit had been repatriated, shipped to Mexico in railcars so they would no longer be competing for "American" jobs.[42]

Between 1918 and 1927 more than two-thirds of the African Americans hired at the Rouge went to work in the foundry, compared to one-quarter of whites. By 1926 the more than 10,000 African Americans at Ford worked largely in that department. African Americans constituted just 10 percent of the new hires in the decade before World War II, and yet in the 1930s half of the new workers being assigned to the foundry were Black. This reliance on African Americans as foundry workers also could account for why Ford hired almost no Black workers in its branch plants where there were no on-site foundries. Thus it is not just that Ford hired African Americans, it is that Ford hired African Americans to work in the foundry.[43] In other words the acclaimed grand achievement of interwar racial liberalism was instead a racial slotting into difficult and deadly jobs.

The studies conducted by Whatley, Wright, and Foote also reveal the profound fact that African Americans in the foundry quit less and stayed longer than workers in any other category. Whites were sent there less, stayed shorter times, and quit more often. They were able to escape "body-killing" work. This, in combination with segregation in hiring, meant that the foundry gradually and then not so gradually became known as a Black department. Through the peak years of production at the Rouge, fewer foreign whites were coming to Detroit and more African Americans were taking those jobs. Even so in the early 1920s the identification of the Black Ford worker with foundry work was far from absolute. Bates, drawing on Whatley, Wright, and Foote's calculations, demonstrates that in 1920 the proportion of Black workers hiring into the foundry was about double the total number of Black workers in the total workforce. But by 1933, that proportion soared, reaching as high as five times the African American percentage of the total Rouge workforce. Since Black foundry workers were also counted as part of the general Ford workforce, such proportions actually understate their concentration in foundry work. Bates describes "a virtually all-Black foundry at the Rouge" after 1933.[44]

That foundry work was devalued because it was associated with African American labor has had a particularly cruel impact on the understanding of the nature of foundry work. In considering the association of dangerous work with masculinity when it was performed by white coal miners, and how that association disappeared when Black miners took over these risky jobs, Robin D. G. Kelley argues, "Once derogatory social meaning is inscribed upon the work (let alone upon the Black bodies that perform the work), it undermines its potential dignity and worth ... racializing the division of labor ... has the effect of turning dirty, physically difficult and potentially dangerous work into humiliating work." Young white foremen who often supervised Black foundry labor were said to harbor bitterness about their own placement in the plant, around heat, fumes, and "n******, wops, and dagoes."[45] The historian of technology Howell Harris argues, "On the face of it, molding [steel] is simple, hot, dirty, dangerous, health-destroying labor. Foundries did provide many entry-level jobs for generations of immigrant and migrant males ... but the molding process was actually extremely complex." Accordingly, Harris held, "there were and could be no 'Gantt charts'" specifying with alleged objectivity the labor processes involved.[46] The degree of intellectual engagement required of the individual worker in many foundries proved labor there to have been more skilled than most of the production jobs on the assembly line at Ford. Foundry skills developed and passed on by enslaved workers remained important in Southern industries after the Civil War. Yet because the work was associated with first Eastern European and then Black American workers in the North, the assumption of its entirely deskilled character has been little questioned.[47]

In assessing Fordist racial liberalism the direct testimony of Black workers and organizers from the interwar years also deserves weight. According to the autobiography of Black Detroit worker Charles Denby, African Americans had long called the Rouge "the house of murder," and the fact that exceptionally deadly foundry work fell increasingly to them did not go unnoticed.[48] African American activists understood better than anyone the symbolic and real significance of the labor of Black workers at the Rouge. They saw the relation of Ford's hiring of Black labor to Ford's obsessive anti-unionism and clearly understood the potential role of Black workers in ending the open shop at Ford. Sometimes the murder was literal. In 1932, well before there was a Congress of Industrial Organizations, Curtis Williams was one of the scores of workers shot by company police in the Hunger March and the only of the murdered workers who was Black. The massive funeral demonstrations that followed the murders at Ford memorialized only those four workers who had been killed on the day of the march. Because Williams died three months later in the hospital his name for decades was not associated with those mourned in the funeral protests attended by tens of thousands in Detroit. Some of the participants in the funeral march carried signs with the slogan "Negro and White Unite." After Williams's death, the workers' committee wanted to bury him alongside his comrades in Detroit's Woodmere Cemetery. But it was a segregated cemetery. In defiance of racial segregation, the workers and their supporters planned to rent a plane from which they would drop Williams's ashes over the Rouge plant. Such defiance of segregation outside the plant was seen by Black organizers as part of the struggle to organize for rights inside the plant.[49]

Alston's *Henry Ford and the Negro People* was the work of a Black radical who had witnessed the murder of the Hunger Marchers. It responded to the anti-unionism being promoted by African American ministers in Detroit by launching a broad attack on Ford. "The price that the mass of Negroes working in the foundry have to pay in order for a few of their brothers to work at skilled jobs is too great," he wrote. But Alston was not content to make his argument just against working conditions and life chances for Black workers in the Rouge plant. He asked his audience to consider the meaning of what Ford published in the *Dearborn Independent.* Alston, aware of the important links between the anti-Semitism and anti-Black racism practiced by white elites in Detroit, was one of the few people to draw attention to such connections and make them relevant to unionism. In an attack on the *Dearborn Independent* he drew attention to the anti-Semitism inherent in blaming a Jewish man for leading "Negroes" to commit crimes which "inevitably" led to lynching. He quoted the *Independent:*

> It turned out that the maker of a brand of "n***** gin" which had spurred certain Negroes on to the nameless crime was one Lee Levy . . . Trace the appearance of this gin as to date and you will find the period when the Negro outbursts and lynchings became serious. Trace the localities where this gin was most widely sold and you will find places where disorders prevailed.

The layers of reactionary ideas expressed in this article run deep, combining contemporary and longer-standing racism in order to excuse lynching as being brought about because of the behavior of Jews and African Americans themselves.[50]

An appreciation of the combination of oppressive labor and sophisticated African American knowledge of that oppression makes even more profound the bedrock question: "Why would Black Detroiters continue to line up for work at the 'house of murder'?"[51] Warren Whatley, writing with Thomas Maloney, gives an answer that is as simple and persuasive as it is eloquent—that Ford was the best choice among extremely limited options. This question underscores not just the immediate tragedy of racism and violence in auto work at Ford and in the larger society. It also points to the need to find more precise and textured analyses of racism in the North of the United States during the Jim Crow period in the South. To describe what happened in Detroit in the limited language of discrimination on one side, or paternalism on the other, fails to account for the vastness of the struggle that faced Black workers in that city, on and off of the job. In 1932, Henry Ford and his managers followed Black workers out of the Rouge plant and into their homes in Inkster, Michigan, one of the nation's first suburban ghettos. In the description below of what ensued in Inkster, the same tensions among reform, profit, paternalism, and colonialism apply.

THE STRANGE CAREER OF PATERNALISM: INKSTER AND THE RACIALIZATION OF REFORM

At the Rouge plant, as we have seen, the company hired African Americans who were more educated and, from the viewpoint of the company's own moral code, far more socially stable than their white peers. Yet, in its internal discourse and public propaganda, Ford consistently spoke about these workers and their families as if "Blackness" itself were a disability. Allan Nevins and Frank Hill's authorized three-volume history describes Ford's allegedly liberal treatment of Negroes as being linked to the "honorable primacy in employing the lame, blind, ailing and other physically handicapped persons." The authors later refer to the "special regard which Ford still paid to the Negro, the physically handicapped and the hope-bereft graduates of the penitentiaries." All of these people in need of redemption and improvement were seen as being especially lucky recipients of Ford's generosity.[52]

That Ford linked what its leaders understand as racial inferiority to physical disability is in many ways not surprising and is a perspective with a long history in racist theory, before and after its embrace of liberal environmentalism. As the social sciences came to be included in the totality of science, new iterations of racial hierarchy came to be practiced in the fields of anthropology, sociology, and biology that could be used to challenge white supremacy and colonialism.[53] As chapter 5 considers, however, such scholarly challenges to the brutalities associated with colonial practices of racial categorization could be made to work within frameworks of racial segregation. Arguments about the need of nonwhite workers to racially catch up to white workers were constructed and relied on the very challenges to biological explanations of social events that exposed the falsity of arguments for racial civility.[54]

Policies that degraded Black neighborhoods were instrumental in making white supremacy into common sense in white Detroit. Ford both accommodated and forwarded such policies. Between 1910 and 1920 the African American population of Detroit grew by 80,000 as the city's overall population doubled, leading to a massive housing crisis.[55] In detailing the life experiences of Detroit's Black workers Shaw Peterson argues that although African Americans had access to jobs and even wages not available to them in other cities, Black Detroiters were still impacted by structural racism. Citing a report on the problem of overcrowding in the city in 1919 she found:

> Not a single vacant house or tenement in the several Negro sections of this city. The majority of Negroes are living under such crowded conditions that three or four families in an apartment is the rule rather than the exception. Stables, garages and cellars have been converted into homes for Negroes. The poolrooms and gambling clubs are beginning to charge for the privilege of sleeping on poolroom tables overnight.[56]

A 1925 investigation of Detroit's Black population found typical a case in which a "Ford worker was the head of a family of three with five lodgers. In his home four adults slept in a room measuring seven by nine feet."[57] Reflecting back on Ford's Sociological Department home-visits of immigrant workers in the 1910s reminds us that one of the company's most pressing concerns was to prevent the practice of taking in boarders. Of course, Ford had never included Black workers in these sociological examinations despite his alleged interest in Black uplift. What had come to be a social crisis in Black residential areas was completely neglected by the company. It is not to argue that Ford should have been intervening into the homes of Black workers. Indeed, the case of Inkster shows that a different set of rules and racist assumptions were applied to African Americans when Ford *did* involve himself and his company in this social crisis. The initial neglect of Inkster and the support of housing segregation by Ford call into question the overall rationale provided for monitoring workers' lives outside of the workplace. In other words, the crisis in Inkster that Ford stepped in to solve was created by social policies that his company endorsed, most especially the racial segregation of the town of Dearborn. The Inkster case also opens to scrutiny the relationship of Ford's interventions into these Black communities as a way of thinking about his company's support for social engineering projects in Brazil and South Africa.

Overcrowding in housing is well documented by social historians as one of the primary experiences of African American migrants to Northern cities. It, along with the poverty that attended it, created concentric circles of social problems: by the early 1930s health officials in Detroit indicated that six times as many African Americans as whites had tuberculosis and that two-thirds of the deaths resulting from pneumonia and half of those caused by tuberculosis could have been prevented with adequate housing and sanitation. While urban realities like these had been a target of Progressive Era activists seeking to redeem immigrant European workers, Detroit reformers never shared quite the same fervor in addressing the needs of African Americans. The crisis faced by Black Detroit existed in poor and working immigrant and white neighborhoods too, but in those areas it was at least minimally addressed. Indeed, over 50,000 single-family homes were built in Detroit between 1923 and 1928 in response to this situation, nearly all of which were in already white areas of the city.[58]

Though something like 15 percent of Black Detroiters owned their homes in 1926 the mayor's Interracial Committee reported that decent, sanitary, and affordable homes in Detroit's Black neighborhoods were "the exception." In Detroit, urban housing in Black neighborhoods resembled rural housing: single, detached wooden homes; in 1925, 30 percent had no indoor bathrooms. Almost half of all Black families shared houses with at least one other family and / or took in lodgers. Lodging was an economic necessity for families and for the single men who became lodgers who simply could not afford to live otherwise.[59]

Racist exclusion meant that African Americans in Detroit suffered the effects of the housing shortage far longer than even European immigrants. In response to this continued crisis the Detroit Urban League tried to help solve the housing crisis in Black Detroit. Though the primary work the league had done with poor African Americans was as a de facto hiring hall, in 1920 league head John Dancy set out to find a piece of land in the Detroit area that was not controlled by restrictive covenants. Dancy also searched for landlords who would cooperate in renting or selling property to African Americans. In 1920, one white realtor worked with the Urban League to acquire a 140-acre tract of land that he was willing to divide into plots and sell to African Americans.[60] This area became the village of Inkster, incorporated in 1926. The original town of Inkster was named after Robert Inkster, postmaster from 1866–68 who would become a substantial landowner in Michigan. It was Robert Inkster from whom Henry Ford bought the land on which the Highland Park plant was built.[61] In spite of the fact that the area offered new residents no paved streets, streetlights, city sanitation, or water, poor Detroiters and especially African Americans saw this as an opportunity that would lead to the building and owning of one's own home. At the time when the celebrated and tragic case of Dr. Ossian Sweet, an African American doctor who defended himself against mobs seeking to remove him from the white neighborhood he had desegregated, separation implied safety as well as exclusion. Drawn to Inkster by the idea that they would be able to become home owners, and with jobs to pay the bills, many Detroit residents were so eager to escape the crowding of the city that they built temporary shelters of tar paper, scrap wood and sheet metal on their newly settled pieces of land.

While African Americans were not the only ones to benefit from the possibilities of tracts in Inkster, the southwest quadrant of the village became nearly all Black. This was the area that would be taken over by Ford in 1931. A population of 150 in 1900 rose to more than 4,400 residents in Inkster by 1930, of which 1,195 were African American and 3,244 were white. In both the 1930 and 1940 censuses African Americans were a large minority but always a minority. Black and white Inkster were fully segregated from one another.[62] The community crossed two township lines, Nankin and Dearborn. Dearborn Township was the home of Ford-dominated Dearborn, which "By legal stratagems and the common consent of its citizens, bar[red] Negroes and Jews from residence." Thus the crisis at Inkster was part of larger patterns of segregation that Ford endorsed. Dearborn was also the site of the Rouge plant, nearly eight miles from the African American settlement in Inkster, though connected by an inter-urban rail line.[63]

The disaster of the Depression hit Inkster fast and furiously. In October 1930 the village had to ask Edison Electric to extend it a promissory note because it could not pay its bill for municipal street lighting. In May 1931, when Edison turned off their service, the village was $8,000 in debt to the electric company. With a village treasury of $2.75 it faced debts of nearly $30,000. In order to pressure the village to make good on its three-year-old debts, in 1931 the first National Bank of Dearborn, the Peoples State Bank of Inkster, Dearborn State Bank, and Edison made the city promise that any taxes collected would go to them first. Garbage collection had already been suspended. The village had sold its lone police car in 1929 and now paid its three police officers $1 per month. Fears of increased street crime after the public lights were turned off led the volunteer police chief to launch a campaign to get shopkeepers to string up their Christmas lights until ten o'clock each night.[64] A survey of Black Inkster found 700 men unemployed in 1931, 500 of whom had worked for Ford. It also revealed the not surprising but staggering fact that 90 percent of those surveyed were buying their homes under land contract, a kind of mortgage payment plan for small plots of land where no houses yet stood. Many of those trying to buy land were living in uncompleted houses they were trying to fund as they continued to pay off their plots of land. When the firings started many people simply could not finish construction on their homes.[65]

Why Henry Ford decided to intervene in Inkster as he did has not been adequately explained. As Sward wrote, one very real possibility is that the "jerry-built community" of Inkster had become "an eyesore to all who beheld it . . . [A] colony . . . too close to the Rouge for comfort."[66] Richard W. Thomas refers to Inkster's Black section as a "satellite" ghetto. It is also likely that the company, which was starting to feel pressure as it continued to lay off workers, benefited from the reams of free publicity garnered through this small project while avoiding the more politically organized and activist neighborhoods in Detroit, also in crisis. Further, intervening in Inkster built goodwill for Ford in the large Black population of metropolitan Detroit at a time when it was badly needed.[67]

But since Henry Ford welcomed opportunities for social experimentation it is probable that Inkster also represented to him another opportunity to try out a project in men-making as well. The *New York Times* seemed to think so. "[Ford] concluded that these people had not learned the lesson which months of idleness should have taught them, that is first to pay off their debts and put their house in order. That was the beginning of the Inkster educational experiment." The *Times* also reported that Inkster "is an ideal ground for this experiment, because its population is almost entirely one race, there being 500 colored families and only 50 white families."[68] Ernest Liebold remarked, "Both Mr. Ford and myself felt that this was an educational thing as well as an economic one."[69]

Ford's approach to solving the problems the people of Inkster faced was to institute a system of debt peonage:

> What we did down there was take over the supervision of these Negroes and employed a number of them at the Rouge plant on the basis of $1 a day . . . the difference in their earning, between the actual wage they were paid, which was probably $6, and the $1 that was given them in case, was placed in a general fund in the Ford Motor Company's books.

With 500 workers back in the plant the company was setting aside a total of about $2,500 per day. Of course, during the Depression most Rouge workers were working a two or at most three-day week. Records do not indicate how many days Inkster residents worked, though there was obvious material incentive on Ford's part to keep them in the plant as many days as possible. The general fund that Ford created from workers' unpaid wages was used to cover the costs associated with feeding and housing the people of Inkster and restoring city services.

Ford's practices in Inkster, and some other Depression-era relief activities, revived the nearly dormant Sociological Department. Yet the department it revived was not the one which sought to make citizen-consumers out of those who worked in the plant. In some small ways the policies Ford insisted on in Inkster mimicked what the company had done at Highland Park fifteen years earlier. But the goal now was to make functioning subjects out of the presumably uncivilized Black Ford workers and Inkster residents. Racist stereotypes shaped the context in which African American workers might qualify for aid from the company, aid which decades before had been virtually guaranteed as part of the wage of any immigrant worker who complied with company rules.[70]

Before any Inkster resident and Ford worker could qualify for home repair he had to be evaluated by a Sociological Department representative. The representative's job was to determine whether or not the potential recipient of help was "worthy" of and qualified for the company's assistance. One of the most important evaluative criteria was cleanliness: "There was no excuse for filth and untidiness just because one was unemployed."[71] Reports described the homes of laid-off workers by listing the number of rooms, number of people living in those rooms, and their condition: "unsanitary"; "incomplete"; "under constr" [*sic*]; "overcrowded but clean." "Liabilities" included "a large expensive car, player piano, or radio costing hundreds of dollars."[72] Of course, Ford is the company celebrated for the idea that every worker should be able to own a car. Moreover, Henry Ford himself encouraged people to avoid the evils of urban culture by staying home and listening to the radio, *his* radio show in fact. Yet here owning cars and radios was described as excessive, though it is likely these workers drove the same cars and listened to the same radios as their white peers. For Ford, not everyone was ready for the responsibility of mass consumption. The *New York Times* followed suit, ridiculing the hungry residents of Inkster: "Investigators found a new washing machine in a home where there was no food. They learned that the housewife had purchased it on easy payments because the company selling it offered a turkey, free, with each machine. They found vacuum cleaners where there were no rugs to be cleaned, waffle irons where there was no batter to bake in them."[73]

Making their homes livable was of course one of the most serious worries of Inkster residents, many of whom had been extended credit to build or expand their small houses when they were working for the Ford wage. Those who did not have credit, who had been building bit by bit, were simply forced to stop when the paychecks did. Ford underwrote the homes of people buying under land contract and out of the fund of workers' wages paid back-rent for others. From 1931 to 1938, 150 homes were built in Inkster; some of those were for people who had been living in tents. All who agreed to accept aid from the company also had to accept the terms of the company's repayment policy. Each worker was required to sign an IOU that would obligate not just himself but his kin to pay his debt in the event that he could not.[74]

Running a commissary for the residents of Inkster was one of Ford's central tasks and the company had multiple objectives in doing it. Striking a blow against the perceived "Jewish control" of shops in Inkster was one of the most important according to Liebold. "The reason that prompted us to make the financial arrangement down there was that there were a couple of Jewish merchants in Inkster . . . some of the Negroes got so involved they were no longer able to make their payments . . . when they found out that these people weren't getting any more than $1 a day they wouldn't give them any more credit."[75] Ford believed that Inkster's crisis was a direct result of its residents' irresponsible handling of money. Thus the commissary operated as the center of a cash-free economy. Not only would Ford be providing for the needs of people, the company would be teaching them lessons in living.

The commissary sold food raised on Inkster farms, dresses sewn by women "volunteers" from the village, shoes cobbled there, and bread baked there. All of that was done with unpaid labor and an "established policy [was] in effect for regulating all the accounts that were being carried and charging the people from the general fund."[76] According to one Ford sociologist Inkster residents were aware that the commissary they relied on was started in part because the company did not want them to use the commissary it had started for white Ford employees in Dearborn.[77]

The unsanitary living conditions of the poor were not a new preoccupation for reformers. Ford and others related the sanitary conditions of Inkster to the behavior and outlook of its residents even though there had been no garbage collection in Inkster for years, and no sewage lines had been extended to Inkster's Black neighborhood. The schools that Ford built also lacked indoor plumbing. A special story to the *New York Times* read, "A hopelessness had seized the village which reflected itself in untidy homes. Every yard was littered with rubbish. Vacant lots were junk piles."[78] Unemployed workers were put to work hauling garbage in trucks from the Rouge; ditches were dug, roads were paved; expenses were covered by the fund of workers' wages. From the point of view of Ford's management, Liebold in particular, problems were capable of easy solution. As they did in the Rouge, the company relied on Donald Marshall to "take care of the direct and immediate supervision of these people."[79] As the chief Ford lieutenant in Inkster, Marshall had the authority to approve or reject credit at the commissary. If Marshall came to Liebold about any "problem people" they had not succeeded in running out, he would "get return railroad tickets and send them back."[80]

Liebold became centrally involved in the schooling of the African American children of Inkster. The Depression exacerbated an already severe problem of classroom shortages in area schools which meant that some children were sent to school in Dearborn. Segregation was nearly total: In 1933, 399 of the 462 students in Inkster's elementary school were African American. In 1932, of the 38 students from Inkster enrolled at Fordson High

School in Dearborn, 37 were African American, though the school itself was overwhelmingly white. African American students were reportedly given grades of "A" in physical education classes without attending so that white students would not have to attend integrated classes where there was a chance of bodily contact. Liebold was also in charge of building schools for African Americans. He wrote, "I had the plan for the building . . . I had some of our men go out and to the building . . . the cost of that service was all charged to the Negroes from the general fund . . . we wanted to confine these Negroes to the area in which they lived in order not to make it necessary for them to have to go too far to school."[81] By 1937 Inkster had its own elementary and high school. Of course, education in Michigan was not legally segregated. But both schools were built in the center of "Black" Inkster. As in the Rouge, Liebold and Ford had a great amount of involvement in the day-to-day operations of the Ford-Inkster Project. Liebold kept close tabs on what happened at the school, and arranged for the African American inventor George Washington Carver, beloved by Henry Ford, to deliver a graduation speech at the new high school.[82]

The practice of withholding wages from African American workers in the Rouge ended in September 1933 with the minimum wage clause of the National Industrial Recovery Act.[83] From then on Ford's sociologists had to try to collect the debts voluntarily. Under pressure from Ford to make this happen, collectors started bribing relatives of Ford workers with jobs if they would agree to sign a portion of their wages to pay off the debt. Sometimes this meant that African Americans could not find employment at Ford through the front door. Instead they had to have a debtor in mind whom they would pledge to support in order to be hired at Ford.[84] Though in the end Ford had to write off some of the expenditures in the Ford-Inkster Project it also managed to run Inkster like an efficient sharecropping system. Ford spent $884,035.37 on the Inkster project between 1931 and 1935; payroll deductions and voluntary payments totaled $788,076.00, leaving a deficit of $96,000. Not only would the company likely have collected this if federal law had not changed, it is also remarkable that Ford, the richest man in the world, could do so little and receive such incredibly positive press.[85]

Here too extremely limited options could make Ford's shouldering of the white man's burden appear beneficent. Set against the inaction and unwillingness of employers to challenge Jim Crow and the clear preference given to white workers that prevailed nationally, Ford's coercive policies and meager

FIGURE 7. Henry Ford was an admirer of George Washington Carver, naming the segregated African American school on his Georgia plantation The Carver School. Ford purchased the cabin where he believed Carver had lived as a slave, moving it to Greenfield Village, where he encouraged Carver, pictured here, to spend the night. Courtesy Collections of The Henry Ford.

support for Inkster could seem those of a "benevolent despot." Ford was lauded nationwide and even in much of the African American press for his company's efforts in Inkster. The *Atlanta World* described the "rehabilitation" of Inkster as "splendid."[86] The *Pittsburgh Courier*'s celebration of Ford centered on the company's philosophy that one did not necessarily have to be earning a wage in order to be working, endorsing Henry Ford's notion that "stimulating" people to work is better than contributing millions to "community chests." The paper added, "There are several hundred families in the little town of Inkster. They were practically destitute and certainly they were out of 'hire.' Mr. Ford set the people to work cleaning up their homes and backyards, as well as the roads of their town . . . everything resembling a handout was abolished and a modern commissary where personal IOUs were accepted was installed."[87] Self-help and bossiness would similarly conspire in Ford's plantation in Jim Crow Georgia.

In 1926, the *Dearborn Independent* ran a two-part series of essays on the post–Civil War Reconstruction of the U.S. South. The articles described Reconstruction with delicious if unwitting irony as "inimical" to the "Anglo-Saxon instinct of fair play." The essays argued that the white South had a responsibility to make the Negro believe that "only an industrious and self-reliant race is worthy of respect." Reconstruction had slowed Negro progress toward that future because it had "helped the Negro acquire a taste for idleness and unearned luxuries"; more importantly it had created illusions, by "putting a semi-barbarian people in political power over white people." These articles echoed what Ford's paper had been saying about African Americans in the North. Such language almost exactly repeated some of what the company would say about its intervention in Inkster. Written near the height of the Ku Klux Klan's 1920s popularity and in the wake of the anti-Reconstruction extravaganza that was the film *Birth of a Nation* the decade before, the articles were remarkably presentist. According to the *Independent,* whites realized that they "would have to take the Negro with us or he would pull us down by the sheer weight of his millions."[88]

The sentiments expressed in these articles reflect the sometimes paradoxical yet firmly held white supremacist views that Henry Ford and company ideologues like Liebold and Cameron shared about race, progress, and what they called civilization. In the Reconstruction example, African Americans were seen as both "semi-barbarian" and incapable of political rule; on the other hand, if ignored, the "Negro problem" would surely doom the white race. Of course, none of these accounts take into consideration the possibility of Black leadership, the realities of workplace skill and knowledge among Black workers, or the history of self-organizing and support among Black laborers. Here again Ford created the historical narrative it claimed described the problem that whites needed to solve.

In 1936, Henry Ford launched a campaign to bring jobs and social improvement to the people living on the land and in the villages of Bryan County, Georgia, south of Savannah. At the center of Ford's 100-mile stretch of land along the Ogeechee River was the 80,000-acre plantation Richmond Hill, where Ford decided to "gamble on the potentialities of the land [and] take a chance with the underprivileged inhabitants."[89] Ford's experiment was aimed at both the African American and the poor white residents of the plantation who were targeted for improvement through work, education, and inoculation. A reporter for *Scribner's Commentary* described this decision as a continued expression of Ford's interest in rehabilitating "sub-marginal" districts and his "fellow-men."[90]

Ford's interest in the region initially had been encouraged by his friends Thomas Edison and H. F. Firestone, who had been his traveling companions on the Ogeechee. Both Edison and Firestone imagined that the area would be ideal for raising giant goldenrod. Edison was already supported by both Ford and Firestone in his experiments to produce rubber in the United States, and believed that goldenrod might be made to produce latex that would be usable for industrial purposes.[91] Ford's interest in ecological experimentation in Georgia, combined with his increased involvement in the lives of the poor people who would come under his patronage as workers and as the subject of experiments in social improvement, is a story which illuminates Ford's programs at Fordlandia and Belterra by comparison.

The management of workers in Georgia and Brazil was understood as requiring a strong medical component. When the industrial surgeon Dr. C. F. Coulton approached Henry Ford in 1937 to propose an experiment in eradicating malaria on and around Richmond Hill, Ford told him "to go ahead with the program, regardless of the cost."[92] The project was two-pronged: to eliminate malaria in the region and to test a new drug called Atabrine. Atabrine was synthesized as a possible replacement for quinine in 1932 by the German company I. G. Farben, a conglomerate deeply connected to Ford and one whose connections to Nazism figure prominently in the historical literature on corporations and reaction in Germany.[93] Farben introduced Atabrine in the United States in 1935 through a partnership with the Winthrop company, which sold it as "made in America" after stamping the tablets in the U. S.[94] When the drug was first tested, regular reports of mental disturbances followed its use. There is no record of either Winthrop or Farben responding to these claims, though by 1941 when the drug was marketed in the United States for national defense purposes, its price had dropped by 90 percent.[95] Because of Japanese control of almost all of the world's sources of quinine, a new anti-malarial drug was needed for U. S. troops in the Pacific. Despite its known side effects, Atabrine was given to those troops, who complained regularly about the problems attending its use. The pill was bitter, it turned the skin a yellow hue, and caused headaches, nausea, and vomiting. It was also reported, as prior studies had documented, to lead to temporary psychosis.[96]

The people living and working at Richmond Hill were compelled to take Atabrine even before its use by U. S. troops. Describing Richmond Hill as "an ideal setup for the real scientific method," Coulton noted: "This was the first mass experiment of its kind." In his oral history, taken by the Ford Motor Company in the 1950s, Coulton described the idea of "making everyone who lived on Mr. Ford's property take a five-day treatment of . . . Atabrine." Delivering a biological judgment and a medicalized palliative at the same time, he summarized the goal as being "to sterilize these human cesspools." Nurses administered the drug to everyone who lived in the community "man, woman or child, white or black." According to Coulton "they had to take it or get out . . . If they refused they were told to either take this medicine or get off the property." Of course people in the community were concerned about malaria, but even according to Coulton there was still some objection to taking the unknown drug: "There were a few who didn't want to do it, but they did. They didn't want to lose their jobs, so they took the treatment just the same."[97]

The administration of Atabrine was accompanied by a massive drainage project funded by Ford, which managed to eliminate malaria in Bryan County.[98] This success led Ford to support Coulton's clinic at Richmond Hill from which the latter conducted other experiments among the people of the region. As someone who did "a great deal of industrial surgery," Coulton knew that people suffering from syphilis had poor coordination and reflexes, and that this may have been why there were an increasing number of industrial accidents in the area. He discovered an unusually high accident rate in one industrial plant in Savannah, where 300 African Americans worked. He decided to test those injured on the job and found that one-third had syphilis. This led Coulton to wonder whether there "was a difference between the city Negro and the country Negro." Of course, his clinic at Richmond Hill provided "an ideal opportunity to test the blood of a large number of colored people who . . . had never lived in the city." The tests came back just the same; about one-third of those tested had syphilis.[99] Following the same protocol established with the malaria treatments, "we made it compulsory that all the people in Mr. Ford's empire who had a positive blood test report at our clinic weekly."[100]

The overseer of the whole plantation was called Mr. Gregory, and he worked alongside Ford manager E. D. Mitchum. Like other Ford supervisors Mitchum believed in the Ford project of saving people from themselves. One of the activities he describes most vividly in his oral history is destroying stills on Ford property. According to Mitchum there were "over 250 whisky stills destroyed on the Ford Farms between 1930 and 1937, some small and some large. Each one of those stills at that time was furnishing anywhere from two to three men with work."[101] The stills were destroyed under orders from Henry Ford.[102] Such an approach echoed Ford's outlawing of drinking on the Brazilian plantations, discussed in the next chapter, and the company's insistence that workers not drink in order to qualify for the five-dollar-a-day wage at Highland Park. In this case, the destruction of the stills also had a decidedly economic impact, making employment on the Ford farms an increasing necessity.

Mitchum was most interested in work on the schools. Because the plantation was privately owned, the schools Ford set up were run by their own trustees, independent of the Board of Education. A reliance on teaching to create discipline and control was a constant part of Ford's men-making projects. This was most profound in contexts, like Richmond Hill, Inkster, or Belterra in Brazil, where there was a direct connection between the workplace and the home. What Ford wanted for the school he ran for African Americans—an institution named after George Washington Carver, who supervised agricultural production at Richmond Hill for a time—was for it to be run by his trustees and "not by the Negroes altogether."[103] After receiving nineteen applications, the company hired H. G. Cooper as principal and head teacher of the Carver School. Cooper graduated from Georgia State University and had a strong commitment to progressive education, although what he meant by progressive education and what Ford meant by it were quite different. As a former director of the Sociological Department at the Rouge said regarding Ford's progressive education: "You hear and read so much about the philosophy Mr. Ford was supposed to have . . . the John Dewey type of philosophy . . . I would consider [his] more of a Nicholas Nickleby type of apprentice training rather than an expression of progressive educational philosophy."[104] According to Mitchum, Ford was a man for education, "but only so far. He told us one day at a meeting, 'Now, I don't want those n****** down there to go no further than the seventh grade. That's far enough. Give them a seventh grade education and that will keep them out of trouble. But *learn* them how to work!"[105] The particular way in which the imperatives of racial capitalism overwhelm reform and even paternalism in this quote suggests that Ford shared with the Southern elite a commitment to what the Black activists and educators Bob Moses and Charlie Cobb have critiqued and explained as "sharecropper education."[106]

At Richmond Hill Cooper seems to have been able to walk the line between Ford's insistence that schoolchildren spend most of their time engaging in productive work and his own interest in teaching academic subjects. He describes being able to prevent manual training for boys and home economic training for girls from dominating school life until 1941. By then, though, much of the school day was taken by instruction in the trades. As Cooper recalled, "Boys took carpentry and diversified farming. The girls took a diversified home economics program consisting of sewing, cooking, family relations and consumer buying."[107] Schooling was instituted at Richmond Hill for Black and white adults too, although the emphasis on adult education seems to have been for African Americans. Adult education courses, recommended though not compulsory, drew 181 out of 500 African American residents of Richmond Hill to night school in 1939. The largest classes were reading, writing, and arithmetic, although Ford tried to get women into sewing classes and men into "manual arts."[108]

One plan for how to make permanent the improvements being made possible at Richmond Hill relied on seeing home and work as spheres of training, which would help restore the pride and traditions that the South—and here the emphasis was particularly on the white South—had lost. As the social investigator Joseph Thornes put it, "With a system based on service—not servitude . . . [and] Richmond Hill plantation setting the example, could not an understanding, benevolent 'massah' regain the glory of the plantation system . . . by precept and example the master would lead not drive and would teach and discipline as he led."[109] From Brazil to Inkster to the U. S. South all the modernity and progress promised by Ford did not keep the company from aspiring to just that role. Even when his colonialist visions failed, Ford and his managers worked diligently to enforce a colonial power structure with racial hierarchy at its core.

One essayist explored Ford's commitment to making the land and the people of the region productive. The author described the "pathetically typical . . . faded gingham . . . work scarred hands, malaria yellowed face" of the white woman to whom he offered a lift in his car on his way to the plantation. But things were changing: rehabilitation and reclamation of the "five hundred whites and thousand or so blacks" was allegedly happening through a fostering of a "we-can-do-it" spirit. Detailing the achievements on the plantation—a sawmill, powerhouse, two schools, a community house, and a firehouse—he made it clear that Ford would be bringing people into the modern age through his use of "chance not charity." In this author's view, it was that unique commitment which the Negroes of the South most needed. It may as well have been 1870, not 1940, as the "lessons" of Reconstruction still applied: "To most of the colored workers, accustomed for generations to being told what to do, a sense of responsibility was strange and uncomfortable at first."[110]

FIGURE 8. Dorothea Lange captured this image in California, 1937. The links between auto modernity, domestic labor, and racial hierarchy were made at home and at work by Ford managers and sociologists and in company propaganda such as this billboard. Courtesy The Library of Congress.

A remarkable report called "Richmond Hill: A Study in Social Trends Where 'The Old Order Changeth'" was written for Ford by an observer of the nighttime adult reading classes. It found that the schooling that was being provided by Ford was appropriate for the particular needs of the South. The author argued that Ford's understanding of the need to balance social improvement and social responsibility would teach the correct lessons to those who were in his care. The author meant to placate whites in Savannah who "shuddered to think" of the problems that would come from educating Negroes. He argued that Richmond Hill was leading a trend in which "as Negroes received more education they will be given more responsibility, thus making practical use of their education and diverting their new energies toward self-control."[111]

Anthropologist Ann Laura Stoler's extraordinary work describing the simultaneity of cultural, racial, and modern forms of colonialism might apply to Ford's activities both globally and in the U. S. South. Her discussion of the "global field" across which "paradigms of progress . . . reverberated" elegantly depicts the global connectedness of colonial managers and elites from the U. S. South to South Africa to the Dutch Indies. In analyzing U. S. management's involvement in colonial plantation projects in the Indies, and the Carnegie Corporation's study of poor whites in South Africa, Stoler conveys the richness that colonialism as a framework can provide to history made static by conventional comparative approaches.[112] The implications of Stoler's perspective for understanding Ford's global presence are multiple. Colonial management, which informed Ford's actions in Inkster and Richmond Hill as well as transnationally, preached a reliance on categorization, regulation, and conformity. In many ways, debates about colonial policy were never more than debates about how to *manage* colonized people, territory, and resources.

How or whether colonized people would be introduced to civilization was basically about how to classify and contain identities in increasingly dynamic commercial worlds. It was about measurement: of color, culture, health, and potential. Managers, like colonizers—and managers *as* colonizers—needed to create stability in some arenas precisely because of the volatility and instability of modernization itself. Ford also shared with colonialists, and for that matter with national elites around the world, a concern with men-making, even as most agreed that some people were more ready for improvement than others. Both production and consumption played a role in shaping the terms of colonial societies, just as each did in Ford's workplaces. The story of Ford's two Souths—Richmond Hill and, in the next chapter, Brazil—reveals the contradictory nature of racial constructions, forged in part through mass production and mass consumption, even as it underlines the place of white supremacy as a unifying ideology. The limited gains made by Black workers at most U.S. Ford Motor Company sites made them peripheral within some contexts and absent from others. Where Black workers in the United States were concerned, and likewise the workers of the world, Ford did not impose a single racial system. The company instead adapted to and experimented with a variety of racial orders.

FIGURE 9. Workers were organized into gangs to clear the rainforest on Ford's Amazon plantations. Like all Ford workers worldwide they were required to wear company badges at all times. Here you can see them pictured on workers' waists. Courtesy Collections of The Henry Ford.

FOUR

Breeding Rubber, Breeding Workers

FROM FORDLANDIA TO BELTERRA

"Shades of Tarzan!" You'd never guess these bright, happy, healthy school children lived in a jungle city that didn't even exist a few years ago.

"THE FORD RUBBER PLANTATIONS"[1]

IN DIEGO RIVERA'S *DETROIT INDUSTRY* frescoes the Rouge assembly line sits at the center of a world of connected but distinct representations of the relationship the artist sought to celebrate between nature and technology. Though commissioned by the Detroit Institute of Arts, the project was underwritten by Edsel Ford, a patron of the arts and decided disappointment to his father, Henry. The main frescoes marvelously portray the intimate processes of mass production on the Rouge assembly line. Smaller panels show doctors and nurses delivering babies and curing disease while in others researchers tirelessly pursue new knowledge in laboratories. Also present, though, are panels that depict war, diseased cells, and destruction. Reflecting Rivera's conviction that knowledge was not neutral but had to be used for correct purposes in order for human society to progress, these frescoes demonstrate the artist's search for balance—between nature and technology, spirituality and science, the past and the future, the primitive and the modern, the physical and the intellectual.

Above the large frescoes on the north and south walls are several round, slightly cartoonish figures. Rivera intended these to be feminine representations of what he called the "four races": white, yellow, black, and red. In their hands the characters each hold what Rivera called the "four elements of the world."[2] These elements formed the basic ingredients in steel, which for Rivera was the key to modern manufacturing possibility, particularly as represented by skyscrapers and cars. Of these differently colored figures Rivera said:

> The yellow race represents the sand, because it is most numerous. And the red race, the first in this country, is like the iron ore, the first thing necessary for

the steel. The black race is like the coal, because it has a great native aesthetic sense, a real flame of feeling and beauty in its ancient sculpture, its native rhythm and music. So its aesthetic sense is like the fire, and its labor furnished the hardness which the carbon in the coal gives to steel. The white race is like the lime, not only because it is white, but because lime is the organizing agent in the making of steel. It binds together the other elements and so you see the white race as the great organizer of the world.[3]

The fantastical yet explicit link between race and industrial production Rivera articulated verbally and through his art was one that Henry Ford made as well. Both used the metaphor of forging when talking about making men and the future. Ford's involvement in Latin America was understood by Rivera as having significance other than as an imperial power, and he believed that the future of the Americas would be found in the unique coming together of the techno-culture of the hyperdeveloped north, or the United States, and the resilience of traditional indigenous cultural practices across the Americas. Indeed, though the enormity of Ford's impact on the planet is evident in Rivera's frescoes, in speaking about them Rivera emphasized not the troubling emergence of U. S. industrial dominance but instead the emergence of a new world.

The only people outside of the United States represented in Rivera's frescoes were *seringueiros,* Brazilian rubber tappers. In the panel where they appear the Amazon is connected to the Rouge plant by water, rubber on one side being tapped from trees, smoothly transported from the Amazon River across the Atlantic Ocean up the Rouge River where it would be transformed—by labor, heat, and technology—into tires. In the frescoes, the *seringueiros* represent the process Rivera wished to celebrate, in which human labor and intellect could transform raw materials into goods whose use would be freeing. They are also suggestive of Rivera's internationalism, learned in the surrealist and communist movements, which saw industry as bringing liberation to people worldwide. Interestingly, however, the rubber tappers find no place in Rivera's imaginary chart of the races of the world, being neither "actually" yellow nor red, neither black nor white. While this may have been an oversight on Rivera's part, the "in-betweenness" the rubber tappers represent is precisely what Ford relied on when it decided to build its rubber plantations in the Brazilian Amazon.[4]

Rivera's evocation of a racial order in which whites represented intellect and organization fits with much of Ford's white supremacist approach to "men-making." So, too, does Rivera's forging metaphor mirror the language that the company used in describing the new men it scooped out of its Americanizing melting pots in Detroit. The use of this industrial metaphor by both Rivera and Ford in relating their visions of social improvement—the transformation of raw materials that forging implied—demonstrates the sensibility each brought to thinking about nature and technology, the old and the new.

In including this depiction of Ford's Brazilian rubber concessions in his Detroit frescoes Rivera offered a research opportunity that went mostly overlooked by scholars for many years. Who were these rubber tappers? Why were they, the only images of workers not in the United States, included in these frescoes? The answer is that Richmond Hill, Georgia, was not Ford's only experiment in running a plantation. The Depression-era projects undertaken there mirror Ford's efforts in another "American South," the company's rubber plantations, Fordlandia and Belterra, in the Amazonian region of Brazil in the state of Pará. As they did in Georgia, Ford managers and doctors in the Amazon sought to construct an infrastructure familiar to its managers as a first step in gaining control of its new environment

The Ford plantations date from July 21, 1927, when a concession of approximately 2.5 million acres was granted the just-incorporated Companhia Ford Industrial do Brasil. The land, which extended approximately 95 miles along the Tapajos River and 50 miles inland, was described in one company report as "an immense and savage wilderness uninhabited except for a few wild Indian tribes."[5] While the history of the plantations can be used to reveal narratives of many kinds, the above quote underlines the importance of racialized ideas about civilization to the company's investment decisions. "Social engineering through spatial engineering" as geographer Andrew Herod has called it, was central to the plan Ford brought with it to Brazil even as the company's built environment would also prove to be a key part of worker resistance and assertions of local control on the plantations.[6]

As places that Ford was inventing from the ground up, the plantations were ideal sites for experiments in men-making, first in the context of single male workers and then by making families. The plantations were, after all, both homeplace and workplace, creating a total atmosphere in which straight lines connecting behavior to work time and leisure time could be drawn. The relationship of racial engineering to social engineering, and the relationship of each to the built environment of the plantation, both underlined and undermined the company's interest in bringing what it knew about factory production to plantation production. Indeed, the desire for and commitment to racial improvement allowed the Ford Motor Company to build common cause with modernizers in Brazil. In pursuit of what Ann Laura Stoler described as the "cultivation of race," company men and Brazilian elites saw possibilities for social engineering in the very materiality of plantation living.[7]

Ford and its supporters proved to be wrong about this and many other things in Brazil. The company's industrially inflected attempts to carve a rubber plantation out of what it perceived as the chaos of the jungle and the savagery of its people led to failures of several kinds—managerial, botanical, and infrastructural—at first one plantation, Fordlandia, and then a second, Belterra. This chapter considers the ways that Ford's "Amazon venture" mimicked the company's initiatives on its U.S. plantation in Richmond Hill and of debt peonage to run the town of Inkster. After Ford was confronted with the militancy of its Amazonian workforce, which took some years to develop, the models of family formation and surveillance Ford implemented through the Sociological Department at Highland Park also made their appearance on the Brazilian plantations. Lacking the dimension of the high wage, Ford's approach to worker control on the plantations looked much more like what the company was pursuing in the name of rehabilitating Black workers in Inkster.

Fordlandia is now better known thanks to Greg Grandin's history of its failures to produce the progress, profit, and predictability that Ford prized. The other subject of this chapter, Belterra, is less fully treated, but similarly analyzed, in Grandin's work. In each case, the exercise of Ford management's habitus of racial development figures little in Grandin's popular and sweeping account of Ford, rubber, and Brazil. Human frailty and imperial hubris are well dramatized, company boldness crossing over into tragicomic failure, showing just how little control Ford had over the world. But the particular arrogance of and violence done by white supremacist race-thinking, which had been tailored to Brazil's population and politics and which shaped both Ford's decision to invest in Brazil and daily life on the plantations, scarcely appear in Grandin's account. In rural Brazil, this chapter will argue, Ford's conviction that the racial character of local people ensured a better prognosis for development made the firm of use to the modernizing Brazilian state. A projected Brazilian self-image was rising to the fore that was wholly consistent with Ford's white supremacist practices in the United States and South Africa even as it differed from both in logistical and local manifestations.

How Ford's luckless history in Brazilian rubber cultivation was specifically an adventure and misadventure in white managerialism becomes clear when considering the plantation experiments as neither exceptional nor purely mimetic. Belterra and Fordlandia were not simply distended examples of a Fordist project that worked in the United States but was defeated by Brazilian politics, tropical vegetation, and imperial hubris. The company tried, serially and simultaneously, a series of styles of race management that had been practiced in different parts of the United States at different times. As concerned the rubber-producing areas of Brazil there was no one system to be exported but instead a combined, uneven, and shifting Fordism within and across national boundaries.[8]

Though the racial calculus that attended Fordist narratives of racial progress mattered greatly to managerial elites and nation-builders, Ford did not invent the search for the perfect match of race, climate, and productivity, or the perfect combination of primitivism and imperial tutelage. In 1913, as Ford was about to inaugurate the five-dollar day and the Sociological Department in Detroit, Major John Finley was already reflecting on the happy results of the U.S. occupation of the Philippines, coining the phrase "race development by industrial means" to describe what had transformed the "Moros and pagans of the Southern Philippines." Finley took "race development" from the title of the periodical in which he wrote, the estimable *Journal of Race Development*. Notably, the *Journal of Race Development* was the founding publication of international relations in the United States, soon to become the repository of the scholarship of American empire and renamed *Foreign Affairs*.[9] Founded in 1910, the *Journal of Race Development* reflected on an international scale an optimism akin to that professed domestically by the Sociological Department regarding the wonders worked by the contact of "advanced" races and their systems with those peoples who lacked the "aptitude or opportunities" to advance. The U.S.-born anthropologist of Latin America Philip Ainsworth Means used the journal's pages to propose an even grander term than race development and one more evocative of connections between American race management, capital accumulation, and imperial expansion that shaped all academic theorizing on such matters. Means named the uplift of those peoples whom history had left behind as "race appreciation." But even within such faith in progress there were limits imposed by the ultimately arbitrary and violent reality of white supremacy. The editor of the *Journal of Race Development* urged scholars to identify the "best primitive races" and work with them, though he was especially skeptical about native people in Brazil. For him, "The mentality of the West European," when contrasted with "the Arawaks of central Brazil," captured the full range of racial difference.[10]

Important differences between the national contexts for these projects exist. The strict Black-white color line that juridically structured race in the United States meant that just one drop of African ancestry of almost any sort made a U. S. citizen a member of the "Negro race." In Brazil the existence of multiple kinds of racially different people of mixed descent was acknowledged, sometimes celebrated and often not. Ford's 1920s move into the Amazon coincided with a deepening social expression of desire in Brazil to believe that the country could be whitened—and indeed that it was in fact whitening. Racial mixture would be (not unproblematically) celebrated at times as a feature of Brazil's national identity rather than being considered a crime as it was in the United States or a sign of crisis and white degradation as it was in South Africa. To be a mixed-race nation did not, however, imply the nonexistence of white supremacy. Indeed mixing was only celebrated when viewed as whitening, which could occur via education and economic mobility as well as biological reproduction.[11]

Ford's decision to go into the business of extracting rubber has been rightly linked to the company's desire to vertically integrate—that is, to own—the sources of all materials necessary to mass-produce cars. As discussed in previous chapters, by the late 1920s the company already owned mines, forests, sheep, cows, and myriad other natural sources of the raw materials that went into making cars. It had also acquired by then many of the infrastructural components needed for transporting these materials, parts, and finished products around the globe and around the United States. An increasingly elaborate network of roads, railroads, ports, and shipping routes linked the inside of Ford's factories to the natural resources the company sought. Digging out its own deepwater port in the Rouge River in order for cargo to come and go had been the last step Ford needed to link this network globally.

Now with direct access—from the River Rouge to the Great Lakes to the Atlantic Ocean to the Amazon River—the decision Ford made to obtain full control of its own rubber production fit within the economic and political framework that drove this company's expansion in the 1920s. On the Brazilian side, the rise and decline of Fordlandia and Belterra between 1927 and 1945 coincided with political and economic dynamics that help us understand both the fact of Ford's decision to locate its plantations there and the welcome given to the company by regional and national politicians.

In the summer of 1928, the Ford-owned *Lake Ormoc* had set sail from Detroit to the latest Ford acquisition, more than two million acres of land in northern Brazil. Signaling the opening of a short but lethal chapter in the history of American imperial adventures, Ford's arrival on the Brazilian coast brought with it commitments to order and progress through which it would assert its capacity to remake the ecology, society, economy, and people of the region.[12] One of 199 decommissioned vessels Ford purchased from the U.S. military, the *Ormoc* took its name, imperially enough, from the lake community of Ormoc in the Leyte province of the Philippines.[13] Following the ship was a barge carrying provisions to house and care for the "American staff" for up to two years and to launch the plantation. In addition to a set of track and ties for laying its own rail, the company brought with it, "[a] filtration plant . . . dock construction equipment . . . medical supplies . . . power house engine room . . . saw mill equipment . . . road machinery . . . tugs and workboats."[14] The *Ormoc* was fitted to function for two years as an engineering and hospital base for the work of developing the plantation.[15]

In part because of their "preparations" for living separately from those recruited to the plantation, Ford managers who traveled on the *Ormoc* were discouraged from learning anything about the region in which they were going to be settling. Ford employees brought with them a sensibility that was not merely racist but also ignored actual history and projected a fantastical narrative of life in the jungle. In describing the launch of the plantation on the "concession of approximately 2,500,000 acres" Ford managers expressed early on the certainty that "in the beginning plenty of laborers can be recruited on the Tapajos and neighboring rivers. These men when well fed and cured of hook worm [*sic*], malaria etc. will make good laborers."[16] As at Richmond Hill, hookworm signified laziness: whether people agreed to Ford's rules for work and life on the plantations was in part understood as signaling whether or not they had been cured.[17]

Of course, Ford's settlers did not bring only the material goods they "needed" to survive in the Amazon; they also came with words, ideas, expectations, and law to back them up. Long before the *Ormoc* was packed, the Brazilian consular representative sent the company a letter reading, "I have in hand a cable gram from the minister of Agriculture of Brazil stating that hereafter American capitalists ready to cultivate rubber plantations in the state of Pará on the valley of the Amazon should pay no more taxes of import."[18] Through the Companhia Ford Industrial do Brasil the U. S. company would import machinery and supplies and export raw materials and rubber. From the outset the company anticipated the need to operate as far more than a rubber-producing firm. Reflecting the colonial sensibility that informed their content, the Articles of Association of the Joint Stock Company describe the company's interest in reshaping the social and economic life of the region it had just purchased. Buying and selling imported produce and "any articles of nature," building hospitals, docks, railroads, mills, and generally transacting business reflected Ford's intentions.[19]

Toward such ends Ford pursued two goals most emphatically in its negotiations with the governors of both the state and the country: the absolute suspension of taxes of import (which it fought to have extended only to itself) and the right to totally control access to the enormous piece of land it now owned. Ford lawyer, manager, and head of Fordlandia, Oz Ide, negotiated the incorporation of the Companhia. His description of the range of authority the company acquired from the government is staggering:

> In the first place we wanted a right to develop this land [though] I don't think we agreed to develop the whole thing but we needed all that land because we didn't want people close to us . . . In addition to that we wanted the right to build railroads, the right to establish banks and our own school system. . . . There would be a lot of Americans down there with their families and they would want their own school system there. We also wanted mineral rights so that if anything developed of value we could exploit it. It gave us the right to any power developed from the waterfalls and to dam up the river in way we needed to do. We had the right to build railroads and airfields and any other means of communication and also to navigate the waters.[20]

Ide's testimony reinforces the perspective that Ford's venture is much more aptly described as a colonial, rather than just a business, one. Schools and banks, in this scenario, were not designed for "the natives." What was on Ide's mind was caring for the arrivals from the United States, whom the company imagined would be settling in what one writer later called an "irradiating center of civilization."[21]

Strikingly, Ford's choice of location for its massive "concession" was not far from an earlier U.S. settlement. In the nearby town of Santarém, at the intersection of the Tapajos and Amazon Rivers, was a community of Southern expatriates from the United States. Part of an exodus of thousands of white and a handful of Black southerners who refused to live in the United States after the Confederate States had been defeated in war, these settlers chose Brazil in part because of their belief that the "plantation lifestyle" of the deep South could be recreated there. *Os confederados,* as they came to be known, built their most famous community south of São Paulo, naming it Americana. The Santarém community furnished at least one future Ford manager.[22]

Ford's plan to exploit the natural resources in the region and the labor of those who lived in it was part of an overall strategy by the United States to gain control from the British of the rubber market. As the overwhelming consumer of the world's rubber, U.S. industry had a particular stake in its price. Ford did not hesitate when he received, in 1923, a letter from H.F. Firestone inviting him to participate in a "conference of international significance." The immediate rationale for the meeting was the 1922 implementation of the British Rubber Restriction Act that had more than doubled the price of rubber on the world market. According to Firestone an increase of over $150 million should be expected as a result of the British move, an untenable situation for those, like Ford, who sought to promote "the use of automobiles and the development of highway transportation." Revealing of the globality of the most nation-based realities, low world prices for rubber would matter in a new way to those who consumed cars in the United States. The democratization of consumption of automobiles began to develop a link to, and to undergird calls for, low world market prices of the commodities from which they were built.[23]

Firestone's goal, of building support among industrialists and political leaders in the United States against British domination of the world rubber market, would be achieved through a campaign conducted via both national and international political channels. Though he sought support from French, Italian, and Dutch colonial companies against the legislation, Firestone mostly relied on appeals to U.S. national interests. His conference would be an opportunity for manufacturers to show the U.S. government that they were serious about investing in rubber production, the intent of which was to "make America independent." Firestone added that Senator Medill McCormick of Illinois, chairman of the Committee on Foreign Trade Relations, would be in attendance, signaling the readiness of the United States to back Firestone's plan.[24]

Ultimately, Firestone's appeal worked. Within five years American firms had acquired land for rubber production across the globe: Firestone launched the Liberian plantations for which it would become notorious, Goodyear began plantation agricultural experiments in both Sumatra and the Philippines, and Ford took possession of the Amazonian land, an area just smaller than the state of Connecticut.[25]

While Ford was said to be moving into a relatively uninhabited land, the region had long been a center of rubber production and had already experienced a spectacular boom and terrible bust that accounted for some of the enthusiasm with which government leaders greeted Ford's investments. From the late nineteenth century through the first decade of the twentieth, the Amazon region of Brazil supplied the overwhelming majority of the world's rubber.[26] Sophisticated networks enabled the extraction of rubber by *seringuieros* (tappers) who worked semi-autonomously and sold their rubber to traders, who in turn sold it to exporters. Historically, individual *seringuieros* did not control prices, but they could control, because of the characteristics and geography of the task, the pace and intensity of their work; *seringuieros* could and did work less or more depending on their own needs and interests. Of course, the work was deadly and difficult, but it did not have literal oversight, or as Ford would call it on its plantations, supervision. But as commercialization of rubber tapping deepened, with the first multinational incursions into the region, "violence and dislocation left large areas nearly depopulated and the Apiaca tribal culture in tatters."[27] A method of harvesting rubber for the world market that had always been accomplished through the pain and sweat of tappers became worse as even small vestiges of control were taken from people in the region.

The words of travel writer Mark Jacobson describe what came together in the Amazon:

> Geography may make history, but in places like the Amazon there is also the unforeseen convergence of botany and commerce. Europeans [in the Amazon] who watched Amerindians extracting a milky substance from tall, skinny jungle trees (*Hevea brasiliensis*), were aware of the springy properties of the Amazonian rubber plant from their earliest exploratory days. However, it was not until 1839, when Charles Goodyear discovered the process of vulcanization (which tempers the rubber so that it doesn't turn sticky in heat or brittle in cold), that the boom began in earnest. With the invention of the automobile in the 1880's and the subsequent demand for rubber tires, the fortunes to be made from the sap were so enormous that steel magnate Andrew Carnegie is supposed to have said, "I ought to have chosen rubber."[28]

The Amazon rubber boom brought what has been described as excess and grandiosity to the region as rubber barons competed to outperform one another in displays of their wealth and power. Increasing world desire and demand for Brazilian rubber had driven the rubber boom from the 1880s onward, bringing the world economy into areas of the Amazon region that decades later would be incorrectly re-narrated as untouched, remote, savage, primitive, and pre-modern. "I found a village and made it a modern city," said Amazonas Governor Eduardo Ribeiro. Jacobson wrote that, "Dreaming of an Oz-like empire in the jungle, Ribeiro presided over the electrification of Manaus's street lamps. He built a system of electrically powered trolley cars, the first in Brazil."[29] In a subsequent article for *Travel and Leisure* Jacobson described Manaus's opera house, completed in 1897, "The crown jewel of this rain-forest Xanadu ... Ribeiro's celebrated opera house, the remarkable *Teatro Amazonas.* The looming cupola (done in the yellow, green, and blue of the Brazilian flag) required 60,000 tiles, ordered from Alsace-Lorraine."[30]

By 1920 Manaus was seen as strange and fantastical, an example of colonial overreach in which the "untamed" jungle had demonstrated its determination and capacity to reabsorb the allegedly cosmopolitan slices that had been carved out of it. The imagined strangeness of the juxtapositions of high culture and primitive conditions laid the basis for representations of colonial absurdity in literary and filmic representations of Brazil from this period forward, most spectacularly in Werner Herzog's film *Fitzcarraldo.*

Ford believed it shared nothing in common with the rubber barons of the past or the (Catholic) decadence that attended their decorative proclivities. What Ford was after was not exploitation but development, not theft but investment. One manager wrote, "In ten years' time the Tapajos will be a principality within the state. Not a principality as in the old days with a happy rich and extravagant prince and slaved [*sic*] people." So certain was this Ford manager of his company's ability to make men he further described the Ford-controlled region as becoming, "A principality without a prince, whose people will be full of health, instructed, aware of their rights, happy with that happiness which incomparable scenery gives and having order without the necessity of an organized force."[31]

THE PAST IN THE FUTURE

In 1910 the price of rubber skyrocketed in response to intensifying industrial demand and market speculation. In the months of April and May, when rubber prices were reaching the exorbitant mark of three dollars per pound, "British investors alone incorporated 163 firms to exploit rubber trees, wild or planted, in 28 different countries."[32] From the viewpoint of tappers in the

Amazon the situation was tragic: just as prices on the world market reached their high point, their own capacity to meet demand was diminishing. By the mid-1920s, the once-booming Amazon was increasingly impoverished, a result of the massive subsidization of plantation rubber economies by the British Empire elsewhere. Tappers, many of whom migrated to the area during the boom, had fled the region, were trying to supplement their incomes with other kinds of work, or were working harder to earn less. Though rubber tapping was still the main source of income in the region, this fact now said more about the area's poverty than its prosperity. The historical specificity of this problem is critical, resulting as it did from the very world market that Ford, later, argued would solve it. In the case of the Amazon region, the poverty that Ford's managers explained in terms of racial failure and the absence of civilization was actually a product of the global economy from which the region had been excised over the previous decade.

Further, the established baseline of global misery in plantation agriculture also made a mockery of the high-wage bargain the five-dollar day had symbolized in the metropole. Ford management decided to pay a quarter, or slightly more than the prevailing wage in the Amazon, fearing that to do more would lead workers to "melt" back in the local terrain and economy after paydays. However, premium pay could hardly even be calculated in a region in which nonwage arrangements and reciprocal obligations often applied. Moreover, the premium was added to a standard wage in one of the world's most depressed regions, making the bargain quite different from that struck for a time in Detroit. Finally, the impoverishment of life in the region following the end of the rubber boom had made people less reliant on the market economy and more capable of sustaining themselves through fishing and planting food for use. Thus the 300 percent turnover rate early in the Ford plantation experiments—a number that mimicked that of Highland Park before the five-dollar day—reflected resourcefulness and self-determination in the context of what was already a crisis caused by global capitalist rubber production. Workers tried to maintain some connection to the wage economy, as well as to production for use, and therefore left to fish and farm seasonally, a reality treated as a problem by labor recruiters in so-called development projects in many imperial sites.[33]

Competing with Britain by using the same seeds—now in their originary environment— seemed sensible to the Ford managers who consulted no botanists in their decision to launch Fordlandia. The "triumph of plantation *hevea*" was recently characterized by historian John Tully as a central feature in the social-historical relationship of rubber to mass production and characterizes the early to mid-twentieth century geopolitical economy of rubber.[34] Seemingly, the time and place were right for Ford's project.

MAKING AMERICAN RUBBER, MAKING RUBBER AMERICAN, AND REMAKING MIXED-RACE BRAZIL

In 1919 Ford had established an industrial presence in Brazil through its assembly plant in São Paulo, and had begun to use this as a continental base for providing the steadily growing Latin American market with cars and tractors. The company thus viewed the Amazon as foreign but familiar. Ford had chosen Pará because its ecology was home to *heveas brasilis* with which the British had had enormous success in developing for plantation growth and expansion. (That Britain had illegally acquired *heveas* seeds at the height of Amazonian dominance of the world rubber market in an historic "seed snatch" from Brazil by a British imperial thief dressed as a botanist has been well documented.)[35] These were clearly factors in Ford's decision to launch its plantations in the Brazilian Amazon. But at least as important as each of these reasons was the company's belief in the racial improvability of its future workforce: Fordlandia was, even before its inception, a racial project. The possibility of recruiting and developing laborers of what Ford believed to be specific racialized types helped tip the scales in favor of Brazil, as compared to other regions with equally favorable climates and geographies. Carl LaRue, a botanist who scouted plantations for Ford, recommended Brazil because, although "labor is somewhat more expensive than in the East . . . labor is also more intelligent than the average labor in the East." LaRue spelled out a solution to the problem of cost, arguing that the use of machines on a modern plantation that Ford intended should offset any advantage that the plantations in "the East" might have.[36] LaRue also believed that the laborers whom Ford would recruit in Brazil were themselves capable of being modernized because of what he saw as their racial characteristics. LaRue's report claimed both racial and historical expertise:

> The dwellers of the Amazon Valley are of three main stocks: Portuguese, Indian and Negro . . . admixture has gone on so long that it is difficult to distinguish the different types. The mixture is not a particularly good one from a racial standpoint but it is by no means a bad one . . . the fate of these people is more tragic because they are not possessed of the stolidity of the

orientals, but have enough of the white race in them to suffer keenly and long intensely for the better things. As it is, their condition is worse than that of any of the coolies in the East, far worse even than that of the average slave in the old days.[37]

Such a hopeful view differed from that expressed by LaRue in a 1924 report that had urged "A million Chinese [workers] in the rubber sections of Brazil would be godsend to that country."[38]

That "race-mixing" could imply improvement, that is, whitening, was a variation on the racism—the literal belief in white supremacy—practiced at that moment in the United States and South Africa.[39] It reflected neither the "one drop rule" that policed race in the United States, nor the then slightly less draconian model in South Africa, where so-called "mixed-race" people were beginning to be acknowledged, even as whites believed "race-mixing" would lead to the "degradation" of those whites who participated in it. The different expressions of white supremacy that Ford embraced in different social contexts did not challenge the company's overriding commitment to racial hierarchies. Indeed the idea that the company believed it could tap the desire for consumer goods they believed flowed in the veins of "Amazonian people" is revealing of Ford's very particular ideology of exploitation. As the story of Fordlandia reveals, such thinking was essential to the company's approach to its workforce: LaRue's final recommendation to the company concluded that extending "help" to the destitute of the region and establishing "profitability" were compatible goals.[40]

On the other hand, the project of racially improving people it described as being the products of "admixtures" left Ford management as leery of using indigenous labor as Herbert Hoover had been in his celebrated development of gold mines in Australia. As secretary of commerce and then president of the United States in the 1920s Hoover was instrumental in forwarding schemes for U. S.-controlled rubber production. In his earlier career as a mine engineer and manager, Hoover zealously catalogued subgroups of Australian aboriginal people before rejecting all of them for mine labor, dismissing them as "n******." (Avoiding "n*****" labor was also one reason Ford management gave for preferring Brazil over Liberia.) Ford managers in Brazil evaluated "tribal" labor in the region and accepted local knowledge from an Oxford-trained Brazilian expert who held that Indians in the region were "not tamed" and concluded that "we should not have any."[41] Labor came from those whom Ford attracted from other parts of Brazil, from West Indian workers in the country on construction projects, and from mixed-race workers who had migrated earlier to the rubber region and remained there, often intermarrying with indigenous people. These local, mixed-race people—*cabaclos*—could have been relied on by Ford managers as "native naturalists" who possessed priceless expertise in rubber cultivation. But this was explicitly rejected by Ford managers who saw them as the objects of improvement rather than as sources of knowledge.[42]

Ford's expansion into the Amazon occurred alongside a social debate that was underway in Brazil about the relationship between scientific management and social progress. In her examination of this process in São Paulo Barbara Weinstein demonstrates how this debate had been developing, "percolating among industrialists, engineers, social hygienists and educators in São Paulo since the 1920s," and insists that it is necessary to understand elite practices as strategies of social control. "By identifying with new currents in rational organization and scientific management," she writes, "these industrialists, engineers, and educators claimed for themselves the professional authority and technical expertise necessary to modernize Brazilian society."[43] These were professionals who, as "advocates of Fordism, while still regarding the factory as the key location for change, believed that the transformation of the workplace required attention to aspects of industrial life beyond the production process."[44]

Ford's arrival in the north could not have been better timed from the point of view of these reformers. As modernizers who seemed to have technology and science on their side, Ford's "American staff" was welcomed by Brazilian elites who hoped to use the company's commitments to menmaking to further their own goals and to address the wreckage in the countryside caused by the changing rubber market. The experiment in the Amazon reveals the inner workings of the corporation, and the connection between the economic and social, the natural and the global, realms it sought to dominate.

Only upon its late fall arrival at the mouth of the Tapajos River did the Detroit crew discover that neither the *Ormoc* nor the barge that followed it could make it upriver, the water being at its seasonal low. Unwilling to be stopped, the crew proceeded to have the entire cargo loaded to smaller boats and carried upriver to the site of the plantation. One writer said, "[I] was told by actual eyewitnesses that the unloading of that cargo would have provided material for a super Charlie Chaplin film."[45] Before operations were even underway Ide quit as the first manager of Fordlandia; he had to be replaced, at Henry Ford's insistence by a "company man" in the first instance, not necessarily someone trained in agriculture or possessing any local or regional knowledge. This compulsion of Ford's absolutely reflects how forceful the company would be in his implementation of "the one best way," even in a natural and social environment with which it was completely unfamiliar. Site selection, which Ide had done through drawing a box on a map with no consideration for the topography of the concession, had resulted in the plantation being placed on hilly terrain particularly poorly suited to rubber cultivation. That the nearest city of any size was a hundred miles away by boat had not seemed to bother him either.

As part of its agreement with the state government in Pará, the company was required to plant at least a thousand trees within one month of the start of the operations. Ide had arranged to have these rubber seedlings planted along the river so that production would be underway before the construction of the plantation began. Upon arrival the crew was informed that the seedlings had actually been planted in the state of Amazonas, not in Pará where Ford had been given permission to cultivate rubber. Local legislation prevented the transport of the trees from one state to the next. Although they tried to reverse this decision in court, the company failed to secure release of the trees.[46]

So they began again. Ide was replaced, again through the urging of Henry Ford, whose hands-on attention bespoke the symbolic import as well as the economic potential of the experiment, by Einard Oxholm. Though as captain of the *Lake Ormoc* Oxholm knew literally nothing about growing rubber, Ford's arrogant belief that "anyone could learn anything" led to his being put in charge of Fordlandia. Oxholm remained at Fordlandia until the end of 1929; his tenure there reflected the swagger of a company intent on absolutely conquering the very ecology that had nurtured the trees it was there to exploit. Ford's willful ignorance in the face of decades of local knowledge of rubber production, held by the indigenous people whom Ford saw as untamed racial others, proved fully disabling. The land that Ford had selected proved completely unsuited to mono-crop plantation. Its hilliness limited mechanization; even what the company knew how to do, running sawmills, floundered in the face of hardwood species that "dulled Yankee saw blades."[47]

By its very structure, plantation agriculture requires a rejection of time-tested knowledge of ecological cultivation and care. Mass production of nature, agri-business as it has come to be called, relies almost entirely on the transformation of ecologies. The rainforest, which had always been necessary to the growth of rubber, was treated by Ford as a problem: "The first obstacle that confronted [us] was the almost impenetrable tropical jungle. But it had to be cleared and for every 40 acres a clearing gang of 20 native workers was organized." As early as summer 1929, 1,500 acres of rainforest had been slashed and burned and planted with rubber saplings. By 1930 3,000 acres were cleared and the infrastructure of the plantation—administrative offices, barracks, a clinic, sewerage and water pipes, railroads, and a sawmill—had been constructed.[48]

It was the rainforest, and the ecosystem that it represented, that enabled the extraordinary growth of latex-producing *heveas brasilis* trees and led to the rubber boom in the Amazon. Because of its refusal to learn this, one of the most significant problems Ford created for itself was blight. Grown in their natural environment rubber trees are protected from the spread of fungus by the shelter of other plant life and the distance between trees. Planting rubber saplings on barren land, in straight rows separated only by a few feet, almost necessarily guarantees the spread of disease from tree to tree. Plantations in the British and French empires dealt with this self-imposed problem through innovations in hybridization and, ultimately, pesticides. Ford, still intent on using the once highly reliable *heveas brasilis* tree, did not learn its lesson until the mid-1930s.[49] It was not until late 1933 that Ford hired its first botanist. Ford historians Mira Wilkins and Frank Hill wrote:

> If [Fordlandia] was a "green hell" for its human inhabitants, it was quite as infernal a habitat for the Hevea. This tree was subject to root diseases, leaf maladies, fruit and flower blights, injuries caused by phanerogamic plants, brown bats, abnormal nodule structure, cortex nodules, abnormal exudations of rubber pad, chlorosis of the leaves, and numerous other hazards.[50]

The initial assumption, that local people would be as amicable to transformation and improvement as the ecosystem, proved equally mistaken. By the mid-1930s the company reported that 3,000 people were employed by Ford.[51] Most of those were engaged in the construction of the physical infrastructure of Fordlandia, which by the early 1930s was sprawling and continued to grow. Work on the construction of barracks, sawmills, roads, and a cafeteria distracted the company from the fact that its primary concern was the cultivation of rubber and, even beyond that, the production of tires. One manager wrote that "a great amount of work has been done . . . and a great deal of money spent [but] very little has been done along the lines of what we came here to do, namely to plant rubber."[52] For all its "progress" the disarray and destruction brought by Ford in at least the initial stages of the project were startling to both American and Brazilian observers, many of whom thought the word Ford was synonymous with efficiency. One troubleshooter sent by the company said, "There is a complete lack of organization at the property . . . Waste is terrible . . . At present it is like dropping money into a sewer." As early as 1930 LaRue was reporting to Henry Ford with some understatement: "Things have not gone forward so well as they should have."[53]

Convincing enough people to live and work on the plantation was the largest challenge Ford faced, and one they were never able to overcome at Fordlandia. The company clearly thought its plan—of creating a waged labor force of single men who slept in barracks, punched time clocks [!], and worked eleven-hour shifts—was not only agreeable but generous in contrast to the quasi-feudal social arrangements on other plantations. The company's particular vision of the men whom they sought to recruit to work on the plantation contributed to the "urgent" need to develop the built environment. Because workers were seen as a threat to the American managers, the structures—hospital, barracks, cafeteria, and mill—increasingly became part of the method of disciplining and modifying the behavior of those who lived at Fordlandia.[54] These places would literally require changed behavior and would also become spaces in which ideas about what constituted social existence were displayed and made manifest.

At Fordlandia workers were paid in money and not company scrip, and thus were not tied as directly by debt to the plantation as Ford workers in Inkster were to the company. However, they still were required to work off the costs of their own transportation to the plantation and to pay for their own food, hammocks, and tools.[55] Despite the company's stated fears that they might at any minute be swamped by workers seeking an easy life, it is evident that Ford was never able to keep people on the plantation. Through November and December, 1,930 more people were fired each week than were hired. In one week 218 were fired while just 42 were hired; another week 188 were fired while 87 were brought on. Though in other weeks the numbers were more well-balanced, those fired outpaced those hired for more than one year.[56]

The company's own racism left little room for it to transcend the sharp limits on its ability to create Ford workers out of the people living in the region and, particularly, on its capacity to get them to stay at Fordlandia. Acting on the deep connection between knowing race and managing workers developed in the United States, Ford managers continued to rank the people they encountered in degrees of "savagery" and "tameness." From a tour of villages he had been sent to inspect, one labor recruiter sent a telegram that read, "Even if they were tame they are lazy and undisciplined." The company replied, "Suggest we only take 100 with the distinct understanding that they are subject to discipline or they will be of no value, they must guarantee to do steady work every day or they would be without value and if they cannot talk Portuguese we might be better off without them."[57] Every colonial administration has its own idea of what it means to "tame savages." In Ford's case the measurement was clearly capitalist work discipline. A "tame" worker wore shoes, lived on the plantation, returned to work the day after being paid, and worked for eleven hours, through the heat of the day. The connection of capitalist production and work discipline, so well developed classically by E. P. Thompson, and ethnically, racially, and regionally inflected in the U. S. histories of Herbert Gutman and Mark Smith, here found another telling variation in which timed agricultural work was sought.[58]

Ford managers projected white supremacist fantasies onto the bodies of the people among whom they now lived. The Americans at Fordlandia seemed to be in a constant state of fear of the tropics and saw threats emanating from both the people and the ecology. This sensibility mirrored the Brazilian eugenicist movement, whose major modernizing projects in the 1920s and 1930s focused on sanitation and disease. Upon arrival at Fordlandia each worker was given a medical inspection. Those with malaria or hookworm were sometimes hospitalized, sometimes turned away, though seemingly never immediately hired. Upon being hired new workers were then photographed for company records. The structured role of the medical department thus became almost immediately integral to the shaping of the workforce, again revealing the link between racist civilizing missions and capitalist labor imperatives, and reflecting a long-standing practice of using the clinic in the control of workers in both colonial and noncolonial contexts.[59] One medical officer at Fordlandia described the medical efficiency of their clinic to his colleagues back home: "By insisting that all sick men go to hospital . . . and by discharging certain men who were just lazy we have been able to practically abolish the former very large list of absentees from work." Increasingly, doctors played a significant role in the management of workers on the plantation; the hospital was the place where sick workers were distinguished from the "just lazy" ones; the latter were fired.[60]

Ford's commitment to its own ideas about how work should be organized and how workers should be managed, learned over decades in its auto factories in Detroit, made little sense in rubber production. Ford managers did not recognize the fact that their techniques had evolved dialectically through the years in which workers had gradually been trained to accept the imperatives that attended the assembly line or at least to not actively resist those imperatives. Managers believed that if they could impose their form of managerial discipline on rubber tappers then plantation production would follow. The less appropriate their ideas were to the task, the more tenaciously the company held to them.

In an exchange of letters with steam whistle manufacturers a manager expressed his concern that the company had not yet found a whistle that could withstand a tropical climate and that was loud enough to allow workers on all sides of the plantation to hear it. The company had scheduled the whistles at 5:30, 6:00, 6:30, 7:00, 11:00, 11:30 a.m.; noon; 3:30, 4:00, 4:30, 5:00, 5:30. But what use, they fretted, is all this precision if no one can hear the whistle? And what good is punching time cards if time is not uniformly understood? As one manager put it, "Owing to the fact that our daily labor are punching time cards it is imperative that time signals be controlled. Otherwise the hours of operation are not uniform throughout the plantation."[61]

Indeed, management thought electric service would be advisable throughout the plantation in order to accommodate time clocks and bells "similar to those in the factory."[62] Electricity, of course, would enable other changes in the lives of those who lived on the plantation. Electricity would make possible, for example, the showing of company-made films to workers. Thus both the intent and the capacity of the company to use consumer forms in its transformation of its workers followed the imperatives of production. At every turn not only the development of loyal and disciplined workers but also the specific transformation of highly suspect and even feared mixed-race workers was the goal.

The company's understanding of the "improvability" of the *cabaclos,* though based on LaRue's reconnaissance, itself drew on the contemporary practices of Brazilian social scientists and, increasingly, politicians and bureaucrats. Commitments to both white supremacy and racial improvement in the interwar years are brilliantly dissected in Jorge Amado's work of fiction *Tent of Miracles,* and Jerry Davila's deeply researched *Diploma of Whiteness.* Both works remind us that race-thinking did not arrive in Brazil with Ford; Davila's focus on the place of educational policy, especially during the regime of Getulio Vargas, in furthering cultural practices and social policies designed to whiten underclass Brazilians, engages the multiple conversations taking place among planners and ideologues of all kinds before and during the period of the *Estado Novo* beginning in 1937. Thus Ford's conviction that those who were "really worse off than slaves" were salvageable precisely because of their "mixed-race" status brought an imperial dimension to a set of processes that were also already local. In Brazil as in the United States white managerialism would complement rather than challenge scientific management as a hallmark of modernity.[63]

As broad and growing support in Brazil for initiatives geared to racial and national improvement in many ways characterized the period coinciding with Ford's projects in Pará, so too did an intense focus on efficiency as an essential plank of modernity and progress. As in other places in this book, white was increasingly becoming the color of management and of modernity in Brazil, where it profited from associations with progressive efficiency. Such realities smoothed the welcome of Ford by state and federal governors and helped the company to win broad autonomy over huge "Ford-lands" from a state increasingly organized around nationalist appeals to national development. Ford managers' image of themselves as possessors of racial knowledge emboldened the company to persist in the Amazon amidst multiple agricultural and managerial disasters.[64]

WHITE MANAGERIALISM RESISTED AND RETOOLED

A 1930 strike revealed the depth of disgust workers felt toward the highly controlled living arrangements on the plantation. On December 22 management announced to workers who had gathered for the evening meal that the structure of food service had been changed. Rather than having food served at tables the men would now line up, cafeteria-style. This message was delivered by a supervisor who had earned a reputation among workers as being especially harsh and unfair. When workers were informed of the new plan they responded by saying they "were not dogs." When they confronted managers about the new policy they were told that "the Company now and then put new rules into effect but it was always for the betterment of the workers." According to a Brazilian foreman, Manoel Caetano, the manager's comments were "Just as putting a match to gasoline." Not satisfied with this so-called betterment program the workers immediately banded together. The managers fled by boat.[65]

When managers returned to Fordlandia they discovered that a good portion of the company's property had been damaged or destroyed. "Most of the time clocks were completely demolished," R. D. Chatfield wrote, fixing on a revealing detail. Also targeted for destruction were the cafeteria, the time card racks, and all the trucks. Managers received a list of demands from the workers. They included the dismissal of a particularly harsh manager, as well as that of the head of the Service Department, Victor Gill, both charged with being arbitrary in relating to workers. Strikers also demanded that men be allowed free access to the dock; that men be allowed to live where they chose; that the rule prohibiting the consumption of alcohol be eliminated; that they be allowed to choose their own recreational spaces and activities; and that no one should be dismissed without being given another chance.[66] What the demands reveal about how life on the plantation was ordered reflects the accumulated practices of Ford, in its Americanization programs at Highland Park, in its strictures regarding consumption at Inkster, and in its repressive system of rules in the Rouge plant.

The stakes of the strike ensured dramatic soul-searching by management. As the labor geographer Don Mitchell has so eloquently paraphrased Marx, "labor makes it own geographies, but not under conditions of its own choosing . . . As long as labor continues to take hold of geographies and continually transforms them in the name of a justice that, while sensitive to 'the local' is also universal in outlook, the geography of capitalism will always be contested." Ford managers saw no justice in the strike, but plenty of threat at the local and global scales.[67]

Even as managers argued about how to make sense of the strike, they shared a paternalistic belief that they knew better than the workers what was good for them. One felt that while the change in the food service plan may have been "the straw that broke the camel's back," it was "no doubt communism, coupled with ignorance," that caused the riot. Another believed that it was the paying of wages in cash rather than company scrip that led workers to push for more, arguing that Ford's "kind treatment of them may be based on weakness." A third felt that the men "naturally" resented the placing of restrictions on their liberties, though "such rules are only intended for the good of their own health." Another explained that it seemed "apparent" that some men could become "Bolshevistic" in their general attitude toward the company and could "quite easily forget that we were providing them with the best living conditions . . . they had known in all their days."[68] The political and ideological explanations of the strike and its attendant violence suggest that Ford believed that at least some of its workers were already "modern," even though the racist fantasies simultaneously held by managers contradicted this. That is, the strike was not blamed simply on savagery, ignorance, and lack of capacity for civility, but on Bolshevism and communism, decidedly modern ideologies. In response to the strike the company called in the Brazilian military, which arrested more than thirty "ringleaders." Following the strike the company agreed to a police proposal to make workers rather than management into Fordlandia's foreigners by creating "passports" for all workers containing their fingerprints and previous police records, a vivid illustration of Ford's willingness to rely on the Brazilian state even as it had a colonial understanding of Fordlandia as its own possession.[69]

Living and working conditions on the plantation changed little as a result of the strike. Not surprisingly, the company continued to have trouble recruiting and retaining a viable workforce. For the next five years, no rubber was exported, few seedlings survived, and what work was done centered on the creation of the "village" for the American staff. In 1934, after clearing 8,000 acres of rainforest, Ford admitted defeat at Fordlandia. Making a radical shift in strategy, the company abandoned virtually the entire plantation, save what it would use for research purposes, and bought more than 700,000 acres of land 80 miles away, creating Belterra. The new plantation promised better growing conditions, easier access to waterways and roads, and the infrastructure that would enable new forms of management.[70]

MEN-MAKING AS FAMILY-MAKING

The move to Belterra coincided with another shift in policy as management decided it would allow some men to bring their families to live on the plantation and would build housing for them. Fantastic fears that the plantation would be overrun by poor women and their children who would require care but could not work had driven past policy. At Fordlandia the company had calculated that "for the opening work it will probably be best to take unmarried men if they can be secured in sufficient numbers. Such men can be housed in primitive quarters and will not need much space . . . whereas the introduction of wives and families means a certain complication in the camp."[71]

But as fewer and fewer men were willing to uproot themselves from communities and families, as more and more single men left after working on the plantation for periods of time, and as militant collective resistance appeared, the company changed its strategy. One manager cabled his field recruiter, "Jovita find out quietly how much it would cost to bring 40–60–70 families . . . labor is so scarce here that we will have to figure on importing families and paying their way stop do this quietly."[72] By this time, although "no likely looking prospect [was] turned away," Ford was still failing to sustain the workforce it needed. Company strategy displayed supreme confidence in its own power despite consistent failure, and managers continued to view those who refused to conform to Ford's many rules as savages. Having succeeded in creating neither a "loyal" nor a "disciplined" workforce, Ford set its sights on the workers of the future: children.[73]

BREEDING WORKERS AT BELTERRA

In a letter to Detroit a manager at Belterra described the "youngsters who are growing up on the plantations . . . who most assuredly are our best prospects for future employees." Again, the metaphoric connection between workers and the natural world was made clear, with new laborers growing up alongside seedlings. Photos of a visit by President Getulio Vargas to the plantation show smiling children waving Brazilian flags (which of course now carried the slogan *Order and Progress*). That these watchwords could also have been Ford's reflects the basis on which a nationalizing, and nationalistic, government and a colonizing corporation could coexist. However, Vargas's urging of recognition of unions, albeit state-influenced ones, at Ford ultimately introduced tensions.[74]

If Fordlandia's project focused mostly on experimentation with *heveas brasilis,* Belterra became the new site for fuller experimentation with people, along lines set out at Highland Park, Inkster, and Richmond Hill. Virtually every activity on the plantation carried within it the potential for Fordist ideas about nationalism, thrift, science, and progress to be shaped into behavior-modifying campaigns. With the introduction of family living at Belterra came the imposition of a multitude of requirements insisted upon by management. School was compulsory for adults—"The night shift [at school] is reserved for adults and the one who refuses—goodbye"—just as for children. Required uniforms were provided partly by the company: "boys wore outfits similar to Boy Scouts and girls neat white pleated skirts and white blouses." Working from a textbook called *Moral Education: My Little Friends* children studied Portuguese, geography, Brazilian history, arithmetic, and geometry.[75] Living in what was described by one writer as a "children's paradise," residents of Belterra learned American folk dancing, a continuing obsession of Henry

Ford's, and were entertained by Ford-made motion pictures. The company was so convinced of the success of the latter practice that Edsel Ford proposed making films about the plantations and then showing them at points along the Amazon and northern Brazilian coast.

From their beginning in the late 1920s until 1940 no significant amount of rubber was exported from the plantations to Detroit for use in tire production. Despite Ford's poor production record the plantations began to receive a tremendous amount of attention in the early 1940s because of the changed global political situation. The U.S. state, beginning to worry that access to rubber was increasingly under threat, popularized arguments made two decades previously by Firestone, Hoover, and others that U.S. industry must control its own sources of rubber. Almost overnight newspapers and magazines started running features on Henry Ford's Amazon ventures. The *Detroit Times* ran a series of articles on Ford and Brazilian rubber, republished as a small booklet in support of the war effort. *Harpers, Cosmopolitan,* and *Business Week* all ran features on the plantations in 1944. The caption under a *Business Week* photo of a time clock reprised after years of failure the article of faith that white managerialism would transform racialized workers: "And time clocks, incongruous devices in the customarily indolent atmosphere of a steaming Amazon jungle—measure the workers' 11 hour days."[76]

In 1941 the company itself published a promotional pamphlet. "The Ford Rubber Plantations" told the story of the lucky Brazilian people who were being civilized through the generosity and vision of Ford. Describing both the natural and built environments at Fordlandia and Belterra, the pamphlet seems designed to lure potential managers and scientists as well as investment by the United States. The little pamphlet says that its purpose is to "give you some idea of the problems that are involved in this vast project and of the methods by which they are being brought to successful conclusion," and reminds the reader that "The Ford Rubber Plantations of Brazil represent but one of many Ford Motor Company projects for the scientific development and utilization of natural resources . . . projects that in no small measure make possible the building of finer and finer cars at low prices within the reach of more and more people."[77]

The spectre of "waste" land and the "jungle" feature prominently in the story of "natives" being brought into the fold of modernity:

> Paved roads, cement walks, comfortable homes, electric lights, telephones—this might be any midwestern town. But it is Belterra, buried deep in the jungle

> of Brazil . . . Yes, There is even a golf course—a sporty 18 holes—at Fordlandia. Beautiful clubhouse, tropical foliage—and 700 miles from civilization.[78]

One journalist was moved to note the participation of the schoolchildren of the plantations in the creation of "Latin-Saxonian unity." Now presumably no longer to be seen as Indian or *cabaclos* but as "Latins," Ford's rubber workers were fighting the good fight, their children described by one journalist as, "Undismayed by isolation these boys and girls are going ahead, playing their part in a great movement that is . . . not only setting an example for satisfied workmen and helping to unify the Western Hemisphere by producing a necessary product for the Americas in the Americas."[79]

In 1941 the company estimated that its plantations "would produce from 30 to 40 million pounds of high quality rubber during the next ten years . . . and thereafter a minimum of 10,000,000 pounds per year." But in 1946 the company left Brazil more abruptly than it had arrived, departing virtually overnight. With the introduction of synthetic rubber in the United States Ford had found a new solution to their production worries. Ford sold the plantations to the Brazilian government for $250,000, a startlingly small fraction of the $20 million it had poured into the project.

"Taming savages" or raising children to be workers were not unlike what Ford did in Inkster and at the Rouge plant. Social control goes with the territory of making people do alienating wage labor. Race proved to be a durable, flexible, and hierarchical language through which discipline and efficiency could be established and legitimized. Recognizing that both social control and nationalization have relied on and promoted racial categorization allows us to begin to think differently about the staying power of racist practice even when laws change. At Ford, "scientific" evaluation was embedded in the quest for constant improvement, and this commitment to improvement was highly racialized.

The line that separates racial from national characteristics in racist thought moves constantly, determined by geography, region, behavior, and timing and not by scientific understandings. In Brazil, Ford managers once felt "it may prove advantageous to hire Chinese laborers, undoubtedly the best of all oriental workmen . . . .as there are many worthless fellows among ordinary Brazilian laborers."[80] Yet in Detroit, Chinese laborers were never considered even as the importation of workers was always on managers' minds—and certainly not as Ford managers supported the political movement that fought for full and continued restriction of Asian migration in

1924. That the overarching goals of production and improvement of men through work could be pursued through such contradictory practices reveals the depth of fantasy that racism requires, the enormous power of those who control wealth to control ideas, and the limits set by national histories and peculiarities on how, but not whether, Ford could continually attempt to manage race.

Insofar as it produced rubber, the short, unhappy history of Ford in rural Brazil continually teetered between failure and farce. As a laboratory for making men, and later families, it was scarcely any more effectual. But as a laboratory for informal, U.S. corporate empire-building, it cannot be written off so easily: the same national narcissism that compromised company attempts to understand the ecology and people of the region would also provide the terms through which Ford would try to categorize those people as uncivilized, malleable racial material that needed, above all, to be managed. Moreover, even during a period of nationalist and populist authoritarian rule in Brazil, Ford had confidence in building its own "land" there, eliciting the aid of local authorities (and, perhaps, *os confederados*) without having to make constant appeals for the backing of the guns of U.S. empire so frequently heard in other parts of Latin America. The projects of racial improvement that it shared with national elites, plus the wealth and promise Ford brought to rural areas devastated by the world market it extolled, could provide a sense that there would be time to develop control over the things it thought consequential: the clock, the school, the clinic and, above all, the pace of labor.

Thus the reformist improvement ethos in Brazil may be described as Fordist.[81] Ford's image inside and outside the United States and its concrete activity in the world ensure as much. However, with social reform as with labor discipline, Fordism named no single system. The distinct mixture of a Brazilian nationalist imaginary that prized "whitening" of the population and that moved toward the embrace of multiracialism as an ideal was as unfamiliar to Ford management as was growing rubber in the rainforest. There could be no set transnational hierarchy on which white supremacy was premised. Instead white managerialism was itself the premise and the promise of the system. Such claims emboldened Ford to promote its "one best way" in varied settings where it sometimes failed spectacularly.[82]

In significant ways differences between Brazil and the United States represent opposite sides of the same racial and political-economic coin. At Fordlandia and Belterra Ford sought to run a productive plantation on its factory model and brought to Brazil ideas about race and reform that it had evolved in the United States. Racist expectations and projected imperial fantasies led to much speculation about the impossibility of Ford creating in the Amazon what it had in the United States. To borrow an idea from the great historian W. E. B. Du Bois, the plantations did fail but not in the ways they were expected to.[83] The failure did not result from the "unreadiness" of local people for modernity or their inability to "adapt" to Fordist behavioral standards. Nor was the failure in any simple way a result of colonial overreach and hubris. The plantations failed for the same reasons that Ford's Sociological Department failed in the United States: the so-called bargain—made in Brazil on the cheap—was not what people desired. Working for Ford did not bring progress or security or self-determination to Brazilian workers any more than it did to those in Highland Park, Dearborn, or Inkster. The promise of improvement through "race development" did not address the problems people in the region actually confronted, nor did it even name them correctly. Despite its centrality to the stated goals of Ford management and of many Brazilian elites, whitening was not the route to the future Ford's plantation workers in Brazil sought.

FIGURE 10. Black South Africans, racially excluded from the town of Port Elizabeth where white workers lived, built a squatter community out of the company's discarded packing crates such as those pictured here being unloaded in India. KwaFord—Zulu for "place of Ford"—is to this day one of the largest districts in the Port Elizabeth metro area. Courtesy Framepool.

FIVE

"Work in the Factory Itself"

FORDISM, SOUTH AFRICANISM, AND POOR WHITE REFORM

The [Carnegie] Corporation funded an investigation by social scientists who drove through southern South Africa in a Model T Ford to determine the extent of white poverty.

"CARNEGIE IN SOUTH AFRICA," CARNEGIE CORPORATION ORAL HISTORY PROJECT.[1]

BY THE EARLY 1980S THE MOVEMENT in solidarity with the struggle against apartheid had become global. In the United States a tireless campaign by trade unionists, students, faith-based organizations, and others seeking to push state institutions to divest all pension money from firms doing business in South Africa came to a head. In the state of Michigan, Ford was at the center of this fight. In 1977 Ford had signed on to the Sullivan Principles, a set of accommodationist commitments that international firms pledged to support in their South African workplaces. As signatories to the Principles, firms promised to desegregate their workplaces, cafeterias, and washrooms—reforms illegal in South Africa. The Sullivan Principles were widely condemned by activists who recognized that those companies who signed on were the very same ones who were being pressured to fully divest their South African holdings but had no interest in doing so; activists rightly saw the Sullivan approach as a way for corporations to avoid meeting the demands for full divestment put forward by the anti-apartheid movement in South Africa. In 1983, John Woodford, a former employee of Ford's Public Relations Department, wrote a letter to the company in which he expressed solidarity with the divestment proposal and the broader struggle by Black workers in South Africa; Woodford targeted all pro-apartheid employers but singled out Ford. In his sweeping condemnation of the Sullivan plan Woodford wrote, "The Sullivan Principles were not designed to lessen apartheid. Rather, the Principles were plainly concocted to deceive public opinion and deflect criticisms of the corporations' continued export of capital from the U.S. to South Africa." Further, he wrote, "Every major Black American religious, labour, political, civil rights and educational organization has officially rejected the Sullivan Principles as an instrument to further the brutal, racist apartheid system."[2] Woodford's targeting of Ford, though connected to his status as a former employee, also reflected a much broader sentiment across the state, the United States, and even the world: Ford had become one of the most conspicuous examples of U.S. firms extracting profits from workers in apartheid South Africa.

The company's long history in South Africa contributed to this dynamic. The first Ford sold outside of North America was bought by Arthur Youldon of Johannesburg in 1903. Model N's and Model T's were sold in South Africa by several dealers based in Natal, Pretoria, and Port Elizabeth, with H.G. Holmes appointed as the company's South Africa agent by Ford of Canada in 1913. It was Holmes who, with future Ford South Africa president Axel Stockelbach, traveled, significantly, to Canada rather than to Detroit to broker the deal that would launch the first Ford assembly plant in Port Elizabeth. Though early automobility was an activity enjoyed by only a small handful of elites, by 1925 Port Elizabeth had become known as the Detroit of South Africa, Ford having steadily increased the assembly, sale, and export of cars, trucks, and tractors to and from the Eastern Cape city: in his first year running the South African operation Stockelbach did business worth $2,578,556, about $36 million in today's dollars.[3]

Ford increased its investment in its Port Elizabeth operations at critical junctures in South Africa's history. In 1948, just as apartheid became the law of the land, Ford nearly doubled its investment in car production in Port Elizabeth. Advertisements in the South African press boasted, "This new factory will be one of the largest of its kind in the Union when completed. It is symbolical of the new era of industrial expansion and prosperity that beckons South Africa . . . it is the function of industry to create the prosperity . . . therein lies the promise of the future and the rich rewards of industrial progress that awaits South Africa."[4] Prime Minister Jan Smuts bragged proudly to his mother about this new, expanded Ford factory: "Just think! On 1 October I am to open the Ford Factory at Port Elizabeth and they will make me a gift of the first Ford made in South Africa."[5]

The revolutionary playwright Athol Fugard memorialized the 1964 opening of Ford's third plant in Port Elizabeth that brought Henry Ford II to South Africa. With his colleagues John Kani and Winston Ntshona (who had worked in the Port Elizabeth Ford plant) Fugard brilliantly captured the meaning of Ford's visit to the PE plant in the play *Sizwe Bansi Is Dead.* The opening scene depicts a Ford worker translating for the English-speaking "Baas" as the latter describes the impending visit from Ford, the "grandfather Baas":

> Tell them Mr. Ford is the Big Baas. He owns the plant and everything in it. He owns everything in this building which means you as well . . . tell the boys that when Mr. Henry Ford comes into this plant I want them all to look happy. We will slow down the speed of the line so they can sing and smile while they are working . . . they must try to impress Mr. Henry Ford that they are better than those monkeys in his own country, those n****** in Harlem who know nothing but strike, strike.

Later, back on the assembly line, Ford's visit is announced by workers who see through the window the arrival of three long black Ford Galaxies, followed by "The General Superintendent, Line Supervisor, General Foreman, Manager, Senior Manager, Managing Director . . . the bloody lot."[6]

Fugard's tale of the everyday violence and indignity that characterized life for South African workers under apartheid drew heavily on the history of Port Elizabeth. *Sizwe Bansi Is Dead* captured the bureaucratic viciousness of rule that was race and class based, experienced by workers in and out of the workplace. White managerialism deepened under apartheid and is particularly visible in the industrial expansion of Port Elizabeth. Fugard and his comrades John Kani and Winston Ntshona who "devised" *Sizwe Bansi* knew that choosing Ford to represent white managerialism more broadly matched how inseparable Ford was from the geographic and political structure of apartheid in that industrial city. Indeed, Henry Ford II's actual 1964 visit to the Port Elizabeth plant coincided with the now infamous Rivonia Trial in which Nelson Mandela, Govan Mbeki, Walter Sisulu, and seven other leaders of the African National Congress were sentenced to lives of hard labor in prison.

This chapter examines the two and a half decades before the apartheid curtain fell in 1948, when white managerialism was promoted first by erecting color bars to prop up and create advantages for white workers. Ford was the first U.S. firm to assemble cars in South Africa, beginning in 1923, and followed by General Motors a couple of years later. The company's reputation for "men-making" was remarked upon early in Ford's tenure in the Eastern Cape. In 1924, a columnist in the South African *Eastern Province Herald* wrote that "the vast industrial works of Henry Ford are not only or chiefly for the output of vehicles demanded in every part of the world, they are mainly for the transformation of human detritus into beings of real economic and social value." The proof for the author lay in Dearborn, Michigan, where "Ford finds employment for a number of men below standard who, but for his combined philanthropy and business acumen, would be on humanity's scrap heap."[7] As a symbol of man-making, industrial growth, mass consumption, and white managerialism, Ford was indeed welcomed in the "other USA."[8]

Nonetheless, there is a paucity of work on the arrival, growth, influence, and meaning of Ford in the years before apartheid, even despite the sophisticated analyses of the role that Ford and Fordism would play in that system's later development. In part because of the history of race and Ford in South Africa, company records on Ford in South Africa are scarcely available.[9] Thus the archival challenges in this case shape any (re)thinking of the significance of Ford's interwar move into South Africa. For the important decades of the 1920s through World War II, when Ford's industrial production developed in Port Elizabeth, the Ford story must be uncovered through other sources. Ford was of great symbolic importance and increasing economic and political importance in these years but was not materially involved in the most important U.S. intervention of the period, namely the Poor White Study of the Carnegie Corporation.[10] This well-funded, multiyear study systematically brought U.S. managerial wisdom to the problems associated with white uplift and industrial development in South Africa. Though Ford itself was not placed to lead broad efforts of reform in the South Africa of the 1920s and early 1930s the company nevertheless represented the connection of factory discipline, men-making, and mass consumption to the racial improvement of underperforming whites. Paired with the Carnegie findings and flexibly undertaken in concert with a variety of enthusiastic state authorities, Fordism provided a model of not just industrial but racial development.

The absence of archival material on Ford's activities specifically does more than encourage creativity in research. It also requires a broad contextualization of Ford at a time when governance in South Africa was preoccupied with both controlling and promoting the expansion of the industrial sector of the economy. Industrial policy took on meaning for politics, for economic development and, perhaps especially, for the relationship of the racial order to the workplace. Because of the absence of company records this chapter turns to alternative sources, in particular the Carnegie Corporation's Poor White Study, as a critical document for situating Ford's arrival in and continued embrace by South Africa's white elite. The Poor White Study, published in

1932, was used as a map for planning industrial policy, education, and social welfare and for deepening already existing arguments about the necessity of liberal reform to save "poor whites" from racial degradation. In its focus on the problems and possibilities presented by the growth of commercial and industrial society, the Carnegie Poor White Study provides a window into how reformers imagined the role of industrial jobs.

South African planners sought lessons from the United States that could be found in the social scientific data of the Carnegie Commission and in factory discipline as practiced by Ford. But these would be put to use in very different demographic situations. Apartheid in some ways came to epitomize a "whites only" Fordism, with all the limits and contradictions the term suggests. But in the 1920s, when first Ford and then the Carnegie researchers began their work, it was not clear that the project of consolidating a singular white racial hierarchy by remaking poor white men and women would lead ultimately to the consolidation of narrow Afrikaner nationalism that underpinned apartheid. The fruition of the Fordist ideal of a vast internal market based on high wages for the mass of the population would ultimately be challenged by the (competing) imperatives of structural white supremacy. But in the interwar period, this chapter will show that new class forces sought new ideological tools and allies in expressing them, enabling the United States to start being seen as an alternative metropole. In appearing as a sort of third way between narrow Afrikaner nationalism on one hand and the British Empire on the other, U.S. institutions filled a niche and found an audience among a growing sector of social scientists and racial liberals.

Just one year after the 1910 creation of the Union of South Africa, the first modern census of South Africa showed a white population of 21.37 percent, a number that would continue to decline. As George Fredrickson's comparative history reminds us, the patterns of race and demography in the United States and South Africa were near opposites, with the U.S. 70 percent or more white in nearly every region and South Africa 70–80 percent nonwhite.[11] The importance of this distinction should not be overdrawn, but neither should it be ignored. South African intellectuals continued to seek input and models from U.S. experts on the patterns, practices, and profits of racial segregation, even knowing that demographic differences would likely translate into economic and social problems that were markedly different. But in the decades after World War I and before apartheid these problems were being identified—and their solutions were far from clear.

To some degree what has been presented in previous chapters helps to explain how Ford became part of South Africa's rehearsals for apartheid in the interwar years. But those factors are worth considering in the context of specific South African conflicts, as Gramsci tried to do for Europe, and for thinking about the prospects of Fordism as a transnational system. First it should be clear by now that racial egalitarianism was not at the heart of the Ford vision developed in the United States and offered for export. The employment of Black workers at the Rouge took place at the intersection of management's demand for labor control and the growing social power of white workers to refuse work that was increasingly understood as racially degraded. "Black work" needed Black workers. The Rouge was also the exception and not the rule for Ford enterprises in the United States. Second, the broad strategies of Ford within the British Empire may have in the first instance made South Africa crucial less as a market itself than in opening markets elsewhere—in India and Australia and the regional networks each of these implied. Third, in the context of the uneven development Ford pursued, South Africa then fit into American imperial schema as a leading economy but on a peripheral continent; its role in the world economy consisted overwhelmingly of raw material extraction and agricultural rather than industrial production. How and to what degree U. S. industry in general and Ford in particular would find fit there was unknowable when the company arrived. Lastly, and most obviously, the Ford empire depended on alliances with elites in host nations: Ford was welcomed in South Africa because of its willingness to pursue a whites-only hiring policy. But the company also found itself confronting debates about protectionism, national development, and the need to move away from past strong links to British imperial trade.[12]

To paraphrase Gramsci, if in the United States hegemony began in the Ford factory, in South Africa it began in the mines and in the maintenance of control by a white minority. As John Saul and Stephen Gelb have demonstrated, because manufacturing capital only gradually challenged mining capital and large landowners politically, and white supremacy limited the development of a large internal market, industrial planning in South Africa would only become so realized through the apartheid period.[13] This is not to say that the whites-only industrial policy that Ford agreed to in South Africa was preordained or somehow based in unchallenged local custom. The early to mid-1920s saw the rise of militance among Black workers across sectors, most importantly through the Industrial and Commercial Workers Union (ICU) whose internal debates about where reform should come from—

employers or the state—reflected those taking place among ruling elites.[14] By the 1920s there was in the mines a substantial tradition of U. S. mining engineers managing giant South African enterprises, Herbert Hoover most famously. Hoover earned his racial managerial expertise in the United States, but because of how he took that "knowledge" into the world Hoover was promoted as a transnational mining engineering expert who also understood day-to-day management of "actual workers." In South Africa Hoover often expanded the roles of African and Chinese miners in ways designed to pit groups against each other in order to ensure production under unsafe conditions.[15] Resistance by white workers played a role in containing these kinds of multiracial but white supremacist initiatives, especially after the Rand Revolt of 1922. Positing new manufacturing jobs as the preserve of whites and as the key to solving the "poor white problem" would become a way, with Ford as a key player, to insist that white workers learn time-work discipline but remain protected from direct competition with so-called subordinate racial groups.

FROM LIVERPOOL TO DETROIT: FORD AND THE REBRANDING OF PORT ELIZABETH

From the mid-nineteenth century, when it enjoyed a momentary competition with Cape Town as the premier port in the Cape Colony, Port Elizabeth had been described as the "Liverpool of the Cape." The town's largest employers were boot and shoe manufacturers, who had profited hugely from demand caused by World War I. Until the postwar years, when the combination of lowering demand and rising mechanization changed the terms of employment in shoe manufacture, apprenticeships in Port Elizabeth and the skilled jobs that followed them had been plentiful for white young men and significant numbers of white women. In 1920 and 1921 the leather shops employed more than a quarter of the white workers in Port Elizabeth and about one-sixth of the Black workers.[16] This industry and others experienced their first major expansions as a result of war production. By 1925, following the arrival of Ford and General Motors, the city had earned the distinction of the "Detroit of South Africa."[17]

In the early 1920s merchants and manufacturers in Port Elizabeth formed an alliance to advance the material and political interests of their city. This development was not unusual for the time, and reflected dynamics that Belinda Bozzoli has thoroughly explored: "During the 1920s, commercial supporters of industries became more and more outspoken, while the merging of the sectors was consolidated on the economic level . . . a powerful alliance had been formed between two highly interdependent forms of capital, and on most issues they were able to act as one."[18] The political expression of such an alliance was most broadly first seen in the creation of the Union of South Africa in 1910. More potentially significant for both the Ford Motor Company and Fordism in South Africa was the creation of a Pact Government in 1924. As instantiations of the deepening need to develop its own national economy to counter British imperial capital, and reflection of the need to shift from a "narrow state" to a "wide state," Pact governance on the one hand and cooperation among previously antagonistic sectors of the economy on the other were two sides of the same coin. Jennifer Robinson argues further for seeing spatial organization as another reflection of the same dynamics: "[T]heir horizons shifted from promoting local conditions facilitative to their own activities to the active encouragement of industrial investment in the town."[19]

The Port Elizabeth City Council launched, in both the national and overseas press and in business magazines, an advertising campaign designed to lure industries to the city. Offering advantages to industrialists revealed a turn to a broader set of interests being reflected in the interest of regional growth. These included:

> A ready supply of (White) labour, especially women; the availability of technically trained workers or the possibility of training them at the PE Technical College; a sizeable local consumer market; the proximity of the harbor to factories dependent on imported raw materials or parts; a good distribution network to the rest of the country . . . it also offered incentives such as cheap, well situated land, electricity and gas.[20]

It is in this context that the first Model T assembled in South Africa rolled off the line on January 19, 1924. For its first six years the company operated in a leased property, where 70 workers assembled about 1,400 cars per year. In 1930 the company opened a new, larger plant and expanded the workforce to 175 workers, making it one of the largest employers in Port Elizabeth. Production increased to 3,658 cars annually. As Ford's commitment not just to producing for a South African market but for a continental export market grew, so did the shop. Within a decade 23,555 Fords a year were being made in Port Elizabeth.[21] Ford South Africa prided itself on being able to claim that its vehicles had been assembled entirely by white labor.[22] The company described its decision to embrace a whites-only hiring policy in its Port Elizabeth plant in no uncertain terms. As a Ford public relations expert in South Africa recalled in 1961, "Up to 1952, the Ford plant in South Africa employed only white labor. When they started operations there was a 'poor white' problem. There was considerable unemployed European labor. Thus, they filled the need by employing only white labor."[23]

Ford's policy was neither singular nor new. By the time of its arrival in Port Elizabeth significant legislation already existed that restricted the movement of so-called "native" and "Asiatic" workers in South Africa. These laws included: the Mine and Works Act (1911). which imposed the industrial color bar; the Native Labour Registration Act (1911), which made "breach of contract" by African farm and mine workers a criminal act and outlawed leaving jobs without their employer's consent; the Native Land Act (1913), which initiated the reserve or Bantustan or homelands system that would be expanded in later years; the Native Urban Areas Act (1923), which confined Africans to segregated townships; and the Pass Laws, laid down in 1922 by the Stallard Commission, which required African men over age sixteen to carry passes that recorded their permission (or lack of it) to work and live in particular "white" areas.[24] Each of these related to the state's desire to limit the interaction of white and Black workers, but only one, the Native Land Act, specifically legislated white movement too, by forbidding the purchase of land in "native" areas by whites.[25]

Ford's relationship to the broader contours of segregation in urban South Africa, expressed through its whites-only hiring policy, was also made visible in the "location" of New Brighton. The oldest existing Black location, or township as they came to be known, New Brighton was celebrated by whites as a "model township" in the progressive city of Port Elizabeth. New Brighton had been designated a location through the terms of the Native Reserve Location Act of 1902 that authorized "the Government to set up and control African residential areas outside towns." Originally the bill had been limited to areas within municipal boundaries and the actual locations themselves.[26] Reflecting the urbanization of the area, New Brighton's status changed in 1923 when it came under the new Native Urban Areas Act. The 1923 act gave the Port Elizabeth municipality responsibility for administering New Brighton where there were no schools until 1928; only in 1930 was electricity extended to it. The population of the city nearly doubled between 1921 and 1936 but manufacturing jobs were overwhelmingly the preserve of whites. Though Port Elizabeth had the highest percentage of white labor of any industrial city in South Africa, through the 1920s and '30s, the growth rate of the African population exceeded all others. African rural migrants still sought employment in Port Elizabeth because of the same kind of desperation that drove rural whites—sometimes displaced from farm labor by the very Fordson tractors Ford sold in South Africa—to the city.

As the population of Africans in Port Elizabeth increased, so did the demand for housing. As throughout South Africa, informal squatters' settlements were constructed adjacent to townships. In New Brighton the largest of these camps was called KwaFord. KwaFord is the Zulu word for "place of Ford" and earned its name because the housing in the settlement was originally constructed from packing crates discarded by the company and stamped with the word "Ford." Built by African migrants from the countryside, KwaFord was not formally incorporated into New Brighton until 1948. By then, the township had been extended more than a few times to incorporate new housing schemes, especially for so-called "coloured" workers (that is, mixed-race people who were also excluded from work at Ford) and other camps brought into being because of the racist exclusion of Africans.[27]

Though the Depression hit Port Elizabeth hard, the 1933 development of a deepwater port meant that the city could materially and directly connect to the world economy and attract foreign investors who required docking. Boosterism in Port Elizabeth, promoted by the Chamber of Commerce, increased when the new port opened it to the global economy in a new way. The chamber's propaganda reflected a commitment to industrial development and white supremacy that specifically appealed to English, Afrikaans and American elite sensibilities. Soon foreign capital accounted for more than half of the investment in local industry, and auto had become the largest employer. 92 percent of those who worked for the auto plants were white, although whites represented just 60 percent of the workforce in other manufacturing concerns. In 1938, of the African population in Port Elizabeth nearly as many were unemployed as were employed in trade and industry, the largest source of jobs.[28]

From the end of the Second Anglo-Boer War in 1902 through the 1930s both white and African farmers left the land in steady numbers, making their differential treatment in cities critical to maintaining white supremacy. A combination of drought, capitalist intensification in agriculture, and the shifting away from a tenant labor (*bywoner* in Afrikaans) system brought many into the burgeoning cities where their presence as semi-employed or unemployed slum dwellers became a source of worry to elites. Increasingly, fears about emerging solidarity and cohabitation between the Black and white poor sped up the state's commitment to legislating and providing for segregated housing and workplaces in growing urban areas like Port Elizabeth. White panic about race-mixing, and the declining ratio of white-to-Black population it would cause, was a central feature of policies that emerged in the late 1920s and 1930s.[29]

By the early 1920s the former *bywoners* were increasingly being referred to as "poor whites" and described as a "problem." Of particular concern was the anachronistic apprentice system in the boot industry, the earliest significant source of manufacturing jobs in Port Elizabeth that drew young women and men from nearby farming areas. The tradition of artisanal apprenticeships, which required white youths to achieve journeyman status before they would be hired, was becoming obsolete in the mechanized and mechanizing boot-making shops in the city.[30] Further, "European" youths were compelled to attend school, which meant employers could get access to "coloured" youths at a younger age. These problems were exacerbated by another: the belief that "white men would not live at the wages that they were paying coloured men."[31] While subsequent study of the poor white problem offered various explanations and solutions, the problem of weighing the imperatives of capitalist competition in relation to the imperatives of white supremacy would remain a central focus. Fordist practice and U.S. social science were both mobilized in mutually reinforcing ways by the South African state.

WHITE ANXIETY, WHITE UNION, AND THE COMING OF FORD AND THE CARNEGIE COMMISSION

Sentiment about the role industry could and should play in post–World War I South Africa found expression with the help of several American enterprises. Teachers College of Columbia University and the Carnegie Corporation of the United States, institutions whose interests and personnel frequently overlapped, provided social-scientific leadership to white South African reformers who viewed a range of social crises also as racial crises. Within a society in which whites ruled and some whites worked, what this study has called "white managerialism" continued to take on new meanings. The most celebrated articulation of the role of these reformers, the five-volume report by the Carnegie Commission on South Africa's white poor produced between 1929 and 1932, coincided with Ford's expansion in Port Elizabeth.[32]

The idea that unmanaged poor whites were a particular problem for governance in South Africa had deep roots in the British hatred of the Afrikaner people. But the emergent social problem of "poor whitism" took on a new meaning after the Second Anglo-Boer War but before the turn to the kind of Afrikaner nationalism that characterized apartheid rule. In the interwar period a segment of the white political elite sought to build a political coalition between British- and Dutch-descended whites. For those at the top this would represent a kind of third way, tilted neither too much toward the British Empire nor toward Afrikaner nationalism. For those at the bottom this meant imagining the future lives of poor whites not as despised peasants but fully civilized citizens. How these tensions played out would have a profound impact on segregationist policy and practice in South Africa.[33]

The 1920s and '30s are critical therefore to understanding both Ford's roots in South Africa and early South African political / cultural interest in Ford, as both were shaped by this complex period of transition. In these years U.S. institutions began to curtail their earlier and overwhelmingly pro-British policy toward South African society. Ford came into the country via its relationship with the British Empire, following on decades in which American commissioners, engineers, and social reformers there had worked in alliance with British South Africa. However, from 1902 forward, shifting dynamics that would deepen because of World War I came to the fore. New Anglo-Boer political and economic formations, emergent class struggles among Black South Africans, and increasing possibilities for competitive tensions between the British Empire and the United States revealed anxieties of many kinds about securing the future of white rule in South Africa.[34]

Not just political relations were changing. U.S. exports to South Africa were ten times greater at the end of the war in 1902 than they had been in 1892. The import of U.S. capital goods and the hiring of U.S. managers meant that imports mattered far beyond the realm of consumption. As early as 1902, *Iron Age* wrote, "there is plenty of room in South Africa for manufacturers of all nationalities and it is only by the clashing of the best of every country that real progress can be affected." Suggesting that Britain should not fear increasing U.S. economic influence in the country, the journal felt certain that the United States would be a logical source of new industrial leadership and capital in South Africa.[35] Operating now in the moment of coalition politics in South Africa—beginning with Union in 1910 and then under the Pact Government of 1924—the limits of a focus on British firms and politicians that the United States had pursued in the past started to become apparent.

Seeking influence in the formerly closed Afrikaner domains of the Transvaal and the Orange Free State meant that relationships with Afrikaner elites had to be forged. Upper-level managers and capitalists in the United States were overwhelmingly Anglophiles, yet as the historian of empire Paul Kramer has wonderfully documented, expressions of solidarity with the Boer frontier narrative had begun as early as 1900 when Boer victories against the British opened space for white critics of Anglo-Saxonism to speak. Politician Williams Jennings Bryan wrote at length on the topic:

> The union of the Anglo and the Saxon formed a new and valuable type, but the process of race evolution was not complete when the Anglo and the Saxon met. A still later type has appeared which is superior to any which has existed heretofore: and with this new type will come a higher civilization than any that has preceded it. Great has been the Greek, the Latin, the Slav, the Celt, the Teuton and the Anglo Saxon, but greater than any of these is the American, in whom are blended the virtues of all.[36]

Though not in fashion in the United States—but soon to be politically mobilized for the purpose of Jewish and Catholic exclusion—such an imagined blend of different white racial stocks appealed to an emergent political and ideological viewpoint in South Africa. Imagined similarities between American settlers and Afrikaner frontier narratives yielded possibilities that could be tapped for political and cultural arguments about the need to move away from an overdetermined focus on British South Africa. That the United States had defeated the British Empire militarily and achieved independence was also a source of cultural connection to Afrikaners, who cherished their own narrative of oppression at the hands of the British. Indeed, a peculiar and new kind of respect for Boer initiative and scrappiness that echoed narratives of American frontier ingenuity in the face of danger from savages and the uncivilized pressures of the frontier emerged early in the twentieth century and became essential to the political moment of Ford's arrival in the Eastern Cape. In exploring the importance of such changes Kramer has documented the significance of "tensions within Anglo-Saxonist ideology and its dynamic construction and reconstruction in light of specifically colonial politics."[37]

A show assembled by Alfred W. Lewis for the 1904 St. Louis World's Fair underlines the shift taking place in U.S.–Dutch South Africa relations. Lewis convinced a number of both British and Boer veterans of the South African war to restage the pivotal battle fought between the British and the

Dutch for control of all of South Africa from 1899 to 1902. In the reenactment, Lewis called upon the world-famous Boer general Piet Cronje to reenact his heroic leadership in the guerrilla war against the British imperial army and his ultimate surrender. Cronje was a perfect fit for American audiences, who would be inclined to express solidarity with a portrayal of resistance to the British while nonetheless seeing themselves as part of an Anglo—and Anglican—tradition.[38]

The defeat of the Boers was celebrated in such a way that recognized both British and Boer strengths. The U.S. army, after all, had only recently switched from fighting *with* Philippine militias to fighting *against* them. Cultural representations like those at the 1904 World's Fair and later at Coney Island in the summer of 1905 did not of course stand in for diplomacy or more material expressions of business across borders. But as popularly oriented historical spectacles, they provide an insight into broader political themes. The common experience of settler colonial expansion permitted further U.S.-Boer affinities to develop. With regard to the particularities of racial categorization, most comparative histories of the United States and South Africa take Black / white relations as their logical starting point and search for apartheid's roots in Jim Crow laws and practices in the U.S. South. That the foundational myths of each as settler colonies also shared glorified accounts of determined whites arriving by covered wagon to vanquish the savages and domesticate the frontier provided another basis for comparison. The South African policy of setting aside small amounts of land—7.5 percent in 1913 and 13 percent after 1936—of land for so-called "natives" echoed U.S. practices in constructing the reservation system. But Ford's outright rejection of African workers—as the company had rejected "pure" indigenous people in Brazil as rubber workers—and the Carnegie Commission's relative disinterest at this time in the problems of the African poor suggest a different link to settler ideas. The determination to remove natives from national narratives of progress thus expressed the unity of English and Boer South Africans, but more fully fit with the latter's self-image as frontiersmen.[39]

Despite the overwhelming history of Anglo-Saxonism and pro-British sentiment that shaped the Anglo-Americanism of the 1920s, U.S. institutions were faced with changing realities in South Africa that would require new sensibilities. Ford brought a certain experience in making both "particularism and universalism" that positioned it as uniquely flexible when it was advantageous and inflexible when it was not. Moreover, the company arrived in South Africa under British imperial auspices to "save" overwhelmingly the Boers.

THE RAND REVOLT AND THE SHIFTING TERRAIN OF WHITE SUPREMACY

The advent of Ford assembly in South Africa followed a period of intense labor struggle and class conflict in the country. In order to understand the state's interest in relying on private capital to help solve the poor white problem, and the articulation of the problem itself, it is necessary to understand the context of turmoil that led to "industrial reconciliation" and, ultimately, to the consolidation of cross-class whiteness in South Africa that shaped that reconciliation.

In early 1922 the gold mines on the South African Witswatersrand exploded in a strike that would only end after more than 250 workers and innocent nonparticipants were killed.[40] The Rand Revolt began defensively, in response to an employers' offensive that would have reduced wages, eliminated jobs, and broken the Status Quo Agreement which set the industrial standard for hiring policy. The Status Quo Agreement protected jobs in the mines for white workers by regulating—that is to say, limiting—the numbers of African workers who would be hired and in what jobs. In late 1921 the mining companies insisted on their right to ignore that agreement and to launch a policy that would replace several thousand white workers with Black workers at lower wages. This announcement from the mining companies, clearly backed by the government, came out of nowhere from the white workers' point of view, considering that negotiations had been underway in which labor representatives were willing to take steps to address the economic downturn that followed the war. It was the combined disrespect of the mining companies for established negotiating processes and the attempt to eliminate protections for white workers that led to the strike.[41]

The Status Quo Agreement acted as the incomplete but effective "Colour Bar" in the mines, a bar that the minority white workers relied on for the preservation of access to mining jobs and for the maintenance of wage scales. Making a far-fetched racist comparison to U.S. history, organized labor after the strike defined the struggle to preserve the Colour Bar as being "the same question as caused the Civil War in the United States . . . for the Colour Bar and the Status Quo Agreement . . . were in substance and effect an occupational Mason and Dixon line, against the spread of what is in substance and effect Negro slavery.[42] There are many things wrong with this comparison and it is most worth noting the obvious: Black workers in twentieth-century South Africa were not slaves. The "fact" of their low-wage status was historically created and contingent, linked to the capacity of all workers to articulate strategies for struggling. Nor of course did the Mason-Dixon line have anything to do with protecting workers, North or South. One of the many tragedies of the 1922 strike is that precisely at a moment of upheaval and extraordinary dynamism, precisely in the midst of taking their lives into their own hands, many white workers would actively and violently seek to deny that possibility to Black workers. Many white workers marched under the banner of Communism, whose internationalist refrain had been distorted by local racism into "Workers of the world unite and fight for a white South Africa."

The Rand Revolt is enormously significant for the role it played in articulating white working-class perspectives and crystallizing white rulers' fears within a society ordered by race *and* class at a moment of new nationalism. Jeremy Krikler, the most trenchant analyst of the multiple historical narratives that the revolt represents, writes:

> It is a commonplace that the Rand Revolt of 1922 exemplified in a stark and extreme way all the paradoxes of the position and consciousness of the white working class in South Africa. On the one hand, the strike on the mines and the rebellion of that year stressed how militant this cohort of the proletariat could be: this remains the only strike in South African history that developed into an insurrectionary attempt to nullify the fiat of the employers and overthrow the government of the day. On the other hand, in the midst of this struggle, in whose cacophony socialist and revolutionary rhetoric was loudly heard, the white working class's hostility to the black working class, indeed to black people generally, was made clear, not merely by the determination of the strikers to keep black workers out of jobs held to be white . . . but also by the murderous racial violence that erupted in March, 1922. That violence, coming in the wake of the many deeply resonant working class revolts occurring internationally after World War I, ensured that the bloody repression of the strike and the increasingly urgent responses to the poor white problem after it would register elite fears of class insurgencies.[43]

Though the political affiliations of the strikers were various, Edward Roux first and most usefully identified the three groupings that were essential to the organization of what would become both a racist pogrom and an armed insurrectionary movement before it was violently crushed: the reformist trade union leadership; the Council of Action, a group of militant miners previously expelled from the miners' union for radical, independent action; and the commandos, Afrikaner strikers organized along military lines akin to those used in the guerrilla phase of the Second Anglo-Boer War. Since 1914 Afrikaners had become the majority of white workers on the Rand, and though not all were politically organized Afrikaner nationalists many were militantly anti-African and anti-British. Commitments to racist policies materially shaped strikers' demands even as they varied by degree among the white strikers. Thus if we cannot understand the strike solely in terms of racism, neither can we understand it without recognizing the central role that the struggle to *protect and extend racial exclusion on the job* played in mobilizing tens of thousands of white South African workers to strike in the name of a "white South Africa." Ford's employment policies would serve those interests.[44]

In considering the simultaneous socialist, nationalist, racist, and gendered dimensions of the strike, Krikler argues that the fight for a white South Africa must be understood as including a perspective in which "white" represented the state and society and, therefore, access to citizenship and legal autonomy. Krikler's attempt to shed light on the complex tangle of race and class identities as, in his words, "the strikers themselves imagined them" is crucial, as is his argument that the panic over competition with Black labor lacked both coherence and reality.[45] Not only were there already Black workers filling semi-skilled positions in the mines and other places, but what was being proposed by the companies, replacing white with Black labor in the jobs on the lowest rung of the ladder, did not necessarily imply the downward mobility of white workers. In Krikler's words white workers seem to have "despised the idea" that they could be viewed as in any way "interchangeable" with Black workers, regardless of the fact that the employers' proposal would have segregated Black workers into the worst jobs and prevented their mobility.[46] Even in the context of a working-class upheaval, that whiteness could come to mean civility and citizenship helps explain how Fordist ideas, as anti-union as they were, would be embraced not just by bosses and managers but by white workers.

The analogy to American slavery put forth by white strikers is also instructive here. Evoking slavery to describe the threat represented by Black workers allowed white workers to express the panic they felt over wage dependency without actually having to describe themselves as dependent. On the contrary, the euphemistic language of slavery and the very direct language of race both worked to deflect attention away from the historically specific misery, danger, and powerlessness white workers themselves experienced every day in the mines.[47] It is impossible to separate an assessment of the situation of white labor from that of Black labor; the despised status of Black workers in the eyes of working-class whites is precisely the sentiment that white elites would rely on to create cross-class allegiance via white identity in coming decades. Thus from an historical point of view we can understand how the articulation of "the poor white problem" in the period following the Rand Revolt revealed the intimately related yet distinct imperatives of capitalist productivity on one hand and white supremacy on the other.

INVESTIGATING THE POOR WHITE: FACTORY DISCIPLINE AND IMPROVING THE MASTER RACE

Following a visit to South Africa in 1927 by Frederick Keppel, president of the Carnegie Corporation of New York, the Dutch Reformed Church submitted an application to the corporation asking for financial support in carrying out the Poor White Study. The Carnegie Corporation had been created with the task of fulfilling the philanthropic vision of Andrew Carnegie. It supported initiatives that linked "science with social progress and the public consumption of institutionalized knowledge with the ideals of modern citizenship."[48] For more than a decade Carnegie monies had been funding the Eugenics Record Office in Cold Spring Harbor, New York, an organization that pursued the scientific study of race with an eye toward effecting policy in American society.

The Poor White Study seemed to fit precisely the goals of the Carnegie Corporation and was accepted when its application was received. The Control Board of the study was selected by a joint committee made up of representatives of the Dutch Reformed Church and the Research Grant Board of the Union Department of Mines and Industries. A striking coalition, the Church and the Mines and Industries were far from being objective scientific bodies, as both were organizations with political and material interests in the outcome of the study.[49] To launch the study, the newly established corporation relied financially on the Dominions and Colonies Fund, earmarked for social and educational research and projects in British dependencies.[50]

Carnegie president Frederick Keppel, who had previously been the dean of Columbia College, made multiple trips to British colonial holdings, especially to the settler colonies of New Zealand, Australia, and South Africa; James Russell, Keppel's co-thinker, assistant, and the former dean of Teachers College at Columbia, traveled with him. Not surprisingly both men were intent on promoting ideas about educational reform as the most important mechanism for the racial improvement of both natives and poor whites.

Russell had a particular interest in bringing the ideas being developed at Teachers College and Columbia into the wider world. As a highly regarded "talent spotter" Russell ran the college during the period when its student body included 4,000 international students. Russell traveled in these years to British colonial Africa, a trip that would be repeated in 1927 by Keppel and would open Carnegie doors to the Poor White Study.[51]

Strikingly, more than 25 percent of the international students at Teachers College were from Canada. Suggestive of another Anglo-American link, the training of reform-minded Canadian educators was intended to provide expertise and skill to the empire, not just to Canada. According to scholar Richard Glotzer, despite or perhaps because of such deep relations to Teachers College, "Canadians, wary of their larger neighbour, emphasized Dominion status and intellectual links with Britain in the face of American cultural and economic power."[52] In recruiting for Carnegie programs from academic institutions, government, and the arts Keppel sought out individuals who shared a worldview he described as reflecting the "Anglo-Saxon tradition."[53] Glotzer argues: "For Keppel, the British Empire was not coincident with Anglo-Saxon tradition. The latter was a cultural phenomenon, and for upper-middle-class Americans like Keppel, that culture had informed American heritage, cultural ideals, and club life."[54]

Clues to the future relationship between Teachers College, Carnegie, and reformers in South Africa can be seen in the early founding of an alumni association among South African graduates of Teachers College called the Teachers College Club, or TC Club.[55] But the role of American social science in the Poor White Study was most clearly represented in the figure of Ernst Gideon Malherbe, a South African reformer whose career exemplifies assumptions about how the modern efficiency of the assembly line and factory discipline could coexist with segregationist planning and educational reform. Malherbe was trained at Columbia University and Teachers College, completing his doctorate in 1924. According to the South African historian Saul Dubow, Teachers College developed a "distinctive outward looking international programme combining a stress on modernization and professionalization through the adoption of 'new' educational methods with a paternalistic culture of concerns for the retarded cultures of backwards people."[56] While at Columbia Malherbe was in contact with the pragmatist and educational innovator John Dewey, who would participate in a conference on educational reform and native education in South Africa in 1932; the psychologist E.L. Thorndike, whose early advocacy of IQ testing would contribute greatly to eugenic arguments for immigration restriction; and the anthropologist Franz Boas. Their various influences on him are revealed in his own commitment to educational reform in South Africa as well as his role in the Carnegie study, the scope of which went far beyond education. Malherbe's time in the United States coincided with the pre-eminence of eugenic ideas in the social sciences, though his own preference was for work that stressed environmental, as opposed to biological, factors. While this set him apart from certain strains of white supremacist thought in South Africa and the United States, it should not be taken to mean that Malherbe's social science did not both promote and rely on a belief in racial hierarchy. Quoting Thorndike, Malherbe would say that "whatever exists at all exists in some amount and anything that exists in amount can be measured." This included "things" like intelligence, color, and potential.[57]

Many of the others on the team that produced the study were either social scientists from American universities or South African psychologists who visited psychology laboratories at Harvard and Yale; most of the South Africans had studied in the United States or Britain. Two U. S. sociologists, Kenyon L. Butterfield and C. W. Coulter, were sent to aid the investigation. Butterfield, a sociologist from Massachusetts had been in West Africa and Portuguese East Africa on a delegation with the Phelps-Stokes Commission previously. He thought that the "poor white question" was one of the key problems facing South Africa. Relying not on biological arguments but rather on environmental ones, Butterfield stressed that "there can be little doubt that if the natives were given full economic opportunity the more competent among them would soon outstrip the less competent whites."[58] Coulter, from Ohio Wesleyan University and also a sociologist, was included because of his scholarly interest in urban areas, a departure from framing white poverty as a rural problem.[59] Coulter argued that South Africa must begin to create "scientifically trained technicians" to do social welfare work, vociferously objecting to the idea that social work could be conducted unscientifically and unprofessionally.

It is likely that Coulter's ideas influenced the South African psychologist Hendrik Frensch Verwoerd, another critical figure whose work reveals the increasing reliance on the United States as a source of modern ideas about race and social life. Because Verwoerd would go on to become, with D. F. Malan, an "architect of apartheid," his political history has been viewed largely through the lens of Afrikaner nationalism. But as Roberta Balstad Miller has demonstrated Verwoerd's work in the 1920s and '30s campaigning against Afrikaner poverty and his commitments to joint British-Afrikaner research reveal that his subsequent and total turn to Afrikaner nationalism was not entirely predictable. Verwoerd studied in both Germany and the United States, becoming professor of applied psychology and psychotechnics at Stellenbosch University in 1927. Verwoerd pioneered classes in business psychology in South Africa in which he taught topics such as the "psychology of sales" and "vocational testing." His course books overwhelmingly drew on American models. In 1932 Verwoerd became head of Stellenbosch's newly formed Department of Sociology and Social Work, the first of its kind in South Africa. As Miller writes, "If Verwoerd had a political vision during the period before 1937 it was not expressed in ethnic separatism but in his attempt to bring the English and the Afrikaners together in local and national social welfare activities." These politics, expressed most directly in his work with poor whites, took for granted that exclusion of Africans would necessarily undergird Anglo-Boer unity.[60]

Malherbe's proposal to Keppel for a research design that covered a broad spectrum of social concerns about poor whites was basically adopted as the model for the Carnegie study. The plan was to examine "the psychological, physiological, sociological, educational and economic phases of the whole question" in order to produce a study that would provide "an objective coverage of the major dimensions of contemporary citizenship."[61] Malherbe's ideas were remarkably consistent with Ford's industrial models for social life and in their commitment to efficiency in reform. Like his colleagues on the Carnegie team Malherbe was preoccupied by the fear of the degeneration of the white race, and wrote in his biography that poverty was "a menace to the self-preservation and prestige of our white people, living as we do in the midst of the native population which outnumbers us 6 to 1." His research agenda benefited from long-standing patterns of inquiry into the diseases (notoriously hookworm), the social deficiencies, and the eugenic incapacities of poor whites in the U.S. South.[62] Panic over the demographic battle that whites had to fight with so-called colored and native people in South Africa permeated discussions of both poor whites and the prospect of "race-mixing." While heredity and biology were never completely absent from the study, its focus remained on the need to *socially* influence and control the behavior of poor white people. If behavior could be changed poverty could be eradicated; if poverty could be eradicated the desire to "mix" with nonwhites would disappear. This was the economistic and behavioral logic behind Malherbe's approach to the investigation.

The problem of making science out of race and race out of science was obvious to the Carnegie team from the very beginning, when it admitted that "for various reasons an exact enumeration [of who is a poor white] is not practicable." The commission went so far as to say that many white people who were "very poor" were "not 'poor whites' in the sense in which the term is used in this investigation." One could be poor and one could be white, but this did not necessarily make one a poor white.[63] Malherbe made this point publicly in an address he delivered to the quarterly meeting of the Cape Branch of the Women's Refranchisement League. Describing the importance of arriving at a "satisfactory definition of poor white" before the study began, Malherbe said that a poor white was "not merely a white person who was poor." He continued, "if that were so there would have been occasions when he would have classed himself in that category," a possibility his audience was sure to recognize as absurd.[64] He did venture to suggest that, although the commission had decided to hold off on defining the poor white until after it had conducted at least preliminary work, a working definition would be, "a white person whose income is not enough to allow him to maintain a *civilized* standard of living and, at the same time, one whose whole attitude of mind prevents him from rising above that level." These were exactly the "problems" that the Fordism of Highland Park had sought to rectify; the Carnegie investigators would ultimately turn to similar, factory-based methods to solve their problems.[65]

Addressing himself to the question of solutions, Malherbe strongly stated that, while sympathy for and intervention in the lives of poor whites was needed, "the white civilization should not be coddled. It was very necessary to bring out the fighting qualities, the energy which makes for success in the race." Malherbe said that getting poor whites to adjust to "the highly organized modern way of life" would be critical in creating the appropriate distance from the less civilized members of society, especially the native. Though focusing almost exclusively on environmental factors in shaping racial identities, here Malherbe evoked the question of heredity and the problems that happen when "marriage with feeble minded persons" is allowed to occur. By way of example, Malherbe cited the case of "an American soldier in the War of Independence who had a child by a feeble-minded woman. 480 direct descendants were traced from this union. Of these 138 had been feeble minded and over 100 had been criminals."[66] In prioritizing environment while not discounting "heredity" Malherbe argued that racial degeneration could be reversed. Walking a political line that sought to appeal to the

British-descended whites who made up most of his audiences, Malherbe simultaneously referenced a proud Afrikaner tradition of independent settlement and imperial defiance. A disaster was in the making but not one of nature and thus one that could be reversed.

Ultimately for the purposes of the study poor whites were defined as "of European descent who gained their livelihood chiefly by farming; as regards their economic condition they constitute a class consisting principally of poor 'bywoners,' hired men on farms, poor settlers, and the growing group of unskilled or poorly trained labourers and workers outside of farming." The report found that a failure to adjust to "modern economic conditions" brought about by the "discovery of diamonds and gold, the capitalistic exploitation of mines, the influx of immigrants with the modern business outlook, [and] the rapid penetration of railways" all contributed to the economic decline of those whites used to living a pioneer, subsistence life. Isolation on farms led to backward business practices, a "certain lack of industriousness," and a decided lack of interest in consumer goods.[67] One solution to this problem? A job at the Ford factory, to be followed by the purchase of a Ford.

FORDISM FOR THE 20 PERCENT?

While clearly the Carnegie team thought that the racial difference between white and Black needed to be made manifest through increased white consumer power, it is also true that this possibility had only recently been extended intraracially among whites across class lines. The role that consumption plays in shaping arguments for racial segregation is a vital, and understudied, component of the history of racism, especially in South Africa where the white working class was so small that it could (and would, ultimately) be incorporated into a structure of privilege that distinguished it from other workers. Indeed, the development of apartheid would insure that "worker" almost certainly assumed the modifier "Black." While historians have focused on the lack of opportunity for and access to consumer goods and services that institutional racism structures for nonwhite people, we less frequently discuss the place that consumption holds in creating white identity through discourses of civilization. For Ford management in a white minority country, maintaining extreme differentials in consumption meant foregoing continuous dramatic market expansion in a way that anxieties about Black spending patterns at Inkster in the United States, for example, had not.[68]

Ford's promise to provide workers a modern future and freedom through consumption found a nice fit with the goals of segregationists in South Africa who wanted to use consumption to civilize poor whites. At least a year before Ford began assembling cars in South Africa the company was intent on developing a consumer market. Advertisements appeared regularly in the pages of the Port Elizabeth papers, each of which revealed the particularly racialized character of this emerging class-based consumer society. One implicitly defines "the people" as white: "Just about half the people have FORD cars, and the other half want them!"[69] Of those attending the agricultural show in Port Elizabeth the company asked, "Are you returning to your home in FORD comfort—enjoying the green fields, sunshine and picnic? Or in a stuffy train?" Targeted at rural or newly urbanized whites, the ad evokes the disgust they were being encouraged to associate with the public space of the train. Though racially segregated, the train nonetheless appeared in the ad as a symbol of the crowded world of the poor, a world in which control of one's own time—say, to stop for a picnic—is impossible.[70]

The equation of efficiency and management with modernity and whiteness was visible in advertising more broadly, as were localized anxieties about class and race status: "What can I give him for dinner? Why worry when AFRICAN MAID is here to help you? There are dozens of dainty dishes that can be prepared with the aid of AFRICAN MAID CORNFLOUR"; "Sunlight Soap: Economy—or the Management of Domestic Affairs—Is the Counterpart of Efficiency"; and "Solving the Problem for the New Poor: Cleghorn's Dress Fabrics."[71]

Anxiety over the consumer habits of poor white people and the psychological conditions that shaped them drove the Carnegie study, but another concern also lay at the heart of the panic. According to the commission: "Long continued *economic* equality of poor whites and the great mass of non-Europeans, and propinquity of their dwellings, tend to bring them to *social* equality."[72] It was not so much the existence of poor whites that mattered, but the behavior their social conditions might engender that was cause for worry. Economic and geographic closeness "impair[ed] the tradition which counteracts miscegenation and the social line of colour [was] noticeably weakening." Even as cases of poor whites "going kaffir" were viewed as "undoubtedly quite the exception," the report stressed that "long-continued contact with inferior coloured races has in some respects had deleterious social effects on the European."[73]

MEN- AND WOMEN-MAKING: GENDER, FAMILY, AND FACTORY DISCIPLINE IN POOR WHITE LIFE

The Carnegie Commission matched Fordist techniques imperfectly on some scores but strikingly well on others. The eugenic inspirations for diagnosis and prescription in the Carnegie study were consonant with Henry Ford's views. The limitations on mass consumption implied in whites-only policies were prefigured in some ways in his treatment of Black workers in the United States, but the demographic differences between the two countries sharply curtailed the furtherance of even the least developed U. S. version of Fordism in South Africa. However, the Carnegie group's emphasis on improving people, orderly social reproduction through interventions into workers' family lives, and relying on factory discipline to produce new men fit perfectly with strategies of Ford management. The identification of family as the key to men-making typified the Highland Park factory regime, and the reliance on the unrelenting pace of the line to produce discipline and so-called steadiness in men was a defining feature of the Rouge.

Maria Elizabeth Rothman was the only woman on the Carnegie investigative team and a member of the South African Christian Association. She conducted interviews with mothers and daughters in 462 "poor white" families that appeared as "The Mother and Daughter in the Poor White Family."[74] The problem of "frequent intermarriage of blood relatives" was examined in the study in part because of the reliance on American models for their work where a eugenic fetish regarding reproduction among Appalachian whites led to scholarly embrace of the term "white trash." However, in South Africa as at Highland Park and in Inkster, it was domestic behavior and attitudes—"the order or disorder in a home"—on which interviewers focused. Stressing as it did environmental as opposed to biological factors, this section of the report found a particular role for women in racial improvement through housekeeping and food preparation. Mirroring Henry Ford's and the American Race Betterment Association's fixation on diet the report concluded that "instruction should be given to mothers and daughters in the proper choice and preparation of various foods, that parents should be encouraged to grow vegetables . . . This instruction should not merely be advisory but should be so organized as to be habit-forming."[75]

Of course, the practice of interviewing poor whites in their homes resembled Ford's practice, by then abandoned, of sending sociological examiners into the homes of immigrant workers in Detroit. Discussed in chapter 1, in those cases Ford insisted that to be treated as an American worker who qualified for his company's five-dollar-a-day wage a particular standard of behavior was required. In the Carnegie model the home and the workplace were less directly linked—behavior at home never became the basis for wages at work—though both were considered essential to the process of racial improvement. However, the commission did recommend that modern management techniques be applied to homekeeping. It urged that the state create schools in which "domestic skills" could be taught, culminating in a "national housewife certificate" upon finishing the course. We can find parallels in Brazil's "diploma of whiteness" or with immigrant workers in Detroit from nationalities whose fitness as fully white citizens was on trial, much as poor whites in South Africa were scrutinized because of their Boer heritage and their poverty.[76]

The gendered division of home and work exemplified by the Carnegie approach exceeded Ford's vision in specific ways. The commission did not conclude that girls and women should be kept out of the workplace; on the contrary the civilizing effect of work and consumption was thought to apply to women too. The study devoted a significant focus to the concern that young women workers in the industrializing towns needed "wholesome" living possibilities. It did not oppose the movement of unmarried white girls to Port Elizabeth and Cape Town, where they were employed in the mechanized boot-making factories, and stressed the importance of their incomes to their families. But it did underline the fear of miscegenation that had resulted in the Immorality Suppression Bill being introduced in 1924. The bill made it illegal for a white woman to have "relations" with a "coloured" man. Strikingly, "native" men were not included in the original language of the bill. This might have reflected the assumption that "natives" shared whites' commitment to racial purity and were not actually seen as threatening in this way, although this was of course contradicted by the forced exclusion of native men from cities. More, though, the bill's wording suggests that the "erosion" of the color line represented by so-called colored people was seen as a threat of a particular kind, a sort of slippery slope. The race-mixing represented by the very existence of so-called colored people was not only the result of past biological reproduction but created a context in which the color line was becoming less sharply drawn.[77]

The commission's emphasis on the poor white family deviated in one important way from Ford's sociological investigations into workers' homes in

Detroit. While in Detroit the company was intent on seeing to it that immigrant men were married, and definitely believed that women would play a central role in policing their behavior, the company still clearly believed that it could better reform the men it employed than any other institution. Indeed, Ford's interest in seeing its workers married was less about an ideological emphasis on family and more about preventing the place and time for homosocial encounters that would lead to union organizing. Preventing men from sharing housing was an important goal of the Sociological Department, even more so than creating families. In his personal involvement with eugenic experimentation Henry Ford expressed interest in the "problem" of biological reproduction. But as an employer this never rose to the level one might expect if in fact his company had been thinking about the "welfare" of its employees and their families.

Carnegie commissioners on the other hand were very interested in white women's welfare, which included support for birth control for poor women. While this is consistent with eugenicist practices regarding poor whites in the United States, it does seem somewhat startling in a place where colonial anxiety over population ratios was ever-present.[78] That white women should be encouraged to limit their reproductive lives in the context of a demographic battle with Africans seems surprising. Yet, "neo-Malthusian" birth controllers believed that if poor whites limited their family size they would quickly and easily mitigate their poverty as well as raise healthier children. Liberal whites expressed the belief, mentioned above, that fewer but better was the more important concern in this moment.[79]

It is revealing that the areas of poor white life most heavily studied were the urban areas of Port Elizabeth and Cape Town even though poor-whiteness was defined largely as a rural phenomenon.[80] Consistent with this, the commission argued that an important solution to the poor white problem lay in finding a way to impose capitalist time-work discipline on poor whites while protecting them from the brutal working conditions to which so-called colored and native workers were subjected. Claiming that unrestricted competition had a demoralizing effect on the European, the report urged that "measures for restricting such competition should aim at counteracting this demoralisation."[81] Promoting the idea that higher wages were necessary for "civilized" workers, the commission offered suggestions on how best to accomplish this. Fordist models of production and consumption fully overlapped with the agenda of the commission for the fifth of the population that was white.

THE PACT GOVERNMENT, THE POOR WHITE, AND THE WELCOME OF FORD AND U. S. EXPERTISE

Embracing a commitment to the role of labor market competition in creating efficiency, as well as a racist worldview, the commission urged that the state intervene to provide white workers with jobs but that it not allow whites to become soft by protecting them too much from competition. The report held, "It will be disastrous for the poor white himself if any protection given him is of such a nature that it results finally in impairing his ability to compete with the non-European."[82] Focusing on the inadequate training being offered in rural training schools, schools which prepared young men for increasingly meaningless apprenticeships, the report stressed that the best training ground for the adult rural poor immigrant was "*work in the factory itself.*"[83]

By the time the report was published the idea of preserving industrial work for whites was being legislated in South Africa. Following the 1924 election of the Pact Government, representing a merger between the Nationalist Party and the South African Labour Party, a "civilized labour policy" had been introduced, inaugurated with the firing of all African workers in government jobs. General Hertzog, prime minister under the Nationalist-Labour Pact Government elected in 1924, sought to create the definition of "civilized standards." "Civilized labour is to be considered as the labour rendered by persons whose standard of living conforms to the standard generally recognized as tolerable from the usual European standpoint."[84]

The Railway Act, which made jobs on the rails the preserve of whites, and the Mine and Works Act followed in 1926, enshrining in law the industrial color bar that had operated contractually in the mines.[85] Among other things the 1926 act legislated that only whites could be in charge of the operation of machinery and codified the categorization of work by race. The idea of white racial improvement, of expanding civilized society through segregation, intensified through the 1920s and '30s and came to thoroughly penetrate progressive, social welfare activities. A host of conferences and committees were organized with the shared goal of creating knowledge about racial segregation. The United States was ever-present in these conversations.

One of the most significant of these conferences was the National Congress on the Poor White Question held in Kimberley in 1934, sponsored by the Dutch Reformed Church and opened by Verwoerd. The call for the conference invited participants to come and "consider the findings of the [Carnegie] investigation, to amend them if necessary and then to appeal to the nation to carry them out."[86] The goal of the conference was to form committees to deal with the "socio-economic, the psycho-educational and the socio-religious" factors that would involve "every important phase of national life." Putting this aspect of the poor white problem into sharp relief the conference planners announced that it had been resolved to nominate a liaison committee of five or six members "who while being thoroughly conversant with the Poor White Problem would also be able to speak authoritatively on the Native and Coloured Question. Their task will be to place the Poor White and the Native Problems in their correct setting... to investigate their mutual relations and interactions and to study to what extent *measures for the solution of the first are likely either to prejudice or enhance the solution of the second*."[87] Indeed, the director of Native Agriculture wrote to the conference planners suggesting that his organization participate in the conference on the grounds that "I realize how very closely the problem you are dealing with touches the Native problem."[88]

Despite such acknowledgments, the emphasis remained firmly on whites and specifically on addressing an ethnic bifurcation in the ruling race that had no direct comparison in the United States. In Verwoerd's opening remarks at the conference he stressed that white poverty was far more prevalent among Afrikaners than British, even as he called on both English and Afrikaners to work together in creating "the beginning of a new era in our participation in social uplift." Though some took this as a sign of Verwoerd relying on the long extant tradition in which British- and Dutch- descended South Africans viewed one another as racially distinct, Balstad Miller rightly reads this as Verwoerd's attempt to appeal to a common whiteness across national (racial) differences. Consistently referencing the need for English and Afrikaner cooperation in attacking the national problem of white poverty Verwoerd, like Malherbe, should be viewed as a racial progressive in the context of pre-apartheid South Africa. Calling "welfare work" the "task of the new democracy" he signaled the emergence of a new kind of South African politics. That politics at times took its cues neither from the British empire nor narrow Afrikaner nationalism. Instead, the United States, represented by the Carnegie Commission and Ford, became a kind of alternative source of leadership in the interwar years. Nevertheless the demographics of race, politics, and class made the two U.S.A.s differ fundamentally in ways that both Ford and the Carnegie Commission had to countenance.

More nearly congruent with U.S. patterns of white supremacy, but not quite distinct from the situation in Brazil, was the South African conception of mixed-race people. In South Africa mixed-race, so-called "colored," residents were objects of exclusion. Thus Ford's Port Elizabeth color bars applied to them, but they were also a distinct category separate from, and separated from, Africans. Among the proliferating conferences and organizations that came into being as a result of Carnegie's intervention and that looked to the United States for leadership on specific social questions was the Committee on Mixed Marriages in South Africa. Commissioned by the Governor General in 1938 the committee was charged with uncovering whether mixed marriages were on the increase, whether they were likely to increase, whether they existed in numbers sufficient to be "seriously detrimental to the welfare of the Union and the future of the composition of the population," and whether it would be necessary to take further steps to discourage such marriages.[89]

The committee began with the same definitional problem that the Carnegie team had: the impossibility of knowing who was white and who was "colored." Given rates of passing and the fact that non-Europeans would have been listed in the records as European if they were able to pass, the committee decided it would have been difficult to "trace the number of such marriages or the degree or 'color' which was present in some of the parties."[90] Outlining the many aspects of segregationist practice and building a case for its logic, the report turned to the question of mixed marriages by claiming that opposition to such unions was a "natural sequence." (Of course, the committee did not note the apparent contradiction that if opposition to this practice were natural it would hardly need a committee to study its existence and outlaw its practice.) Tracing the genealogy of anti-miscegenation legislation through the various acts of immorality suppression, the committee noted the importance of the 1927 move to criminalize white men who lived with native women. Though they had enjoyed historic immunity, in the view of the committee white men needed to be held responsible if in fact miscegenation was to be treated as a social evil.[91]

The committee turned to U. S. models to address the inadequate methodology for determining race. "Coloured" people who may have looked white were in fact not white in the eyes of these social reformers, but no standards of testing existed that could make this legislation practicable. For the solution to this problem the committee looked to the United States where "a situation very much like our own brought about legislation prohibiting mixed marriages in 30 out of 48 states."[92] About the United States the committee wrote, "There, too, a small population of whites originally settled among a large coloured native population of American Indians and the position was soon complicated by the introduction of a prolific race of Negro slaves and later by the immigration of other coloured races." The committee was pleased to note that in more than a few cases the U. S. statutes attempted to define what they meant by white, colored, or Negro down to one-sixteenth of Negro blood. They noted the significant legislation that attended these laws: the crime of printing, publishing, or circulating material that urged or presented arguments in favor of social equality; the harsh penalties levied against those who would perform such a marriage; and the criminalization, in six states, of illicit sexual relations.[93]

When the committee members asked for an explanation as to why mixed marriages were criminalized they were told:

> Of the 30 states which prohibit inter-racial marriages, sixteen may be designated as Southern or border states where the Negro problem is, generally speaking, most serious owing to the presence of Negroes in large numbers . . . statutes in [Delaware and Indiana] are explained by racial prejudice . . . or the dogma of white superiority.

From its assessment of U. S. legislation the committee concluded:

> Manifestly the white population of the United States has never had cause to apprehend the danger of being swamped, whereas in South Africa there has always been an overwhelming majority of natives. The motives which prompted Americans to legislate also actuate those who support legislation on the subject in South Africa, but the latter are also compelled by a much more cogent motive—the desire to keep the white population intact as the dominant and ruling race.[94]

The lessons the committee wanted to take from the United States for policy in South Africa included developing a more precise science of racial classification, registering people based on that racial classification, and more stridently policing transgressions of the racial order. Already under construction, within a decade that structure would be in place.

In adopting the rhetoric and posture of scientific rigor, proponents of segregation shifted gears after World War I called into question European moral superiority in the colonized world. This posture both recalled Ford's Sociological Department at Highland Park, and differed from it. Ford's "sociologists" were deliberately not professionally trained, but instead drawn from the ranks of the company's own white-collar workforce.[95] They generated data for very limited management purposes, not to construct theory and still less to claim transnational racial knowledge. Contrastingly, Morag Bell argues, "The inter-war years marked a new phase of colonial occupation in Britain's African domain in which scientific survey became integrated with colonial administration."[96] As white elites in South Africa looked to new, "objective" justifications for white colonial rule, they increasingly turned to the United States for these new ideas. Ford's reputation as scientific and progressive, far more than its precise techniques (in any case long disused in Detroit), shaped the political and cultural embrace of American capital and cultural influence in the interwar period.[97]

Saul Dubow's study of Malherbe and the meaning of his work should inform our understanding of the contours and limits of what South African white racial progressives in the era of segregation shared with Ford. Insisting that these white supremacists were also reformers, Dubow details the rise of the political movement of "South Africanists" in the interwar years, a movement to which Malherbe was central. Describing it as a "centrist" political tradition Dubow argues convincingly that South Africanism is an especially useful lens onto the formation of white identity and the racialist politics that attended it before Afrikaner nationalism came to dominate. Following on the heels of postwar conciliation between the Dutch and British, which also entailed a class dimension, South Africanism "embraced a broad spectrum of opinion and its tonal midpoint shifted over time." In spite of those shifts South Africanists consistently held the position that parliamentary democracy and liberal policies toward civil society were the appropriate governmental forms for white citizens. As modernizers and racists they embodied those contradictions: on the one hand they tended to stress culture and not biology as the basis for racial policies; on the other they were hereditarians, staunchly opposed to race-mixing, believing it would only lead to white racial degeneration. Their commitments to segregation reflected in part the idea that the development of white civilization required the private spaces that segregation afforded whites (though of course the reliance on African domestic labor meant that few white domestic spaces were, in fact, all white). South Africanists sought to bring like-minded Afrikaner and English South Africans together under the rubric of white nonracialism. Some of the most activist segregationists and policy makers in interwar South Africa did so as they denounced racialism. This helps us understand how the category of white was being redefined to include Britains and Boers in the Union and Pact Government years. The segregation of work and the promise of increased consumption were keys to the creation of a South African white identity. Ford's practice and reputation symbolized both.[98]

Evidence of Ford's specific impact on cultural practices in pre-apartheid Port Elizabeth is fragmentary, though what exists suggests the powerful impact the company had on structures of race and class in the city. In 1929 Autosite was founded as the clubhouse of the Port Elizabeth automobile club and became a gathering spot for the managerial elite of the many transnational auto companies doing business there. The Ford Motor Company, as mouthpiece of the National Association of Automobile Manufacturers, was a key sponsor of the club. After functioning for nearly a decade Autosite acquired a liquor license in 1937 and was reborn as the Port Elizabeth Country Club.[99] Ford's intimate link to the space where class privilege and white managerialism was performed and reproduced is not surprising; it underlines the potency of the company's presence in South Africa.

As much as Ford appealed to South African reformers for its progressive and American mantle, however, its practices there were also impeccably South Africanist. As Gramsci observed regarding Europe, the company's Americanism could only penetrate different social contexts so far. In Brazil's Amazon, Fordism was likewise a "Brazilianist" and not only an "Americanist" force. The color line and the assembly line intersected in such distinct national and international contexts that at least as a racial project transnational Fordism in the interwar years is best considered a process of flexible accumulation. Ford management assumed that it possessed commanding racial knowledge to be adapted, not imposed, as capital moved. As they were filtered through a discourse derived from Fordist efficiency, American social science, and racial modernism, the contradictions and conflicts of white managerialism did not go away but became central features of twentieth-century intellectual and industrial production in South Africa.

CONCLUSION

From the One Best Way to The Way Forward to One Ford

STILL UNEVEN, STILL UNEQUAL

AS THE FORD MOTOR COMPANY'S PLACE in multiple national economies deepened in the decades after World War I so, too, did analysis and assessment of the political and cultural implications of Ford's various presences. No one offered greater insight into the promise and peril represented by Ford than Antonio Gramsci, despite the stark limits imposed on him by incarceration and the multiple deprivations that attended it. In "Americanism and Fordism" Gramsci described the process through which the United States had relatively easily "made the whole life of the nation revolve around production" through a combination of "force . . . and persuasion."[1] Central to this book's arguments is acceptance of Gramsci's observation that possessing the most rationalized labor process in the world enabled Ford to rule workers and reshape society in the interwar years. In arguing that "hegemony [in the United States] is born in the factory and requires for its exercise only a minute quantity of professional and political and ideological intermediaries" Gramsci gave as evidence for this assertion the notion that " the 'structure' dominates the superstructures more immediately and . . . the latter are also 'rationalized' (simplified and reduced in number)."[2] This combination was for Gramsci achievable in the United States in ways it could not be in Europe because of the specificity (not exceptionalism) of United States history and the emergence of Ford.

In arguing, as this book does, that patterns of U.S. racialization, as manipulated by Ford, were critical to this specificity it also challenges Gramsci's claim that "only a minute quantity of professional and political and ideological" intervention was needed. Gramsci's willingness to see the cultural superstructures produced in the early Fordist period as being as rationalized as the workplace itself reflects his sense of a kind of juggernaut of power creating a world with no outside. This is understandable, and makes his intent to interpret the world from his location in a fascist prison even more admirable. But it misses the mark on what was actually happening in Ford factories and among Ford workers. Some ideas were being promoted while others were violently repressed. Gangsterism and Klan organizing flourished in relative terms as workers were gunned down during protests against poverty and hunger. Colonialist ideas about savagery and civilization were fed to Ford workers not just as propaganda in the pages of the *Dearborn Independent* but every time another car rolled off the assembly line allegedly representing modern progress and a vanquishing of the past. One tragedy of this story is that the defeat of unionism at Ford for so many decades was closely accompanied by white supremacist narrations of history and community. Yet and still, the lines between force and persuasion, structure and superstructure, class and race were blurred, not eliminated.

At its most basic level the linking of hegemony and factory enables a vital broadening of analytical possibilities, supplementing scholarship that places the United States in the world by stressing the spread of its culture of mass consumption. Important as those matters were, it was the discipline of mass production at Ford, as well as its advertised ability to transform "backwards" workers through regimented labor, that first made Ford so attractive to foreign leaders and that slowed its spread to countries with stronger industrial unions. The significance of Gramsci's insight for purposes here has been to demonstrate the very close relationship between the mass production of cars and the mass production of men, the cultural forms Ford pursued, promoted, and endorsed, and the imperatives of mass production. The dialectical relationship between these dynamics—often ignored or dismissed by historians seeking to render Henry Ford enigmatic or paradoxical for his promotion of "traditional" cultural forms even as his firm obliterated the material basis for their continuance—is of utmost importance. In promoting cultural practices allegedly retrieved from bygone times and bygone places Ford promoted a past that had never existed. It was not a disappearing past but the future that Ford sought to bring into being, a contemporary and future reality of a white supremacist social order for workers that would not be thwarted by the cosmopolitan, transnational, and transgressive possibilities his massive global workforce embodied.

In seeking to present a holistic treatment of Henry Ford and the company he built, this study has offered insight into the workings of white supremacy as a set of ideas and practices that went with Ford into the world. As these chapters have shown, that process was challenged by different realities in each social context it confronted, focusing on uneven development and modern racial regimes that made Brazil and South Africa different from one another and from the United States, a country which itself produced and encompassed uneven development across regions. Yet despite the differences in application of the terms of white supremacist rule, we can nonetheless perceive affinities across national imaginaries that saw in Ford's method of production a way to build what political scientist Robert Vitalis has recently called a "white world order."[3]

The substantive catalogue of historical studies that have consistently compared Brazil, South Africa, and the United States established one important basis for their selection here. Within those studies, histories of slavery, settlement, and the weight of subsequent white supremacist structures lay the basis for comparison. Largely because of that, most of these studies use not the United States as a whole but the U.S. South specifically as the place that produced the history linking it to Brazil and South Africa. In bringing Ford's practices in the U.S. North and South into the frame, this study interrupts that practice and argues for a broader understanding of how white supremacy was institutionalized in the United States nationally despite regional differences.

Such a consideration of a more nationally consistent white supremacy in the United States is made possible by thinking dynamically rather than statically about these three countries. Making Brazilian and South African elites decisive actors in U.S. history because of their impacts on the Ford Motor Company is a hallmark of what transnational rather than comparative national approaches to history can accomplish. It also allows us to use analytic tools such as internal colonialism, uneven development, dependency, and state-formation that historians of the global South turn to on a regular basis but which many historians of the United States have preferred to avoid.

By using the Ford Motor Company as a lens through which to look at the globalization of American capital during and after World War I this book sheds light on various aspects of that moment: ideology, production, consumption, the state, and the growth of U.S. empire. Studying Ford has allowed us to consider firm-specific characteristics such as the company's authoritarianism, racism, profound anti-unionism, and its managerial structure as well as the broader themes that described how U.S. firms went into the world in this era, particularly through accessing British Empire rights, setting up branch plants, promoting new social scientific knowledge, exporting U.S. capital goods, dominating transportation and communication structures, and innovating how products would be moved around the world.

By considering how Ford's claim to desire a universal worker in his company's pursuit of a universal product was undermined by the political and social relationships that Ford promoted, this study has tried to offer one way into understanding the staying power of racist ideology and practice. It has argued that it is not enough to say that Henry Ford was powerful and wealthy and also an anti-Semite and a white supremacist. Rather this book has examined a set of practical applications of Ford's wealth and power as connected to the ideology that his workplaces made material. And while some of the specific dimensions of those practices have been demolished by decades of social and workplace struggles, the contours of men-making in the service of car-making continue, as does the practice of producing difference in the pursuit of both goals. This is most visible in China, where city after city wishes to become the new Detroit.

EXCAVATING DETROIT'S FUTURE IN HANGZHOU—A BRAVE NEW WORLD

This book was researched and written during the most recent phase of the prolonged destruction of the city of Detroit and, sadly, as cities across China poignantly sought to earn the title "The Detroit of China." During this time the Ford Motor Company marked three major centenaries: the founding of the company, in 2003; the launch of the first auto assembly line, in 2008; and the introduction of the five-dollar day, in 2014. Each of these milestones highlighted events described over the years by scholars, publicists, and pundits as being "revolutionary" in the scale of their impact on world history. But considering the grandiosity of such claims the celebrations of these anniversaries were curiously muted. Of course it could just be bad timing. At the same time Ford would have celebrated these transformative events it was in the process of a global restructuring of its operations at a scale not seen since the 1970s.

Ford's global plan to cut costs by cutting spending on what it calls "the human side" of its operation and to create new markets is nothing new, and these reforms have meant and continue to mean more misery in and around Detroit and other Ford towns. In the opening weeks of 2006 Ford announced that its North America operations would be closing fourteen plants and eliminating 30,000 jobs. This "rightsizing" plan was described by CEO Bill Ford as "painful but . . . necessary" and branded—*Brave New World*–style—as *The Way Forward* by the head of North American Operations Mark Shields. Shields had previewed *The Way Forward* a full year earlier at the company's December 2005 board meeting. In announcing the cuts and closings, which totaled a loss of 20–25 percent of Ford's North American workforce of 122,000, Shields still hoped to blur the real impact of this news by referring to its North American rather than its U. S. workforce. The number 122,000 represents *all* North American workers, which of course includes Mexico, though the cuts and closings applied only in the United States and Canada.[4] The distinction is important insofar as it describes the company's willingness to appeal to transnational framings when they worked in its favor—suggesting here how devoted an employer Ford still is while blurring the lines about the national contexts in which jobs are created (Mexico) or lost (the United States and Canada). This is not to suggest that auto jobs in U. S. firms are the natural property of U. S. workers or that the crime of job destruction is made greater because the work crosses a national border. On the contrary, it is to point out the hypocrisy in Ford's appeals to its Americanness while deriving profits from the uneven and unequal conditions of investment it helped to create not just in North America but worldwide.

That growing worldwide terrain certainly reveals that much has changed with regard to the place of Ford, and auto production generally, but we might usefully focus as well on continuities. Thus the frequently used shorthand of "post-Fordist" to describe the changed world economy of the last half-century needs to be tempered by an examination of how much the world of neoliberal, lean, and just-in-time production looks like the Ford of the interwar period. Those parts of Fordism that promised unprecedentedly high wages in order that mass consumption would compensate for alienated and concentrated labor are largely gone—*though across the vast span of Ford enterprises they were never universally present.* Gone too are the postwar "Fordist" social and economic contracts in some large industrial economies, where states were sometimes committed to maintaining well-paying jobs in mass production and a social safety net for their workers (though always pressed to do so by strong unions). But the necessity to produce new bodies of workers available and able to do repetitive and sometimes deadly labor very much remains, as does the reliance on uneven development of the world economy and the production of difference within nations to secure and discipline those workers.

So let us be more precise about what post-Fordism might connote and, more importantly for the purposes of this book, about what early Fordism did include. Popular understandings of the Ford Motor Company celebrate the advent of the auto assembly line, the five-dollar-a-day wage, and the mass consumption that this wage is said to have enabled. The implementation of Ford's wage scale is treated as the great equalizer—allowing masses of workers to buy what they built for the first time in history. Neglected in the story of freedom through consumption is attention to the always exhausting and often brutal or deadly working conditions that have characterized auto work for people all over the world. More important still is the overlooked reality that Henry Ford and the Ford Motor Company promoted and / or accommodated ideas and practices that promoted race, gender, and national and cultural difference, which taught people in the United States to view some people as deserving industrial jobs, access to consumer goods, and the "civilization" those goods represented, and others as being not ready, temporarily or permanently, for such things. The racial hierarchies that are used to explain such difference are thus naturalized by way of temporal analyses.

We can examine continuities in "uneven Fordism" despite changes by looking briefly at Mexico, as it becomes the largest exporter of cars to the United States, and at China, now the largest manufacturer of automobiles in the world.[5] A well-intentioned example of the use of temporal scale to underline the differences between the United States and Mexico comes in the 1991 film produced by anti–North American Free Trade Agreement (NAFTA) activists, *$4 a Day? No Way! Joining Hands across the Border.* The film was one of the first to draw attention to the horrific living and working conditions on the Mexican side of the U. S.-Mexico border. The narration begins: "For U. S. corporations, crossing the border into Mexico is like going back in time." This description of relative development is strikingly common; these ideas—that progress is measured in terms of temporality, that some people are living in what might one day become another people's future, or that places like Mexico represent the past of the United States—permeate comparisons of these two countries. (For the Ford Motor Company, which started making cars in Mexico in 1925, it is particularly noteworthy, as Ford had been promising to bring civilization and progress to Mexico for nearly nine decades by the time the film was made.) As evidence for their claim, the filmmakers point to the four-dollar-a-day wages paid by transnational companies in 1991 to their workers in Mexico. In a context considering neoliberal political economy and its precursors, it is indeed striking to point out that it was "Fordism" in the United States that, in 1914, brought about the five-dollar-a-day wage.[6] What accounts for the eighty-year and dollar-a-day difference between the United States and Mexico is far more complicated than can be detailed here. But what does matter is how meaning is made and explained out of such differences.

As John Smith has recently written, "In 1995 [the United States] imported four times as much automobile-related value-added from Canada as from Mexico, just 10 percent more in 2005, and, by 2009, Mexico was the source of 48 percent more value-added than Canada." Twenty years after NAFTA, the 2014 "Site Selection" bulletin of the Barber Business Advisors group reported that Mexico had tripled its share of North American auto production on the strength of holding the autoworker's average daily wage to $16 per day, "$4 less than what the average U.S. autoworker makes per hour."[7] The twentieth anniversary of NAFTA, which automakers celebrated in 2014, also saw Ford positioned to celebrate the hundredth anniversary of its founders' introduction of the five-dollar-a-day wage—though it was not at all clear what such a celebration could mean. Unlike the years that immediately followed the introduction of the wage, when Ford's productivity, which is to say profitability, skyrocketed, today's Ford argues for increased profitability by lowering wages. In the United States the company specifically means to replace older, "more expensive" workers with newer, cheaper ones. This was indeed a key component of *The Way Forward*. Other aspects of the company's announced restructuring in 2006 in fact echoed past practice, including outsourcing, constantly innovating with tooling and technology, and moving work closer to markets. Although the last of these is not unrelated to the others, it is perhaps the most critical facet of the "new" Ford and one that brings us full circle to the dynamic role of the production of difference and unevenness that is the concern of this book.

NEW CHINA, OLD FORD

A 2014 study prepared by Alex Covarrubias Valdenebro under the auspices of the Friedrich Ebert Foundation remarked that Mexico was soon to become the "China of the West" where auto production was concerned. The reference applied equally to its boom in production and its harsh labor conditions.[8] Though Ford arrived late in China in comparison to its U.S. and global competitors, the company is making up for lost time. In March 2015 the Ford

Motor Company brought online a new, $760 million factory in Hangzhou, China. South of Shanghai, the plant is one of seven Ford will open as joint ventures under the name Changan Ford Hangzhou. In the Hangzhou plant, more than 50,000 workers build cars entirely for sale in China. When all seven plants are in operation Ford's capacity will be an annual production of 1.4 million vehicles for the Chinese market.

Questions of difference, citizenship, and men-making are not posed in quite the same way that they were in Brazil, South Africa, and Detroit but they are nonetheless posed. The context in which Ford opens its seven state-of-the-art auto production facilities is the extraordinary growth of the Chinese auto industry that has expanded at an exponential rate over the past two decades. Annual output has increased seventeenfold from about 1.3 million in 1993 to more than 22 million in 2013. As the largest automobile manufacturing nation, China produces 25.3 percent of automobiles worldwide. By way of comparison China made more vehicles in 2013 than the second- and third-largest vehicle producing nations, the United States at 11 million and Japan at 9.6 million, combined.[9]

In the context of the global economic crisis of 2008, average profitability in the Chinese auto assembly sector rebounded quickly. Industry analysts largely attributed this growth to the government's stimulus policies, China's optimized production capacity, and reduced manufacturing costs—in other words, by the exploitation of assembly line workers through increased work intensity and excessive overtime, as well as stagnating pay and use of temporary workers. According to the sociologist Lu Zhang, who has conducted the most far-reaching research into shop-floor conditions in China's auto industry:

> Working conditions are characterized by heavy workloads, long working hours (usually ten to twelve per shift), and excessive overtime . . . The results of the industrial and labor restructuring are significant—an increase of production of 680 percent within ten years. Meanwhile, the total numbers of manufacturing employees declined from almost 2 million in 1994 to 1.5 million in 2001 and increased only to 2.2 million in 2010.[10]

Cars and exhaustion among workers were once again produced together.

So too were cars and social difference. Being classified or described as a temporary worker does not mean in today's China and much of the world that one does not have constant and even long-term work. Rather, it means that a system is in place that ensures vulnerability by denying workers any claims over their jobs or working hours. The reasons for using temporary workers are straightforward—to cut labor costs, increase flexibility, discipline labor, and reduce the possibility of collective labor struggle. In China, the cost of hiring a formal worker, which includes social insurance contributions and fringe benefits, is the same as that of hiring two or three temporary workers. Most temporary workers are hired through labor dispatch agencies, making it easy for auto employers to fire these workers by simply returning them to the labor hiring agencies.[11]

Such terms of work are not structured only by the factory but also by the broader social and political reality that shapes life in China. At the heart of China's productivity increases and increased rates of exploitation—its hospitality to transnational capital and direct investment—is the reality of the internal migration system that leaves tens of millions of workers vulnerable. Through the system of residential registration, or *hukou,* movement in China has historically been prevented, controlled, and carefully regulated. Reforms in the new China that have enabled tens of millions of rural residents to migrate to urban areas for work have importantly not included reform of this system. Where once mobility was stridently restricted, now capital benefits from an internal migration and pass system that enforces only parts of the residency system. The result of this is that millions of workers live in constant states of illegality. Those who possess a rural *hukou* but live and work in an urban area exist objectively outside the structure that offers any degree of social welfare or protection.[12]

Though rural residents are encouraged in virtually every way to leave their villages and become workers, often becoming what the British sociologist Satnam Virdee calls "racialized outsiders," in urban areas and the industrial parks that surround them the state has refused to do away with the system that links one's legal existence to one's official residence. Control over freedom of movement and over the domicile of those people holding a rural *hukou* has not been rescinded. Despite the great risks attached to becoming internal migrants seeking work sometimes thousands of miles from their homes, tens of millions of peasants from poor inner provinces, trying to escape poverty and subsistence livelihoods, have surged out in search of jobs. Estimates are that Beijing has 1.6 million migrant workers, Shanghai has 3.3 million, and that in Guangdong Province there are 12 million. From within these millions of people come the students and small farmers who work as "temporary" and vulnerable employees with rural *hukou* that prevent them from collecting the benefits that are owed them by virtue of their official place of residence.

The promise of high wages continues to bring people into developing auto production centers like Hangzhou despite what it costs them in terms of state benefits and a social safety net. While the contradictions of this system are increasingly evident, as the Chinese state overtly encourages internal migration it also has become clear that the state and the foreign investors it attracts rely on the *hukou* system to keep workers vulnerable. That workers should be considered temporary migrants while coming from one part of their own country to another describes not the promise of a universalized workforce but a divided and vulnerable one on whose existence foreign auto companies like Ford rely for the massive productivity increases described above. It also finds parallels in the histories of Black workers in the United States and African workers in South Africa.

So defined by violence and uncertainty is the *hukou* system in China that scholars Peter Alexander and Anita Chan argue for the essential commonalities between it and the pass laws that prefigured and then came to centrally structure apartheid South Africa. The details of the two systems are remarkably similar. Both require that permission must be obtained before rural people leave for the towns. Both ban taking children to the towns and, for the migrant workers, discourage urban births and institute prohibitions on urban family life. With both, there is also some form of housing linked to employment, separating migrant workers by sex and segregating them from workers who possess an urban *hukou*. In both countries there is periodic migration, generally annual, back to the rural areas. Far from the pro-family labor discipline of Ford in historic Highland Park, such patterns are very like those of early Fordlandia in Brazil.

In apartheid South Africa the maintenance of the system depended on the authorization of passes as it does in China today. Policing of these documents leads to further similarities, such as bribery, harassment, fines, and deportations to rural areas.[13] This vast panoply of measures is actually incapable of stopping the influx of rural people into urban areas and in fact it is not meant to actually do so. As under the apartheid system, Chinese rural dwellers face economic pressures in the rural areas that are too great, people are resourceful, officials are corruptible, and many employers are only too happy to accept the most vulnerable workers. The outcomes are very similar. Pass systems produce a large underclass of less-than-full-citizens living in constant insecurity, accompanied by daily discrimination, suppression, hardship, and denial of human dignity.[14]

Indeed, in Lu Zhang's magnificent study of automobile factories in contemporary China, she found that what was significant about the hiring of vulnerable, temporary workers was that they had not replaced formal, more costly workers in anything close to 100 percent of cases. Why, she asks, would management "retain a segment of more expensive and privileged formal workers whose work could be done by temporary workers" for one-third or one-half of the cost? She argues that management sees difference between workers on the shop floor as valuable, in that formal workers tend to be more loyal and cooperative and to regard temporary workers as their problem. She further suggests that it is not so much antagonism between workers that matters as what she calls "detachment," a social distance "made greater by segregated living spaces and unequal living conditions."[15]

Even at the level of the built environment of the car itself, inequality in China is being established as cultural fact. At the Shanghai Auto Show in June, 2015 Ford unveiled its new model Taurus as the leading edge of its sales strategy in China. The Taurus peaked in popularity in the United States as the best selling car in 1988 but has been reintroduced as a "new premium business sedan for China." A senior analyst at *Autotrader* says, "The Ford Taurus is a storied name in U. S. automotive history, but the fact is, the full-size car market has been in decline in the States with no end in sight." The new Ford Taurus illustrates how the needs of Chinese car buyers are leading design and decisions on product development by global automakers. In the Shanghai unveiling, Ford emphasized how carefully it had studied what it called Chinese culture and use patterns before crafting the China Taurus. The result was six inches shorter than the current U. S. Taurus, but it rides on a wheelbase four inches longer, which opens up more leg room, especially in the back. The company's explanation for this it that in China, owners often ride in back, rather than driving themselves as is typical in the United States, even among executives. Ford notes that the China Taurus has "more than 25 intelligent stowage spaces throughout the cabin," including cup-holders "designed to securely hold different-sized tea bottles . . . Reflecting the importance of second-row passengers in China—where the owner of a premium vehicle is often a passenger rather than a driver—the second row has been designed with an emphasis on comfort."[16] Likewise, Ford will bring back the Lincoln Continental as a storied luxury vehicle for the Chinese market, again focusing on innovations for the consumer. At New York's International Auto Show Ford announced that the new "Lincoln's back-seat amenities will include a laptop table that motors itself into position, electric sockets to power a laptop and other devices, and a champagne cooler in the center console."[17]

The long-standing view of Fordism as producing a new sameness of work and of wants is thus contested in these pages. For all of the homogeneity it sought and generated, Ford also actively and self-interestedly produced difference. Further, Ford did not simply fail to eradicate difference but flourished via unevenness at the scales of the factory, of the plantation, of the neighborhood, of the household, of the nation, and of the globe. Rather than dissolving historically rooted colonial categories, Ford in fact helped consolidate a twentieth-century hierarchy of racial and national realities around the world; despite Ford's professed interest in a universal system, and despite convergences of interest in this idea across the political spectrum, unevenness and difference were central to the company's success. Those inequalities persist and are being remade today, perhaps nowhere more evidently than in China. To the extent that such is the case the recent past and present of auto production and much else are in important ways not so fully "post-Fordist" as we often imagine.

NOTES

INTRODUCTION

1. W. E. B. Du Bois, *The Souls of Black Folk* (Mineola, NY: Dover, 1994, originally 1903), vi, 9. On Du Bois's usages of the term see David R. Roediger, "To Be Continued: The 'Problem of the Color Line' in the Twenty-First Century," in *Twenty-First Century Color Lines: Multiracial Change in Contemporary America*, ed. Andrew Grant-Thomas and Gary Orfield, 281–82 (Philadelphia: Temple University Press, 2009).

2. W. E. B. Du Bois, "The Color Line Belts the World," in *The Writings of W. E. B. Du Bois in Periodicals Edited by Others*, 4 vols., ed. Herbert Aptheker, 1:330 (Millwood, NY: Kraus, Thomson, 1982).

3. Ida Tarbell, *All in the Day's Work: An Autobiography* (Urbana: University of Illinois Press, 2003, originally 1939), 287–92, on the origins of Ford "making men"; Henry Ford, in collaboration with Samuel Crowther, *My Life and Work* (Garden City, NY: Doubleday and Page, 1922), 91–102. See also Stephen Meyer, *Manhood on the Line: Working-Class Masculinities in the American Heartland* (Urbana: University of Illinois Press, 2016); and chapter 1 herein.

4. The nineteenth-century history of eugenic thought in the world is thoroughly explored by Daniel Kevles, *In the Name of Eugenics: Genetics and the Uses of Human Heredity* (Cambridge, MA: Harvard University Press, 1998). For an account of the repopularization of these ideas after World War I in multiple European contexts, see Mark Adams, ed., *The Wellborn Science: Eugenics in Germany, France, Brazil, and Russia* (New York: Oxford University Press, 1990). Also on Brazil and Latin America more broadly, see Nancy Stepan's excellent *"The Hour of Eugenics": Race, Gender, and Nation in Latin America* (Ithaca, NY: Cornell University Press, 1996).

5. Diary of the Day, "The Ford Idyll," *Eastern Province Herald*, February 11, 1924, holdings in the Port Elizabeth Public Library, Port Elizabeth, South Africa.

6. Jerry Davila, *Diploma of Whiteness: Race and Social Policy in Brazil, 1917–1945* (Durham, NC: Duke University Press, 2003).

7. Mae Ngai, *Impossible Subjects: Illegal Aliens and the Making of Modern America* (Princeton, NJ: Princeton University Press, 2004). See also Rachel Ida

Buff, ed., *Immigrant Rights in the Shadow of Citizenship* (New York: New York University Press, 2008).

8. Antonio Gramsci, "Americanism and Fordism," in *Selections from the Prison Notebooks* (New York: International, 1971), 279–318; David Harvey, *The Condition of Postmodernity* (London: Blackwell Books, 1990), 224–39; David R. Roediger and Elizabeth D. Esch, *The Production of Difference: Race and the Management of Labor in U.S. History* (New York: Oxford University Press, 2012); Lisa Lowe, *Immigrant Acts: On Asian American Cultural Politics* (Chapel Hill, NC: Duke University Press, 1996), 27–28.

9. On Taylor and Ford, see Daniel Nelson, *Managers and Workers: Origins of the Twentieth-Century Factory System in the United States, 1880–1920* (Madison: University of Wisconsin Press, 1996), 56–135; David Montgomery, *The Fall of the House of Labor: The Workplace, the State, and American Labor Activism, 1865–1925* (Cambridge: Cambridge University Press, 1987), 216–56.

10. Ralph Bunche, *A World View of Race* (Port Washington, NY: Kennikat Press, 1968, originally 1936).

11. For a particularly sanguine view regarding markets, modernity, and corporate support for integration, see Jennifer Delton, *Racial Integration in Corporate America, 1940–1990* (Cambridge: Cambridge University Press, 2009).

12. John R. Commons, *Races and Immigrants in America* (New York: MacMillan, 1907), 150; Samuel Haber, *Efficiency and Uplift: Scientific Management in the Progressive Era, 1890–1920* (Chicago: University of Chicago Press, 1964), 148. See also Yngve Ramstad and James L. Starkey, "The Racial Theories of John R. Commons," *Research in the History of Economic Thought and Methodology* 13 (1995): 1–75; James R. Barrett, *Work and Community in the Jungle: Chicago's Packing House Workers, 1894–1922* (Urbana: University of Illinois Press, 1987), 20–31; and chapter 3 herein.

13. Howard Segal, *Recasting the Machine Age: Henry Ford's Village Industries* (Amherst: University of Massachusetts Press, 2008), 45.

14. Karl Marx and Friedrich Engels, *Manifesto of the Communist Party* (1848), www.anu.edu.au/polsci/marx/classics/manifesto.html; Dipesh Chakrabarty, "Universalism and Belonging in the Logic of Capital," *Public Culture* 12 (2000): 652–76; Harry Braverman, *Labor and Monopoly Capital: The Degradation of Work in the Twentieth Century* (New York: Monthly Review Press, 1975), 85–138, 146–50. C. L. R. James, *American Civilization,* ed. Anna Grimshaw and Keith Hart (Cambridge, MA, and Oxford: Blackwell, 1993), 173–79, offers a more critical view of Fordism than Gramsci's, but similarly without sustained attention to race and nationality. See also Moishe Postone, *Time, Labor, and Social Domination: A Reinterpretation of Marx's Critical Theory* (Cambridge: Cambridge University Press, 1993), and note 8 above.

15. Grace Kyungwon Hong, *The Ruptures of American Capital: Women of Color Feminism and the Culture of Immigrant Labor* (Minneapolis: University of Minnesota Press, 2006). See also the commentary on what has been translated as "primitive accumulation" and the longer run of capitalism in Massimiliano Tomba, "Historical Temporalities of Capital: An Anti-Historicist Perspective," *Historical*

Materialism 17 (2009): 51–56; Michael A. Lebowitz, "The Politics of Assumption, the Assumption of Politics," *Historical Materialism* 14 (2006): 38–40; David Kazanjian, *The Colonizing Trick: National Culture and Imperial Citizenship in Early America* (Minneapolis: University of Minnesota Press, 2003), esp. 15, 227n33.

16. Alexander Saxton, *The Indispensable Enemy: Labor and the Anti-Chinese Movement in California* (Berkeley: University of California Press, 1975); Ronald Takaki, *Pau Hana: Plantation Life in Hawaii, 1835–1920* (Honolulu: University of Hawai'i Press, 1983); Bruce Nelson, *Divided We Stand: American Workers and the Struggle for Black Equality* (Princeton, NJ: Princeton University Press, 2001); Moon-Kie Jung, *Reworking Race: The Making of Hawaii's Interracial Labor Movement* (New York: Columbia University Press, 2006). On the New South, see the acute work of Brian Kelly, *Race, Class, and Power in the Alabama Coalfields, 1908–21* (Urbana: University of Illinois Press, 2001).

17. Lowe, *Immigrant Acts*, 27–28; Chakrabarty, "Universalism and Belonging in the Logic of Capital," 652–76. For an innovative, interdisciplinary study of difference and power in the production of knowledge in the late twentieth-century United States, see Roderick Ferguson's fascinating *The Reorder of Things: The University and Its Pedagogies of Minority Difference* (Minneapolis: University of Minnesota Press, 2012). For all of the fierce critique of Chakrabarty in Vivek Chibber's *Postcolonial Theory and the Specter of Capital* (New York and London: Verso, 2013), on this point the differences between the two authors are slight.

18. Neil Smith, *Uneven Development: Nature, Capital and the Production of Space* (New York: Basil Blackwell, 1991); Michael Lowy and Jarius Banaji, *Theory as History* (Chicago: Haymarket, 2011); Michael Lowy, *Politics of Combined and Uneven Development: Theory of Permanent Revolution* (London: Verso, 1987). For a trenchant critique of globalization, see Frederick Cooper, *Colonialism in Question: Theory, Knowledge, History* (Berkeley: University of California Press, 2005), 91–122.

19. Henry Ford with Samuel Crowther, *Today and Tomorrow* (Garden City, NY: Doubleday, 1926).

20. Ford, *Today and Tomorrow*, 84.

21. Stanley Greenberg, *Race and State in Capitalist Development: Comparative Perspectives* (New Haven, CT: Yale University Press, 1980); John W. Cell, *The Highest Stage of White Supremacy: The Origins of Segregation in South Africa and the American South* (New York: Cambridge University Press, 1982); George Fredrickson, *White Supremacy: A Comparative History of American and South African History* (New York: Oxford University Press, 1981); Anthony Marx, *Making Race and Nation: A Comparison of South Africa, the United States and Brazil* (Cambridge: Cambridge University Press, 1998); Carl Degler, *Neither Black nor White: Slavery and Race Relations in Brazil and the United States* (Madison: University of Wisconsin, 1991); Charles V. Hamilton, ed., *Beyond Racism: Race and Inequality in Brazil, South Africa, and the United States* (London: Lynne Rienner, 2001); Peter Alexander and Rick Halpern, eds., *Racializing Class, Classifying Race: Labour and Difference in Britain, the USA and Africa* (New York: St. Martin's Press, 2000); Institute of Commonwealth Studies, University of London, *Beyond White Supremacy: Towards*

a New Agenda for the Comparative Histories of South Africa and the United States, Collected Seminar Papers, Issue 49 (London: School of Advanced Study, 1997).

22. Robert Stam and Ella Shohat, *Race in Translation: Culture Wars around the Postcolonial Atlantic* (New York: New York University Press, 2012), xiv; Michael Hanchard, "Acts of Miscegenation: Transnational Black Politics, Anti-Imperialism, and the Ethnocentrisms of Pierre Bourdieu and Loïc Wacquant," *Theory, Culture, and Society* 16 (2003): esp. 6.

23. Marilyn Lake and Henry Reynolds, *Drawing the Global Colour Line: White Men's Countries and the International Challenge of Racial Equality* (Cambridge: Cambridge University Press, 2008). See also Tony Ballantyne, *Orientalism and Race: Aryanism in the British Empire* (Basingstoke, UK: Palgrave, 2002); Marilyn Lake, "The White Man under Siege: New Histories of Race in the Nineteenth Century and the Advent of White Australia," *History Workshop Journal* 58 (Autumn 2004): 41–62. On the world movement of Pan-Africanism in these years see Minkah Makalani, *In the Cause of Freedom: Radical Black Internationalism from Harlem to London, 1917–1939* (Chapel Hill: University of North Carolina Press, 2011).

24. James Campbell, *Songs of Zion: The African Methodist Episcopal Church in the United States and South Africa* (New York: Oxford University Press, 1998). The quote comes from Andrew Zimmerman, "Three Logics of Race: Theory and Exception in the Transnational History of Empire," *New Global Studies* 4, no. 1 (2010): article 6. See also his excellent *Alabama in Africa: Booker T. Washington, the German Empire and the Globalization of the New South* (Princeton, NJ: Princeton University Press, 2010).

25. See Thomas Bender, *A Nation among Nations: America's Place in World History* (New York: Hill and Wang, 2006).

26. Frederick Cooper and Ann Laura Stoler, *Tensions of Empire: Colonial Cultures in a Bourgeois World* (Berkeley: University of California Press, 1997), 3.

27. David Montgomery, "Empire, Race and Working-Class Mobilizations," in Halpern and Alexander, *Racializing Class, Classifying Race*, 5.

28. David Roberts, *In the Shadow of Detroit: Gordon M. McGregor, Ford of Canada, and Motoropolis* (Detroit: Wayne State University Press, 2006).

29. The most expansive and influential consideration of this idea is Michael Hardt and Antonio Negri, *Empire* (Cambridge, MA: Harvard University Press, 2001). Walmart is the biggest contemporary example of a transnational firm said to be able to function without a state, functioning basically as one itself. See especially Bill Quinn, *How Walmart Is Destroying America (and the World): And What You Can Do about It* (New York: Crown, 2005), and Nelson Lichtenstein, ed., *Wal-Mart: The Face of Twenty First Century Capitalism* (New York: New Press, 2006).

30. See especially Jana K. Lipman and Daniel E. Bender, eds., *Making Empire Work: Labor and United States Imperialism* (New York: New York University Press, 2015). Examples of earlier transnational work that energizes the method of this book include Jefferson Cowie, *Capital Moves: RCA's Seventy-Year Quest for Cheap Labor* (Ithaca, NY: Cornell University Press, 1999); Peter Linebaugh and Marcus Rediker, *The Many Headed Hydra: The Hidden History of the Revolutionary Atlantic* (Boston:

Beacon Press, 2000); Naila Kabeer, *The Power to Choose: Bangladeshi Women and Labour Market Decisions in London and Dhaka* (London and New York: Verso, 2000); essays by Marilyn Young, Robin Kelley, Walter Johnson, and Daniel Rodgers in *Rethinking American History in a Global Age*, ed. Thomas Bender (Berkeley: University of California Press, 2002). See also Elaine Tyler May and Reinhold Wagnleitner, eds., *Here, There, and Everywhere: The Foreign Politics of American Popular Culture* (Hanover, NH: University of New England Press, 2000). A smaller body of excellent literature on the specific cultural, transnational, and comparative history of automobile production and consumption has also shaped my thinking about the meaning of Ford. These include Huw Beynon and Theo Nichols, *The Fordism of Ford and Modern Management: Fordism and Post-Fordism* (Cheltenham, UK: Edward Elgar, 2006); Joel Wolfe's excellent *Autos and Progress: The Brazilian Search for Modernity* (New York: Oxford University Press, 2010); David Gartman, *From Autos to Architecture: Fordism and Architectural Aesthetics in the Twentieth Century* (New York: Princeton Architectural Press, 2009); Stefan Johannes Link, "Rethinking the Ford-Nazi Connection," *Bulletin of the German Historical Institute* 49 (Fall 2011): 138–50.

31. KwaFord means "place of Ford" in Zulu.

32. David Roediger, "Americanism and Fordism—American Style: Kate Richards O'Hare's 'Has Henry Ford Made Good?'" *Labor History* 28 (Spring 1988): 241–52; Stefan Link, "Transnational Fordism: Ford Motor Company, Nazi Germany and the Soviet Union in the Interwar Years" (unpublished dissertation, Harvard University, 2012).

33. Ferruccio Gambino, "A Critique of the Fordism of the Regulation School," trans. Ed Emery, 1996, www.wildcat-www.de/en/zirkular/28/z28e_gam.htm; Mark Rupert, *Producing Hegemony: The Politics of Mass Production and American Global Power* (Cambridge: Cambridge Studies in International Relations no. 38, 1995), 44–45, 172 ("golden age"), 192–201. For a similar analysis and periodization, see David Harvey, *The Condition of Postmodernity* (Oxford: Blackwell, 1989), 125–40, esp. 133–35 on unions; Mike Davis, *Prisoners of the American Dream* (London: Verso, 1986), 105–17; Michel Aglietta, *A Theory of Capitalist Regulation* (London: Verso, 1987), 90–208.

34. A number of the texts that address Americanization through consumption usefully without fully linking it to production include Lizbeth Cohen, *Making a New Deal: Industrial Workers in Chicago, 1919–1939* (Cambridge: Cambridge University Press, 2008) and her *A Consumers' Republic: The Politics of Mass Consumption in Post-War America* (New York: Vintage, 2003); Victoria de Grazia, *Irresistible Empire: America's Advance through 20th Century Europe* (Cambridge, MA: Harvard University Press, 2006); Richard Hull, *American Enterprise in South Africa: Historical Dimensions of Engagement and Disengagement* (New York: New York University Press, 1990); Robert W. Rydell and Rob Kroes, *Buffalo Bill in Bologna: The Americanization of the World, 1869–1922* (Chicago: University of Chicago Press, 2005). For works that seek to locate the expansion of American influence in material contexts and other than just via consumption, see Mary Nolan, *Visions of Modernity: American*

Business and the Modernization of Germany (New York: Oxford University Press, 1994); Daniel Guerin, *Fascism and Big Business* (New York: Pathfinder Press, 1994); Ann Laura Stoler, *Carnal Knowledge and Imperial Power: Race and the Intimate in Colonial Rule* (Berkeley: University of California Press, 2002); Emily Rosenberg, *Spreading the American Dream: American Economic and Cultural Expansion, 1890–1945* (New York: Hill and Wang, 1982) as well as her *Financial Missionaries to the World: The Politics and Culture of Dollar Diplomacy, 1900–1930* (Durham, NC: Duke University Press, 2004).

35. Gramsci, "Americanism and Fordism," 285;

36. Roediger and Esch, *Production of Difference*, 170–204.

37. Herman Feldman, *Racial Factors in American Industry* (New York: Harper & Brothers, 1931), cited in David R. Roediger, *Working toward Whiteness: How America's Immigrants Became White: The Strange Journey from Ellis Island to the Suburbs* (New York: Basic Books, 2005), 75.

38. For Marx and the capitalist "personality" as against labor, see Karl Marx, *Pre-Capitalist Economic Formations* (New York: International, 2000), 118. On the "industrial army" of managers see Marx's *Capital: A Critique of Political Economy*, 3 vols. (Chicago: Charles H. Kerr, 1906), I:364.

39. Allan Nevins and Frank Ernest Hill, *Ford: Expansion and Challenge 1915–1933* (New York: Charles Scribner's Sons, 1957); Keith Sward, *The Legend of Henry Ford* (New York: Rinehart, 1948); Upton Sinclair, with an introduction by Stephen Meyer, *The Flivver King: A Story of Ford America* (Chicago: Charles Kerr, 1987); Stephen Meyer, *The Five Dollar Day: Labor Management and Social Control at the Ford Motor Company, 1908–1921* (Albany: State University of New York Press, 1981); David Gartman, *Auto Slavery: The Labor Process in the American Automobile Industry, 1897–1950* (New Brunswick, NJ: Rutgers University Press, 1986).

40. There are of course many, many biographies of and works about Henry Ford. This list is not comprehensive but means to touch on a few works of history that deal with "the two Henry Fords" in some capacity: David Lewis, *The Public Image of Henry Ford: An American Folk Hero and His Company* (Detroit: Wayne State University Press, 1976); Ford Bryan, *Friends, Families and Forays: Scenes from the Life and Times of Henry Ford* (Dearborn, MI: Ford 2002); Richard Bak, *Henry and Edsel: The Creation of the Ford Empire* (New York: Wiley, 2003); Robert Lacey, *Ford: The Men and the Machine* (New York: Little, Brown, 1986); see also Robert Casey, *The Model T: A Centennial History* (Baltimore: Johns Hopkins University Press, 2008). Greg Grandin's *Fordlandia: The Rise and Fall of Henry Ford's Forgotten Jungle City* (New York: Metropolitan Books, 2010) offers some more critical evaluation of the relationship between Ford the ideologue and Ford the inventor but still accepts the idea of Ford as a paradoxical and perhaps even anachronistic figure. For three admiring recent accounts see Douglas Brinkley, *Wheels for the World: Henry Ford, His Company, and a Century of Progress, 1903–2003* (New York: Penguin, 2003); Richard Snow, *I Invented the Modern Age: The Rise of Henry Ford* (New York: Scribner, 2013); Steven Watts, *The People's Tycoon: Henry Ford and the American Century* (New York: Vintage, 2005).

41. Charles Denby, *Indignant Heart: A Black Worker's Journal* (Detroit: Wayne State University Press, 1978), 5.

1. FORD GOES TO THE WORLD; THE WORLD COMES TO FORD

1. Ferruccio Gambino, "A Critique of the Fordism of the Regulation School," trans. Ed Emery, 1996, www.wildcat-www.de/en/zirkular/28/z28e_gam.htm. On the project begun by Henry Ford in about 1908, Upton Sinclair, *The Flivver King: A Story of Ford-America* (Detroit: United Automobile Workers of America, 1937), 23.

2. William Trufant Foster and Waddill Catchings, "Must We Reduce Our Standard of Living?" in *America Faces the Future,* ed. Charles Austin Beard (Boston and New York: Houghton Mifflin, 1932), 53; cf. Foster and Catchings, *The Road to Plenty* (Boston and New York: Houghton Mifflin, 1928); Aldous Huxley, *Brave New World* (London: Chatto and Windus, 1932); Antonio Gramsci, "Americanism and Fordism," *Selections from the Prison Notebooks* (New York: International, 1971), 279–318.

3. Mira Wilkins and Frank Ernest Hill, *American Business Abroad: Ford on Six Continents* (Detroit: Wayne State University Press, 1964), 1.

4. "Knudsen Report and Related Materials," Accession 6, Box 260 FF, Benson Ford Research Center, The Henry Ford, Dearborn, Michigan. Hereafter BFRC.

5. Sidney Lens, *The Forging of the American Empire: From the Revolution to Vietnam, a History of US Imperialism* (New York: Thomas Crowell, 1971), 276. Lens stresses, "At the turn of the century the U. S. exported more minerals and raw materials than it imported. By 1930 the situation was reversed."

6. Ford's reliance on the colonial networks established by the French and especially the British empires is suggestive of one challenge to the American exceptionalist idea that because the United States had not possessed colonies, it was different from its European rivals in a fundamentally democratic kind of way.

7. David Roberts, *In the Shadow of Detroit: Gordon M. McGregor, Ford of Canada, and Motoropolis* (Detroit: Wayne State University Press, 2006), 6.

8. "Knudsen Report and Related Materials," Accession 6, Box 260 FF, BFRC.

9. As early as the Monroe Doctrine in 1823 the United States was claiming a unique proprietary relationship to Latin America and "the Western Hemisphere," which it claimed was not a colonial one but, at worst, a paternal and always a mutually advantageous economic and political relationship designed to advance prospects for self-determination. This did not prevent U. S. firms from investing in other parts of the world, even those under the colonial control of competitors, namely Britain. But Latin American countries were an early and continual site of U. S. agricultural exploitation, raw material mining, and industrial production. For an excellent collection of essays dealing with the broad cultural and social meaning of this proprietary relationship over time, see Gilbert Michael Joseph, Catherine Carlisle

LeGrand, and Ricardo Donato Salvatore, eds., *Close Encounters of Empire: Writing the Cultural History of U.S.–Latin American Relations* (Chapel Hill, NC: Duke University Press, 1998).

10. On the Liberian plantations see Ibrahim Sundiata, *Black Scandal: American and the Liberian Crisis, 1929–1936* (New York: Institute for the Study of Human Issues, 1980), and Alfred Lief, *The Firestone Story: A History of the Firestone Tire and Rubber Company* (New York: McGraw Hill, 1951).

11. Howard Wolf and Ralph Wolf, *Rubber: A Story of Glory and Greed* (New York: Convici-Friede, 1936), 503. See also John Tully's excellent chapter on the 1913 strike in Akron in his *The Devil's Milk: A Social History of Rubber* (New York: Monthly Review Press, 2012), 149–60.

12. This of course was never meant to include those employed in Firestone's worldwide plantations where the settling of strikes, particularly in British Malaya, would involve far more paltry concessions to the needs and demands of workers who worked in near starvation conditions to begin with. Following a massive and brutally suppressed 1940 strike on its Malayan plantations Firestone did grant some concessions in a conscious effort to claim that the company cared more about its workers than the union did. Tully, *Devil's Milk,* 161, 273.

13. Daniel T. Rodgers, "An Age of Social Politics," in *Rethinking American History in a Global Age*, ed. Thomas Bender (Berkeley: University of California Press, 2000), 257.

14. Allan Nevins and Frank Ernest Hill, *Ford: Expansion and Challenge 1915–1933* (New York: Charles Scribner's Sons, 1957), 356.

15. Joan Hoff Wilson, *Herbert Hoover: Forgotten Progressive* (Long Grove, IL: Waveland Press, reprint edition, 1992), 79.

16. Nevins and Hill, *Ford: Expansion and Challenge,* 279–93. For broad contours of Ford's extractive industries see Mira Wilkins and Frank Ernest Hill, *American Business Abroad: Ford on Five Continents* (Detroit: Wayne State University Press, 1964). For broad contours of American control of extractive industries see Lens, *Forging of the American Empire,* 248–82.

17. "Letter from Henry Ford to the Honorable Judge Davis," Vertical File, *Mining-Iron-Coal,* BFRC.

18. Emily Rosenberg, *Financial Missionaries to the World: The Politics and Culture of Dollar Diplomacy* (Cambridge, MA: Harvard University Press, 1999).

19. Nevins and Hill, *Ford: Expansion and Challenge,* 357.

20. Ibid., 359.

21. Ibid., 542. See also Part One of the excellent Public Broadcasting Corporation documentary, *The Great Depression,* "A Job at Ford's." The distinction between "automotive vehicles" and "cars" is significant in that Ford was the largest producer of tractors during and immediately after World War I. Given that periods of capitalist intensification, which arguably describes the postwar period, result in "new enclosure" and the reorganization of agricultural work it would be fascinating to look at consumption of the Fordson tractor in relationship to land privatization in the United States and United Kingdom and in colonial contexts. Ford was producing

tractors in Ireland during the war and built a tractor production facility in the Soviet Union in 1932.

22. Nevins and Hill, *Ford: Expansion and Challenge,* 376.

23. Ibid., 375.

24. Mary Nolan, *Visions of Modernity: American Business and the Modernization of Germany* (New York: Oxford University Press, 1994), 3–57, and chapter 2 herein.

25. David Lewis, *The Public Image of Henry Ford: An American Folk Hero and His Company* (Detroit: Wayne State University Press, 1976), 129. The vast majority of the publicity and promotion of the Ford empire was done in association with the massive Ford Rouge plant, which more than 100,000 people per year toured after 1927. The place of the Rouge at the center of the company's global empire, and the centrality of the *Dearborn Independent* to its propaganda machine, is dealt with in chapter 2. On "self-advertising" and Ford's genius, see also Samuel S. Marquis, *Henry Ford: An Interpretation* (Detroit: Wayne State University Press, 2007, originally 1923), 15–24.

26. *The Ford Industries* (Detroit: Ford Motor Company, 1924), v.

27. *The Ford News,* April 15, 1922; January 1, 1927; October 15, 1923; BFRC.

28. *The Ford News,* VII, January 1, 1927, 2, cited in Nevins and Hill, *Ford: Expansion and Challenge,* 357.

29. Dr. Joseph Collins, "Sigmund Freud: A Man and His Methods," *Dearborn Independent,* January 2, 1926, 4–6; V. A. Cazalet, M. P., "England as an Englishman Sees It," *Dearborn Independent,* January 9, 1926, 22–23; William Lee Calnon, "The Lure of the South Seas," *Dearborn Independent,* January 30, 1926, 8 and 18; C. F. Freeman, "Bolshevism in the Philippines," *Dearborn Independent,* February 13, 1926, 6–7; Henri Galland, "At Home with the African Black," *Dearborn Independent,* January 9, 1926, 24. For the anti-Semitism of the publication see chapter 2.

30. "United Effort," Vertical File, *Exhibition—Chicago World's Fair,* BFRC.

31. "Huge Ford Exhibit to Show Processing of Raw Materials," Accession 629, Box 3, BFRC.

32. Lewis, *Public Image of Henry Ford,* 162 ("civilization"); "A Visit to the Ford Rouge Plant," Accession 44, Box 16, BFRC. On the connections between attacks on waste, transnational U. S. business, and U. S. public culture in the 1920s, see Hoff Wilson, *Herbert Hoover: Forgotten Progressive,* 90.

33. One woman interviewed as an adult about Depression-era Detroit describes the experience of touring the Rouge plant as a child during those years. She remembers seeing the assembly line from the catwalk in the plant, first thinking the men seemed likes marionettes in their motions and then seeing them as part of the machinery. See *The Great Depression,* "A Job at Ford."

34. "A Visit to the Ford Rouge Plant," Accession 44, Box 16, *Rouge Plant Trips,* BFRC.

35. Gramsci, *Prison Notebooks,* 571; Raymond Williams, *Keywords: A Vocabulary of Culture and Society* (New York: Oxford University Press, 1983), 145, 144–46; Perry Anderson, "The Antinomies of Antonio Gramsci," *New Left Review* I / 100 (November–December 1976): 5–78.

36. Immanuel Wallerstein, The *Modern World System II: Mercantilism and the Consolidation of the European World-Economy, 1600–1750* (New York: Academic Press, 1980), xxii–xvii; the best description of hegemony in this global sense in scholarship on the United States is Thomas J. McCormick, *America's Half-Century: United States Foreign Policy in the Cold War and After* (Baltimore: Johns Hopkins University Press, 1995), 4–10; on Arrighi and for useful interventions on hegemony and scale, see Lorenzo Fusaro, "Gramsci's Concept of Hegemony at the National and International Level," August 2010, www.iippe.org/wiki/images/0/09/CONF_IPE_Fusaro.pdf, esp. 2–7, 22–36; Giovanni Arrighi, *The Long Twentieth Century: Money, Power, and the Origins of Our Times* (London: Verso, 1994), 28.

37. Mark Rupert, *Producing Hegemony: The Politics of Mass Production and American Global Power* (Cambridge: Cambridge Studies in International Relations no. 38, 1995), raises this question interestingly but with very different disciplinary concerns.

38. Gramsci as quoted and discussed in Fusaro, "Gramsci's Concept of Hegemony at the National and International Level," 27; cf. David Harvey, *The Condition of Postmodernity* (London: Blackwell Books, 1990), 127.

39. Stephen Meyer III, "Adapting the Immigrant to the Line: Americanization in the Ford Factory, 1914–21," *Journal of Social History* 14 (Autumn 1980): 69; Rupert, *Producing Hegemony,* 113; for "House of Corrections," see David Roediger and Philip Foner, *Our Own Time: A History of American Labor and the Working Day* (New York: Verso, 1989), 191; Jack Russell, "The Coming of the Line: The Ford Highland Park Plant, 1910–1914," *Radical America* 12 (May–June 1978): 39.

40. "Proceedings of the Third Race Betterment Conference," *National Conference on Race Betterment* (Battle Creek, MI: Race Betterment Foundation, 1928), xv; Mark Adams, ed., *The Wellborn Science: Eugenics in Germany, France, Brazil and Russia* (New York: Oxford University Press, 1990); Nancy Stepan, *"The Hour of Eugenics": Race, Gender and Nation in Latin America* (Ithaca, NY: Cornell University Press, 1991); Daniel Kevles, *In the Name of Eugenics: Genetics and the Uses of Human Heredity* (Cambridge, MA: Harvard University Press, 1998, originally 1985); and chapters 2, 4, and 5 herein.

41. For the 38 percent figure, see Alan McKinlay and James Wilson, " 'All They Lose Is the Scream': Foucault, Ford, and Mass Production," *Management & Organizational History* 7 (February 2012): 50. On gang labor and race, see David Roediger and Elizabeth Esch, *The Production of Difference: Race and the Management of Labor in the United States* (New York: Oxford University Press, 2012), 52–54, 62.

42. Russell, "Coming of the Line," 38–42; Meyer, "Adapting the Immigrant to the Line," 69, 72 (60 percent); Martha May, "The Historical Problem of the Family Wage: The Ford Motor Company and the Five-Dollar Day," *Feminist Studies* 8 (Summer 1982): 410. Stephen Meyer, *The Five Dollar Day: Labor, Management and Social Control in the Ford Motor Company, 1914–1921* (Albany: State University of New York Press, 1981), 72, 37–89 passim.

43. Meyer, "Adapting the Immigrant to the Line," 69.

44. John R. Lee, "The So-Called Profit Sharing System in the Ford Plant," *Annals of the American Academy of Political and Social Science* 65 (May 1916): 300; Meyer, *Five Dollar Day,* 95–122. The Lee reforms and the five-dollar day are well cast as parts of a broad package attacking turnover; May, "Historical Problem of the Family Wage," 411.

45. Melvyn Dubofsky, *We Shall Be All: A History of the Industrial Workers of the World* (Urbana: University of Illinois Press, 2000), 166, and for the context, 132–67; Meyer, *Five Dollar Day,* 158–59; Meyer, "Adapting the Immigrant to the Line," 77; on the "Detroit experiments" in Americanization and their reach, see Roediger and Esch, *Production of Difference,* 178, and Edward George Hartmann, *The Movement to Americanize the Immigrant* (New York: Columbia University Press, 1948), 129–30; Russell, "Coming of the Line," 40–41.

46. Foner as quoted in May, "Historical Problem of the Family Wage," 423; Dubofsky, *We Shall Be All,* 166.

47. "Henry Ford Gives $10,000,000 in 1914 Profits to His Employees," *Detroit Journal,* January 6, 1914; Lewis, *Public Image of Henry Ford,* 7, includes the company's statement announcing the reforms; the best account remains Meyer, *Five Dollar Day,* 95–122; see also Nevins and Hill, *Ford: Expansion and Challenge,* 296. For the logic of the reforms and the claimed results of spectacular gains in productivity, see Lee, "So-Called Profit Sharing System in the Ford Plant," 297–307, esp. 308.

48. David Hounshell, *From the American System to Mass Production, 1800–1932* (Baltimore: Johns Hopkins University Press, 1984), 257.

49. Meyer, *Five Dollar Day,* 72.

50. Ibid., 156.

51. "Labor Turnover in Cleveland and Detroit," *Monthly Labor Review* 7 (January 1919): 12–13; Meyer, "Adapting the Immigrant to the Line," 77; Joyce Shaw Peterson, *American Automobile Workers, 1900–1933* (Albany: State University of New York Press, 1988), 58; Daniel Nelson, *Managers and Workers: Origins of the Twentieth-Century Factory System in the United States, 1880–1920* (Madison: University of Wisconsin Press, 1996), 157. For contemporary regard for Ford, see also Howard Hill, "The Americanization Movement," *American Journal of Sociology* 24 (May 1919): 633.

52. Georgios Paris Loizides, "'Making Men' at Ford: Ethnicity, Race, and Americanization during the Progressive Period," *Michigan Sociological Review* 21 (Fall 2007): 114–15, including the quotations.

53. J. Herkel, "Employment Department to F. Dolson, September 16, 1920," Accession 284, Box 10, BFRC.

54. Loizides, "'Making Men' at Ford," 122; Meyer, *Five Dollar Day,* 155; Meyer, "Adapting the Immigrant to the Line," 73–74.

55. Gramsci, "Americanism and Fordism," in *Prison Notebooks,* 280–87, particularly 281, 284, and 291 on "parasitic" elements. Gramsci based this generalization on his knowledge of the landed class in Italy and on his attempts to understand why "bourgeois reforms" had not been achieved of any substance in czarist Russia. For a

useful critique of Gramsci on this "rational demographic composition" and an attempt to consider relations of race and culture, see Sergio Bologna, "The Factory-Society Relationship as an Historical Category," trans. Ed Emery, 1991, http://libcom.org/library/factory-society-relationship-historical-category.

56. Gramsci, "Americanism and Fordism," in *Prison Notebooks,* 281 ("demographic"), 285 ("intermediaries"), and also 302–3.

57. Ida Tarbell, *All in the Day's Work: An Autobiography* (Urbana: University of Illinois Press, 2003, originally 1939), 287–92; Meyer, "Adapting the Immigrant to the Line," 70; Meyer, *Five Dollar Day,* 124–26, 127 ("unlearn"); Richard F. Snow, *I Invented the Modern Age: The Rise of Henry Ford* (New York: Scribner, 2013), 290. On the earlier venture in Colorado, see Roediger and Esch, *Production of Difference,* 88; Frank J. Weed, "The Sociological Department at the Colorado Fuel and Iron Company, 1901–1907: Scientific Paternalism and Industrial Control," *Journal of the History of the Behavioral Sciences* 41 (Summer 2005): 269n1 and 269–84; Loizides, "'Making Men' at Ford," 110.

58. Meyer, "Adapting the Immigrant to the Line," 72; Meyer, *Five Dollar Day,* 152 for the Bureau of Labor Statistics quotation.

59. David R. Roediger, *Working toward Whiteness: How America's Immigrants Became White* (New York: Basic, 2005), 65 and 57–92; Meyer, *Five Dollar Day,* 114–15 and 144 for the quotations; Lee, "So-Called Profit Sharing System in the Ford Plant," 303, counted four categories used by investigators along the same lines.

60. Meyer, *Five Dollar Day,* 113–15. For the quotations see Georgios Paris Loizides, "Families and Gender Relations at Ford," *Michigan Sociological Review* 25 (Fall 2011): 22 ("working for him" and useful commentary on that phrasing).

61. Lee, "So-Called Profit Sharing System in the Ford Plant," 304–5; McKinlay and Wilson, "'All They Lose Is the Scream,'" 52 and 45–60.

62. On remigration, see Loizides, "'Making Men' at Ford," 118, 120–21, and for the compulsory nature of the English School see 126; see also Hartmann, *Movement to Americanize the Immigrant,* 130, on the films; Meyer, *Five Dollar Day,* 156 ("industry and efficiency").

63. Jeffrey Eugenides, *Middlesex: A Novel* (New York: Farrar, Straus, and Giroux, 2002), 104; Lee, "So-Called Profit Sharing System in the Ford Plant," 307.

64. George F. Pierrot, *An Illustrated Guide to the Diego Rivera Frescoes* (Detroit: Detroit Institute of Arts, 1934). See also Linda Bank Downs, *Diego Rivera: The Detroit Industry Murals* (Detroit: Detroit Institute of Art, 1999).

65. Sarah Terrill Bushnell, "Give Men a Chance—Not Charity," *National Magazine,* July 1920, 155–56.

66. *The Ford Times,* November, 1916, Vertical File, *Ford English Schools,* BFRC; Lee, "So-Called Profit Sharing System in the Ford Plant," 306; Loizides, "'Making Men' at Ford," 126; for Roberts, see Meyer, "Adapting the Immigrant to the Line," 78.

67. See David R. Roediger, "Americanism and Fordism—American Style: Kate Richards O'Hare, 'Has Henry Ford Made Good?'" *Labor History* 29 (Spring 1988): 249 ("melting pot"), 250 (for the quotations), and 241–52.

68. John Reed, "Industry's Miracle Maker," *Metropolitan Magazine* 46 (October 1916): 12; Snow, *I Invented the Modern Age,* 222 ("revolutionist"), 267–68 ("saint"); Steven Watts, *The People's Tycoon: Henry Ford and the American Century* (New York: Vintage, 2005), 197–98, 212, 219.

69. Snow, *I Invented the Modern Age,* 234 ("advisors"); Meyer, *Five Dollar Day,* 143 ("ungentlemanly"), 114 (on the department's naming).

70. Ida Tarbell, *All in the Day's Work,* 287–91 on Ford, 292–94 on Taylor. See also Snow, *I Invented the Modern Age,* 235.

71. Loizides, "'Making Men' at Ford," 119–20; Lee, "So-Called Profit Sharing System in the Ford Plant," 305. On labor contracting and capital, see Gunther Peck, *Reinventing Free Labor: Padrones and Immigrant Workers in the North American West, 1880–1930* (Cambridge: Cambridge University Press, 2000).

72. Lee, "So-Called Profit Sharing System in the Ford Plant," 309.

73. Ibid. On redlining, maps, and home loans, see Roediger, *Working toward Whiteness,* 224–34; Kenneth Jackson, *Crabgrass Frontier: The Suburbanization of the United States* (New York: Oxford University Press, 1985), 196–201.

74. Loizides, "Families and Gender Relations at Ford," 25–27. Andrew Zimmerman, "Three Logics of Race: Theory and Exception in the Transnational History of Empire," *New Global Studies* 4 (2010): 7.

75. Meyer, "Adapting the Immigrant to the Line," 76. For especially vivid evidence on profit sharing and patriarchy see Loizides, "Families and Gender Relations at Ford," 20. See also Tarbell, *All in the Day's Work,* 290.

76. Peterson, *American Automobile Workers,* 58 (quoting Ford); Meyer, "Adapting the Immigrant to the Line," 73 ("smile"); Meyer, *Five Dollar Day,* 116 ("domestic"). On the sexual exploitation of immigrant working women by supervisors, see Roediger, *Working toward Whiteness,* 186.

77. Alice Kessler-Harris, *A Woman's Wage: Historical Meanings and Social Consequences* (Lexington: University Press of Kentucky, 1990), 25, quoting Couzens; Wayne A. Lewchuk, "Men and Monotony: Fraternalism as a Managerial Strategy at the Ford Motor Company," *Journal of Economic History* 53 (December 1993): 829–30.

78. Peterson, *American Automobile Workers,* 57–58; Roediger, "Americanism and Fordism," 250–51; May, "Historical Problem of the Family Wage," 413–16; Lee, "So-Called Profit Sharing System in the Ford Plant," 303.

79. Steve Meyer, "Workplace Predators: Sexuality and Harassment on the U.S. Automotive Shop Floor, 1930–1960," *Labor: Studies in Working-Class History of the Americas* 1 (Spring 2004): 79 ("densely masculine") and 77–93; Meyer, "Work, Play, and Power: Masculine Culture on the Automotive Shop Floor, 1930–1965," *Men and Masculinities* 2 (October 1999), 115–34. On intensity of expressions of hypermasculinity in the plants in later years, see also Meyer, "Rugged Manhood: The Aggressive and Confrontational Culture of Male Auto Workers during World War II," *Journal of Social History* 36 (2002): 125–47.

80. Meyer, *Five Dollar Day,* 169–94; Meyer, "Adapting the Immigrant to the Line," 78 (on the declining share of compensation formed by the profit), 79; Rupert, *Producing Hegemony,* 125, 130.

81. Meyer, "Adapting the Immigrant to the Line," 77–78; Meyer, *Five Dollar Day,* 196; Lee, "So-Called Profit Sharing System in the Ford Plant," 308–9; Watts, *People's Tycoon,* 197–98; Loizides, "Families and Gender Relations at Ford," 29.

2. FROM THE MELTING POT TO THE BOILING POT

1. George Seldes, with Helen Seldes, *Facts and Fascism* (New York: In Fact, 1943), 138.

2. Allan Nevins and Frank Ernest Hill, *Ford: Expansion and Challenge 1915–1933* (New York: Charles Scribner's Sons, 1957), 124; "Berlin Hears Ford Is Backing Hitler," *New York Times,* December 20, 1922; Michael Dobbs, "Ford and GM Scrutinized for Alleged Nazi Collaboration," *Washington Post,* November 30, 1998.

3. Albert Lee, *Henry Ford and the Jews* (New York: Stein and Day, 1980); Neil Baldwin, *Henry Ford and the Jews: The Mass Production of Hate* (San Francisco: Public Affairs, 2001); Max Wallace, *The American Axis: Henry Ford, Charles Lindbergh and the Rise of the Third Reich* (New York: St. Martin's Press, 2003).

4. Antonio Gramsci, "Americanism and Fordism," in *Selections from the Prison Notebooks* (New York: International, 1971), 285.

5. Wayne A. Lewchuk, "Men and Monotony: Fraternalism as a Managerial Strategy at the Ford Motor Company," *Journal of Economic History* 53 (December 1993): 838–48; Tim Mason, "The Origins of the Law on the National Organization of Labour of 20 January 1934," in *Nazism, Fascism, and the Working Class,* ed. Jane Caplan (Cambridge: Cambridge University Press, 1995), 80, 93 (on factory communities); Stefan Johannes Link, "Rethinking the Ford-Nazi Connection," *Bulletin of the German Historical Institute* 49 (Fall 2011): 138–50. See also Tim Kirk, *Nazism and the Working Class in Austria* (Cambridge: Cambridge University Press, 1996), 109; Mark Rupert, *Producing Hegemony: The Politics of Mass Production and American Global Power* (Cambridge: Cambridge Studies in International Relations no. 38, 1995), 144–46.

6. Eleni Varikas has written one of the most compelling explorations of how the modern technology and ideology associated with Ford combined with older traditions of anti-Semitism in the moment of Nazism to make possible some of the specific grotesqueries of that moment. "The implicit or explicit assumptions behind [analyses of German history and identity], which posit the existence of a causal and automatic link between economic liberalism and political liberalism, or between capitalism and democracy, prevent us from understanding the undeniably modern elements that make Nazism different from earlier forms of barbarism. Antisemitism (not merely the hatred of Jews), imperialism (not merely conquest), totalitarianism (not merely dictatorship)" for Varikas create the context in which "the hellish alliance between racist scientism and the efficiency of modern technology" occurred. "The Burden of Our Time: Hannah Arendt and the Critique of Political Modernity," *Radical Philosophy* 92 (November–December 1998): 18.

7. Charles Sorensen Papers, Accession 285, BFRC.

8. Waldemar Kaempffert, "The Mussolini of Highland Park," *New York Times,* January 6, 1928.

9. A. R. Panic, "Deeds, Few Words, Mark Advance of Fascism in Taking over Italian Power," *Dearborn Independent,* November 11, 1922.

10. Mary Nolan, *Visions of Modernity: American Business and the Modernization of Germany* (New York: Oxford University Press, 1994), 3–57 and passim.

11. See Joseph Kip Kosek, "Henry Ford for President!" History News Network website, n. d., http://hnn.us/node/138750.

12. Daniel Guerin, *Fascism and Big Business* (New York: Pathfinder Press, 1994, originally 1973).

13. Sayers wrote for the periodical *Friday* in 1940 and is quoted in Seldes, *Facts and Fascism,* 123. Interestingly Sayers adopted Gramsci's pairing of "Americanism and Fordism" in his analysis but argued that American values threatened the continued sway of Fordist practices.

14. Nevins and Hill, *Ford: Expansion and Challenge,* 201.

15. Ibid.

16. Ibid., 203.

17. Ibid., 216.

18. Federico Bucci, *Albert Kahn: Architect of Ford* (New York: Princeton Architectural Press, 1993), 61; John H. Van Deventer, "Mechanical Handling of Coal and Coke," *Industrial Management* 64 (October 1922): 196.

19. Nevins and Hill, *Ford: Expansion and Challenge,* 288.

20. Stephen Meyer, *The Five Dollar Day: Labor Management and Social Control at the Ford Motor Company, 1908–1921* (Albany: State University of New York Press, 1981), 49–50.

21. R. L. Cruden, "Ford's Flimflammery," *Labor Age,* June 1928, 15; Henry Ford, *My Life and Work* (Garden City, NY: Garden City, 1922), 99–100, 103–9.

22. See David R. Roediger, *Working toward Whiteness: How America's Immigrants Became White: The Strange Journey from Ellis Island to the Suburbs* (New York: Basic Books, 2005), 239, 245.

23. Speech by Ellison DuRant Smith, April 9, 1924, *Congressional Record,* 68th Congress, 1st Session (Washington DC: Government Printing Office, 1924), vol. 65, 5961–62.

24. Richard Gid Powers, *Not without Honor: The History of American Anticommunism* (New Haven, CT: Yale University Press, 1998), 48; Jonathan Spiro, *Defending the Master Race: Conservation, Eugenics, and the Legacy of Madison Grant* (Lebanon, NH: University Press of New England, 2009), 252, 379; Stefan Kuhl, *The Nazi Connection: Eugenics, American Racism, and German National Socialism* (New York: Oxford University Press, 1994), 18–19; "John Harvey Kellogg to Mr. E. C. Liebold (May 10, 1937)," in *History of Soy Yogurt, Soy Acidophilus Milk and Other Cultured Soymilks,* ed. William Shurtleff and Akiko Aoyagi (Lafayette, CA: Soy Info Center, 2012), 72. On Ford and the future, see "The Jew in Character and Business," *Dearborn Independent,* May 22, 1920, reprinted in *The International Jew: The World's Foremost Problem. Being a Reprint of a Series of Articles Appearing in*

The Dearborn Independent from May 22 . . . 1920 [to January 14, 1922], vol. 1 (Dearborn, MI: Dearborn, 1920–22), n.p. The *Dearborn Independent* is quoting and mis-citing Werner Sombart's "pro-Jewish" *The Jews and Modern Capitalism* in the passage in question.

25. Douglas Baynton, "Disability and the Justification of Inequality in American History," in *The New Disability History: American Perspectives*, ed. Paul K. Longmore and Lauri Umansky (New York: New York University Press, 2001), 45–49; Baynton, "Defectives in the Land: Disability and American Immigration Policy, 1882–1924," *Journal of American Ethnic History* 24 (Spring 2005): 31–44.

26. Ford, *My Life and Work*, 106, 107.

27. John R. Commons, in collaboration with A.P. Haake, O.F. Carpenter, Malcolm Sharp, Jennie McMullin Turner, Ethel B. Dietrich, Jean Davis, and John A. Commons, "Henry Ford, Miracle Maker," *The Independent*, May 1, 1920, 160.

28. Ford, *My Life and Work*, 106, 107. Regarding the general interest of management in disabled workers, see C. Stanley Raymond, "Industrial Possibilities of the Feeble-Minded," *Industrial Psychology* 2 (September 1927): 473–78; Charles Bernstein, "How Small-Town Industry Makes Use of the Feeble-Minded," *Industrial Psychology* 2 (June 1927): 305–10; Emily Burr, "Adapting the Feeble-Minded to Industry," *Industrial Psychology* 2 (March 1927): 132–38; Florence M. Teagarden, "Are We a Nation of Morons?" *Industrial Psychology* 1 (August 1926): 535–43. For "dismemberment," see Mark Seltzer, *Bodies and Machines* (London: Routledge, 1992), 157.

29. Ford, *My Life and Work*, 108; see also Lewchuk, "Men and Monotony," 831.

30. Ford, *My Life and Work*, 109, 110. Cf. Henry Ford, *Today and Tomorrow* (New York: Scribner, 1926), 92–100; *The Ford Industries: Facts about the Ford Motor Company and Its Subsidiaries* (Detroit: Ford Motor Company, 1927), 42, but see also 47 for a suggestion that some jobs were capable of "getting on [the] nerves" of workers.

31. Gregory Wood, *Retiring Men: Labor and Growing Old in America, 1900–1960* (Lanham, MD: University Press of America, 2012), 33–51, with the quote (from labor radical Robert Dunn) on "young men's game" at 45; Wayne A. Lewchuk, "Men and Monotony: Fraternalism as a Managerial Strategy at the Ford Motor Company," *Journal of Economic History* 53 (December 1993): 838–48, esp. 842 ("ribbons") and 843 ("sweat").

32. Lewchuk, "Men and Monotony," 847.

33. Commons, "Henry Ford, Miracle Maker," 160, 161,.

34. Harry Bennett as told to Paul Marcus, *We Never Called Him Henry* (Greenwich, CT: Fawcett Gold Medal Books, 1951), 11, 60 ("eyes and ears"); on Ford and prisons, sees his *My Life and Work*, 209.

35. Lewchuk, "Men and Monotony," 829–830; Steve Meyer, "Workplace Predators: Sexuality and Harassment on the Automotive Shop Floor, 1930–1960," *Labor: Studies in Working-Class History of the Americas* 1 (Spring 2004): 79 ("densely masculine") and 77–93; Steve Meyer, "Work, Play, and Power: Masculine Culture on the Automotive Shop Floor, 1930–1965," *Men and Masculinities* 2 (October 1999): 115–34.

36. Lewchuk, "Men and Monotony," 850; Ford, *Life and Work,* 114; Meyer, "Work, Play, and Power," 117–24.

37. Moore's oral history is at www.youtube.com/watch?v = lpTecAeYvGU. (I choose not to spell out the derogatory racial term in quoted material, regardless of who is using it or in what context.)

38. Glen Jeansonne, *Gerald L. K. Smith: Minister of Hate* (Baton Rouge: Louisiana State University Press, 1997, originally 1988), 73; Seldes, *Ford and Fascism,* 133; Meyer, "Work, Play, and Power," 131–32; Steven Meyer, "Rugged Manhood: The Aggressive and Confrontational Culture of Male Auto Workers during World War II," *Journal of Social History* 36 (2002): 126–34.

39. Eliot as quoted in John P. Diggins, *Mussolini and Fascism: The View from America* (Princeton, NJ: Princeton University Press, 1972), 122.

40. Edmund Wilson, *The American Jitters: A Year of the Slump* (New York: Charles Scribner's Sons, 1932), 52–53.

41. Ford, *Today and Tomorrow,* 158; Alan McKinlay and James Wilson, " 'All They Lose Is the Scream': Foucault, Ford, and Mass Production," *Management & Organizational History* 7 (February 2012): 56–57 and 45–60.

42. B.J. Widick, *Detroit: A City of Race and Class Violence* (Detroit: Wayne State University Press, 1989, originally 1972), 36–37.

43. Charles Denby, *Indignant Heart: A Black Worker's Journal* (Detroit: Wayne State University Press, 1989, originally 1952), 35.

44. J.S.S., "Close-Ups: C.E. Sorensen—He Makes 'Em!," *Fordex Digest,* January 28, 1935, 9; Nevins and Hill, *Ford: Expansion and Challenge,* 15 ("legends").

45. Ford, *Today and Tomorrow,* 9; *A Job at Fords: The Great Depression* (Blackside Documentary for Public Broadcasting Service, 1993).

46. Pedro Caban, "Subjects and Immigrants during the Progressive Era," *Discourse* 23 (Fall 2001): 24–29. Meyer's *Five Dollar Day* remains the most thorough analysis of Ford's shift from what he calls paternalism to repression in the Highland Park plant. On the melting pot pageant see the powerful description of this event in Jeffrey Eugenides's novel, *Middlesex* (New York: Farrar, Straus, and Giroux, 2002).

47. Keith Sward, *The Legend of Henry Ford* (New York: Rinehart, 1948).

48. Samuel Marquis, *Henry Ford* (New York: Little Brown, 1923), 176.

49. "Reminiscences of Mr. P.E. Haglund," Accession 65, BFRC, 103.

50. Ibid., 105.

51. "Reminiscences of Logan Miller," Accession 280, BFRC, n.p.

52. Sward, *Legend of Henry Ford,* 185–86; Ford, *My Life and Work,* 103–30.

53. Nevins and Hill, *Ford: Expansion and Challenge,* 274.

54. Ford, *Life and Work,* 93 ("alone controls us"), 111 ("expect the men"), 109–15 passim; Nelson Lichtenstein, "Life at the Rouge: A Cycle of Workers Control," in *Life and Labor: Dimensions of American Working Class History,* ed. Charles Stephenson and Robert Asher (Albany: State University of New York Press, 1986), 239; David Gartman, *Auto Slavery: The Labor Process in the American Automobile Industry, 1897–1950* (New Brunswick, NJ: Rutgers University Press, 1986), 97 (including Nash quote), 99 ("bowels"); C.L.R. James, *American Civilization,*

edited and introduced by Anna Grimshaw and Keith Hart (Cambridge, MA: Blackwell, 1993), 176 (for the ratios) and 173–79.

55. Ford, *My Life and Work,* 110–11; Guerin, *Fascism and Big Business.* Of course, it is a tragedy that it was precisely militancy in the auto unions in Italy and their defeat that paved the way for Mussolini's rise to power.

56. Robert Cruden, *The End of the Ford Myth* (New York: International, 1933), 4–5.

57. Sward, *Legend of Henry Ford,* 18; *Wall Street Journal,* July 4, 1929; Denby, *Indignant Heart,* 36; Ford, *My Life and Work,* 106–9.

58. Paul Boatin interview in *The Great Depression: A Job at Ford's;* Denby, *Indignant Heart,* 35–37.

59. "Reminiscences of H. S. Ablewhite," Accession 280, BFRC, 68.

60. Nevins and Hill, *Ford: Expansion and Challenge,* 297.

61. *A Job at Ford's.*

62. Nevins and Hill, *Ford: Expansion and Challenge,* 377.

63. For a magnificent representation of trickery of this kind, and the impact on workers, see Upton Sinclair's *The Flivver King: A Story of Ford-America* (Detroit: United Automobile Workers of America, 1937).

64. Nevins and Hill, *Ford: Expansion and Challenge,* 294; Unsigned, "Ford Facts: Harry Bennett's Service Department," *The Monitor* (Ford Service Managers Association, n. d.), www.fmanet.com/montart/bennett.htm; Bennett as told to Marcus, *We Never Called Him Henry,* esp. 8–11.

65. Bennett as told to Marcus, *We Never Called Him Henry,* 8, 12 ("brawling"), 33 ("stupid waste"), 34–38.

66. Accession 572, Box 30, Folder "Radicals," BFRC; Nevins and Hill, *Ford: Expansion and Challenge,* 592. Nevins does not name the person he is quoting; Bennett as told to Marcus, *We Never Called Him Henry,* 34, 65 ("morbid"), and 64–85.

67. "Reminiscences of H. S. Ablewhite," Accession 280, BFRC, 65.

68. Ibid.

69. Sward, *Legend of Henry Ford,* 298.

70. Ibid.

71. *A Job at Ford's.*

72. Ibid.; Francisco E. Balderrama and Raymond Rodríguez, *Decade of Betrayal: Mexican Repatriation in the 1930s* (Albuquerque: University of New Mexico Press, 2006), 163.

73. Gramsci, *Selections from the Prison Notebooks,* 344. See also Gartman, *Auto Slavery,* 182–95.

74. *A Job at Ford's.*

75. Widick, *Detroit: City of Race and Class Violence,* 51.

76. Ibid., 49; Seldes, *Facts and Fascism,* 128; James C. Scott, *Seeing Like a State: How Certain Schemes to Improve the Human Condition Have Failed* (New Haven, CT: Yale University Press, 1998).

77. Guerin, *Fascism and Big Business,* 106. See also David Abraham, *The Collapse of the Weimar Republic: Political Economy and Crisis* (New York: Holmes and Meier, 1986).

78. Nevins and Hill, *Ford: Expansion and Challenge,* 559.

79. "Henry Ford Boosts Klan," *Montreal Star,* August 27, 1924.

80. Kenneth Jackson, *The Ku Klux Klan in the City* (Chicago: Ivan R. Dee, 1992, originally 1967), 274n21 (including Detroit press in 1925); "Berlin Hears Ford Is Backing Hitler," *New York Times,* December 20, 1922; H. I. H. Browne, "Ford Gets Backing of Klansmen," *Chicago Defender,* June 3, 1922; Craig Fox, *Everyday Klansfolk: White Protestant Life and the KKK in 1920s Michigan* (East Lansing: Michigan State University Press, 2011), 10, 49, 90, 127, 222–23n40 (quoting Stidger). The best general account remains David Chalmers, *Hooded Americanism: The History of the Ku Klux Klan* (Durham, NC: Duke University Press, 1981), with the membership estimate at 109.

81. Michael Phillips, *White Metropolis: Race, Ethnicity, and Religion in Dallas, 1841–2001* (Austin: University of Texas Press, 2006), 85; Seldes, *Facts and Fascism,* 123–24.

82. "Ford and Race Prejudice," *Pittsburgh Courier,* August 4, 1923; Bennett as told to Marcus, *I Never Called Him Henry,* 47, 118–19; Chalmers, *Hooded Americanism,* 197; see also Nahum Daniel Brasher, "Negro America Fifty Years Hence," *Dearborn Independent,* November 6, 1926, 18; "America's Jewish Enigma: Louis Marshall," *Dearborn Independent,* November 26, 1921, reprinted in *The International Jew,* vol. 3, n. p.; Howard Segal, *Recasting the Machine Age: Henry Ford's Village Industries* (Amherst: University of Massachusetts Press, 2008).

83. The four volumes of *The International Jew* were published as Vol. I: *The World's Foremost Problem;* Vol. II: *Jewish Activities in the United States;* Vol. III: *Jewish Influences in American Life;* Vol. IV: *Aspects of Jewish Power in the United States.* For background, see Victoria Saker Woeste, "Insecure Equality: Louis Marshall, Henry Ford, and the Problem of Defamatory Anti-Semitism," *Journal of American History* 91 (December 2004): 877–905.

84. Seldes, *Ford and Fascism,* 125, 138; Wallace, *American Axis,* 186; Link, "Rethinking the Ford-Nazi Connection," 145–46.

85. "Reminiscences of Ernest Liebold," Accession 65, BFRC, 488.

86. Ibid., 489–90.

87. *The International Jew,* vol. 1, 6. "Jewish Liquor Trust and Its Career," *Dearborn Independent,* November 26, 1921; "Jewish Gamblers Corrupt American Baseball," *Dearborn Independent,* September 1921, reprinted in *The International Jew.*

88. Bennett as told to Marcus, *We Never Called Him Henry,* 56, 128–31; Smith's recollections are reprinted in his "Henry Ford's Forged Apology," n. d., www.biblebelievers.org.au/ford.htm. Elizabeth Dilling, an anti-Communist, anti-union, and pro-Nazi investigator paid by Ford, similarly claimed knowledge that Ford "never changed his mind about the role of Jewry." See Powers, *Not without Honor,* 129; on Ford and Smith, see Jeansonne, *Gerald L. K. Smith,* 73–75. See also Neil

Baldwin, *Henry Ford and the Jews: The Mass Production of Hate* (New York: Public Affairs, 2001).

89. Henry Ford, *My Life and Work,* 250–51.

90. Accession 285, Box 2, Folders 4, 1; Box 18, Folder 2, BFRC.

91. Accession 285, Box 1769, Folder 272 "Franklin." See also "Reminiscences of Ernest Liebold," Accession 65, vol. 6, 470, BFRC.

92. "Reminiscences of Ernest Liebold," 470.

93. John Patrick Diggins, *Mussolini and Fascism: The View from America* (Princeton, NJ: Princeton University Press), 1972.

94. As quoted in David L. Lewis, *The Public Image of Henry Ford: An American Folk Hero and His Company* (Detroit: Wayne State University Press, 1976), 152.

95. Link, "Rethinking the Ford-Nazi Connection," 140 ("thrillers"), 146–47 (Volkswagen), and 138–50 passim.

96. Peter Hayes, *Industry and Ideology: I. G. Farben in the Nazi Era* (Cambridge: Cambridge University Press, 2001), 81–115.

97. Powers, *Not without Honor,* 129; Seldes, *Ford and Fascism,* 121; Wallace, *American Axis,* 19; Jeansonne, *Gerald L. K. Smith,* 73–75.

98. "Red Russia Turns Pink," *Dearborn Independent,* November 6, 1926, 10.

99. Link, "Rethinking the Ford-Nazi Connection," 146–47; Diggins, *Mussolini and Fascism,* 299.

3. OUT OF THE MELTING POT AND INTO THE FIRE

1. Henry Ford, *My Life and Work: An Autobiography of Henry Ford* (New York: Classic House Books, 2009), 178–91. The later idea of "constant improvement" is the English translation of *kaizen,* the Japanese managerial term popularized in the 1980s. See Mike Parker and Jane Slaughter, eds., *Choosing Sides: Unions and the Team Concept* (Boston: South End Press, 1988).

2. Personal papers of Henry Ford, Accession 23, Box 14, BFRC.

3. W. E. B. Du Bois, *The Souls of Black Folk* (Mineola, NY: Dover, 1994, originally 1903), vi, 9–10.

4. Beth Bates, *Black Detroit in the Age of Henry Ford* (Chapel Hill: University of North Carolina Press, 2012), 5

5. David L. Lewis, "History of Negro Employment in Detroit Area Plants," 1, as cited in Bates, *Black Detroit,* 41; Georgios Paris Loizides, "'Making Men' at Ford: Ethnicity, Race, and Americanization during the Progressive Period," *Michigan Sociological Review* 21 (Fall 2007): 116–17; Joyce Shaw Peterson, "Black Auto Workers in Detroit, 1910–1930," *Journal of Negro History* 64, no. 3 (Summer 1979): 178–80.

6. For the 1939–40 figures, Warren C. Whatley and Gavin Wright, "Getting Started in the Auto Industry: Black Workers at the Ford Motor Company, 1918–1947," 1990, available at the Cliometric Society, http://cliometrics.org/conferences/ASSA/Dec_90/Whatley-Wright_Abstract/unpaginated.

7. "Ford Says Race Unemployed Freed of Debt by His Plan," *Pittsburgh Courier*, June 4, 1932, 1.

8. "Henry Ford's Motto Leaves Race People Skeptical," *Chicago Defender*, November 17, 1923; Herbert Hill, *Black Labor and the American Legal System: Race, Work and the Law* (Madison: University of Wisconsin Press, 1985), 268.

9. The table is from Whatley and Wright, "Getting Started in the Auto Industry," n.p.; Henry Ford with Samuel Crowther, *My Life and Work* (Garden City, NY: Doubleday and Page, 1922), 143. On village industries and branch plants see Allan Nevins and Frank Ernest Hill, *Ford: Expansion and Challenge 1915–1933* (New York: Charles Scribner's Sons, 1957), 298; Henry Ford and Samuel Crowther, "Village Industries Prove Real Success; Solve Big Problem," *Milwaukee Sentinel*, May 12, 1926, 4; Ford Richardson Bryan, *Beyond the Model T: The Other Ventures of Henry Ford* (Detroit: Wayne State University Press, 1997), 45–57; Howard P. Segal, *Recasting the Machine Age: Henry Ford's Village Industries* (Boston: University of Massachusetts Press, 2008), 45–47.

10. James Loewen, *Sundown Towns: A Hidden Dimension of American Racism* (New York: Touchstone, 2005). Among the more well-known of the Ford-towns near Detroit whose populations have remained entirely white are Westland, Wyandotte, and Cherry Hill. Historically recognized towns that excluded nonwhites along the Rouge River where Ford built mills include Nankin Mills, Schuyler Mill, Phoenix Mill, and Dundee.

11. Segal, *Recasting the Machine Age*, 45.

12. Shaw Peterson, "Black Auto Workers in Detroit," 177; Joyce Shaw Peterson, *American Automobile Workers, 1900–1933* (New York: State University of New York Press, 1987).

13. Shaw Peterson, "Black Auto Workers in Detroit," 178–80.

14. Ibid., 180; August Meier and Elliott Rudwick, *Black Detroit and the Rise of the UAW* (New York: Oxford University Press, 1979), 19–21. For a careful account of the Urban League's growing orientation nationally toward fostering a Black trade union presence—a stance not followed by the Detroit chapter where Ford was concerned—see Touré Reed, *Not Alms but Opportunity: The Urban League and Politics of Racial Uplift* (Chapel Hill: University of North Carolina Press, 2008), esp. 81–138.

15. Kenneth Jackson, *The Ku Klux Klan in the City* (New York: Oxford University Press, 1967).

16. Meier and Rudwick, *Black Detroit and the Rise of the UAW*, 7–9.

17. Lorenzo J. Greene and Carter G. Woodson, *The Negro Wage Earner* (Washington, DC: Association for the Study of Negro Life and History, 1930), 253, 140–41; Lloyd H. Bailer, "The Negro Automobile Worker," *Journal of Political Economy* 51 (October 1943): 417, 419, and 415–28; see also T. J. Woofter, "The Negro and Industrial Peace," *Survey* 45 (December 18, 1920): 420–21; Herbert R. Northrup, *Organized Labor and the Negro Worker* (New York: Harper & Brothers, 1944), 187–92.

18. Loizides, "'Making Men' at Ford," 134 (for the quotations); David R. Roediger and Elizabeth D. Esch, *The Production of Difference: Race and the Management of Labor in U.S. History* (New York: Oxford University Press, 2012), 203–4; Angela

Dillard, *Faith in the City: Preaching Radical Social Change in Detroit* (Ann Arbor: University of Michigan Press, 2007), 64, 65–70.

19. Bradby's daily presence in the plants is significant not just because of what it suggests about Ford's use of Black professionals to "teach" Black workers but also because contact between Black and white workers in the workplace was minimal. Lewis, "Negro Employment," 17.

20. Meier and Rudwick, *Black Detroit,* 5; Bates, *Black Detroit,* 5–8, 55–57, 75–78 (including denials by Bradby that his congregation was built through access to Ford employment). For the quote, see Richard W. Thomas, *Life for Us Is What We Make It: Building Black Community in Detroit, 1915–1945* (Bloomington: Indiana University Press, 1992), 273.

21. Elizabeth Anne Martin, "Religion and the Migrant," *Detroit and the Great Migration, 1916–1929* (Ann Arbor: Bentley Historical Library Printing Services, University of Michigan, online resource, n. d.), n. p.; Dillard, *Faith in the City,* 32 ("laboring classes").

22. Martin, "Religion and the Migrant."

23. Lewis, "Negro Employment," 21. According to Lewis, Ford wrote an undated comment in one of his notebooks about a visit to Reverend Daniel's church, St. Matthew's: "we are going out in society . . . to a nigger church." Beth Bates's recent comprehensive study of African Americans in the era of Henry Ford provides great biographical detail about Detroit's Black clerical leadership and its relations with Ford, Sorensen, Bennett, and Marshall. On this see Bates, *Black Detroit,* 113–14, 138–40, 247–48.

24. Lewis, "Negro Employment," 23, 25; Bates, *Black Detroit,* 189–90; "Reminiscences of Mr. H. E. Ablewhite," Accession 65, BFRC, 86.

25. Meier and Rudwick, *Black Detroit and the Rise of the UAW.* On paternalism and the question of worker loyalty to employers because of it see John Brueggemann, "The Power and Collapse of Paternalism: The Ford Motor Company and Black Workers, 1937–1941," *Social Problems* 2 (May 2000); Eugene Genovese's *Roll, Jordan, Roll: The World the Slaves Made* (New York: Vintage, 1972) famously put forth the idea that paternalism explains the relationships that slaveholders had with their slaves, a relationship enslaved people were able to shape in the context of the hegemonic power of owners. As a revisionist explanation for the dynamics of exploitative relationships between whites and Blacks that allow for the existence of Black humanity even in a racist context, it relied on white historians' past practice of at best debating and most often denying the existence of Black humanity and subjectivity. As an explanatory paradigm for racist power dynamics Genovese's paternalism has been challenged from the point of view of the enslaved African American, but very much less so as an explanation of the behavior of white elites.

26. "All Races Get Slice of Ford Motor Co. Melon," *Chicago Defender,* June 12, 1915; "Henry Ford's Motto Leaves Race People Skeptical," *Chicago Defender,* November 17, 1923, including quote from Ford; Robert Crump, "Negro Workers Given 'Breaks' by Henry Ford, Writer States," *Los Angeles Sentinel,* April 17, 1947.

27. "Henry Ford—Fictionist," *Pittsburgh Courier,* April 21, 1928.

28. Christopher Foote, Warren Whatley, and Gavin Wright, "Arbitraging a Discriminatory Labor Market: Black Workers at the Ford Motor Company, 1918–1947," *Journal of Labor Economics* 21 (2003): 2.

29. Christopher Alston, *Henry Ford and the Negro People,* issued by the National Negro Congress, 1940, 4. On Alston, see Robin D. G. Kelley, "Christopher Columbus Alston: Organizer, Fighter, and Historian," *Solidarity* website (originally 1996), www.solidarity-us.org/node/2514.

30. Robert Cruden, "The Great Ford Myth," *New Republic* 70 (March 16, 1932): 116. Payroll Department report, October 7, 1937, Accession 38, Box 82, BFRC.

31. Shaw Peterson, "Black Auto Workers in Detroit," 78; Roediger and Esch, *Production of Difference,* 25, 185–95. See also Karen E. Fields and Barbara J. Fields, *Racecraft: The Soul of Inequality in American Life* (New York: Verso, 2012).

32. Foote, Whatley, and Wright, "Arbitraging a Discriminatory Labor Market," 493–531.

33. Ibid.

34. Ibid., 10. See also Whatley and Wright, "Getting Started in the Auto Industry."

35. James Barrett and David Roediger, "Inbetween Peoples: Race, Nationality and the 'New Immigrant' Working Class," *Journal of American Ethnic History* 16 (Spring 1997): 3–44.

36. Du Bois, *Souls of Black Folk,* 2–3.

37. Nevins and Hill, *Ford: Expansion and Challenge,* 283.

38. Ibid., 284–85.

39. Oliver J. Abell, "The Making of Men, Motor Cars, and Profits," *Iron Age,* January 7, 1915, 37; Loizides, " 'Making Men' at Ford," 132 ("punitive" and quoting *Auto Workers' News*); Nevins and Hill, *Ford: Expansion and Challenge,* 549. On foundry labor generally, see Zachary Sell, " 'A Jungle to Work In': Race and the Social Terrain of Foundry Production" (Senior thesis, University of Wisconsin–Milwaukee, 2009).

40. Robert Dunn, *Labor and Automobiles* (New York: International, 1929), 69.

41. On heat, see Shaw Peterson, "Black Auto Workers in Detroit," 179; Roediger and Esch, *Production of Difference,* 154–58, 187, 204.

42. Bailer, "Negro Automobile Worker," 416; Roberto Munoz interview, "A Job at Ford's," *The Great Depression,* Public Broadcasting Service, film, 1996. See also Zaragosa Vargas, *Proletarians of the North: A History of Mexican Industrial Workers in Detroit and the Midwest, 1917–1933* (Chapel Hill: University of North Carolina Press, 1993) and Elena Herrada's 2001 documentary film, *Los Repatriados: Exiles from the Promised Land.*

43. Bailer, "Negro Automobile Worker," 417; Foote, Whatley, and Wright, "Arbitraging a Discriminatory Labor Market," 493–532; Bates, *Black Detroit,* 167.

44. Foote, Whatley, and Wright, "Arbitraging a Discriminatory Labor Market," 493–532; Bates, *Black Detroit,* 167.

45. Robin D. G. Kelley, "We Are Not What We Seem: Rethinking Black Working Class Opposition in the Jim Crow South," *Journal of American History* 80, no.

1 (June 1993): 101; Loizides, "'Making Men' at Ford," 133–34 ("wops," quoting the notes of the Communist auto organizer Robert Dunn from 1926).

46. Although later regarded as a common charting technique, Gantt charts were considered revolutionary when first introduced in and after 1910. Coming into being alongside the time and motion studies of Taylor the charts were used to break down a production schedule into a widely accessible explanation of the work involved, claiming to be able to do so objectively. They were most valuable to early transnational firms seeking ways to standardize production across obstacles of language and literacy. That they could not apply even in Ford's advanced foundry underlines how much human intellect was still required to accomplish the day-to-day work of foundry production. Howell Harris, "The Rocky Road to Mass Production: Explaining Technological Conservatism in the U.S. Foundry Industry," seminar paper, Center for the History of Business, Technology and Society, Hagley Museum and Library, September 12, 1996, 12. See also Bailer, "Negro Automobile Worker," 417.

47. On the more complex history of skill and Black steelworkers see James Catano, *Ragged Dicks: Masculinity, Steel and the Rhetoric of the Self-Made Man* (Carbondale: Southern Illinois University Press, 2001); Dennis C. Dickerson, *Black Steelworkers in Western Pennsylvania, 1875–1980* (Albany: State University of New York Press, 1986); Henry M. McKiven Jr., *Iron and Steel: Class, Race and Community in Birmingham, Alabama, 1875–1920* (Chapel Hill: University of North Carolina Press, 1995); Roediger and Esch, *Production of Difference,* 63; Brian Kelly, *Race, Class, and Power in the Alabama Coalfields, 1908–21* (Urbana: University of Illinois Press, 2001), 12, 22–24, 56.

48. Charles Denby, *Indignant Heart: A Black Worker's Journal* (Detroit: Wayne State University Press, 1978), 5.

49. There is no full published account of Curtis Williams's story. Internet sources include www.laborheritage.org/IALL-MI.html and www.forgottenshow.net. The latter is the site for Steve Jones, *The Forgotten,* a jazz opera about the organizing efforts and murder of Lewis Bradford, a minister and radio host who went to work at the Rouge in order to help organize the plant. Its representation of the Hunger March does include Curtis Williams, thanks to the efforts of local activists. Thanks to Detroit revolutionary General Baker for connecting me with this information and for his efforts in getting Curtis Williams's story into the historic record. See also Dave Moore's testimony about Williams, whose shooting he witnessed, on this important history.

50. Alston, *Henry Ford and the Negro Worker,* 5.

51. Thomas N. Maloney and Warren C. Whatley, "Making the Effort: The Contours of Racial Discrimination in Detroit's Labor Markets, 1920–1940," *Journal of Economic History* 55 (September 1995): 472.

52. Nevins and Hill, *Ford: Expansion and Challenge,* 354, 539.

53. See Douglas Baynton, "Disability and the Justification of Inequality in American History," in *The New Disability History: American Perspectives,* ed. Paul K. Longmore and Laura Umansky (New York: New York University Press, 2001);

Vernon Williams, "What Is Race?: Franz Boas Reconsidered," in *Race, Nation and Empire in American History*, ed. James T. Campbell, Matthew Pratt Guterl, and Robert G. Less (Chapel Hill: University of North Carolina Press, 2007), 40–54.

54. Perhaps most significantly in this regard are the many complex and contradictory ways that the ideas of Frank Boas were put to use by liberal segregationists. I develop this argument further in chapter 5.

55. Olivier Zunz, *The Changing Face of Inequality: Urbanization, Industrial Development, and Immigrants in Detroit, 1880–1920* (Chicago: University of Chicago Press, 1982), 372–98.

56. *Pipp's Weekly*, June 5, 1920; Report on Mayor's Housing Conference, Accession 940, Box 5, BFRC; "Negro in Detroit," vol. 5, 1 (citing 1919 report made for Research Bureau of Associated Charities), cited in Shaw Peterson, "Black Auto Workers in Detroit," 182.

57. "Negro in Detroit," vol. 5, 6, 10, cited in Shaw Peterson, "Black Auto Workers in Detroit," 183.

58. "Report to the Health Officer on Housing and Health in Detroit," 1916, 5–6, cited in Shaw Peterson, "Black Auto Workers in Detroit," 183.

59. Shaw Peterson, "Black Auto Workers in Detroit," 190; Kevin Boyle, *Arc of Justice: A Saga of Race, Civil Rights, and Murder in the Jazz Age* (New York: MacMillan, 2004).

60. Victoria Wolcott, *Remaking Respectability: African American Women in Interwar Detroit* (Chapel Hill: University of North Carolina Press, 2001), 138–40; see also Bates, *Black Detroit*, 101–2.

61. John Inkster, *Robert Inkster, 1828–1914*, Inkster Historical Commission, 1954, in the Inkster Historical Commission archive.

62. James Loewen, *Sundown Towns: A Hidden Dimension of American Racism* (New York: New Press, 2005); Lindsey, *Fields to Fords*, 34 (see following note). Lewis, "Negro Employment," 35.

63. Howard Lindsey, "Fields to Fords, Feds to Franchise: African American Empowerment in Inkster, Michigan" (unpublished PhD diss., University of Michigan, 1993), 28. I am indebted to Dr. Lindsey for the stories he uncovered in his interviews with Inkster residents. Wolcott, *Remaking Respectability*, 138–42, makes the connection to the Sweet case. On Sweet, the classic study is Boyle, *Arc of Justice*. Henry Ford's personal secretary, Ernest Liebold, was president of the Dearborn Realty and Construction Company, with Edsel Ford serving as vice president.

64. Lindsey, "Fields to Fords," 43. See also "Inkster in Darkness without Policemen," *Dearborn Independent*, May 8, 1931, 1.

65. Lindsey, "Fields to Fords," 44.

66. Keith Sward, *The Legend of Henry Ford* (New York: Rinehart, 1948), 229–30.

67. Ibid.; A. M. Smith, "Inkster Showing World How to Banish Poverty," *Detroit News*, December 27, 1931; "Ford Acts to Aid Debt-Ridden Workers; Begins Rehabilitation of a Whole Village," *New York Times*, December 16, 1931; Thomas, *Life for Us*, 66, 99 ("satellite"), 275–77, 284–85.

68. "Ford Acts to Aid Debt Ridden Workers," *New York Times,* December 16, 1931.

69. "Reminiscences of Ernest Liebold," Accession 65, BFRC, 1430. Liebold is wrong about the wage, though; in 1931 wages at the Rouge had already been dropped back down to four dollars a day.

70. Ibid., 1420.

71. "Reminiscences of H. S. Ablewhite," Accession 280, BFRC, 111–12.

72. Inkster Commissary Report, n.p., BFRC. See also Lindsey, "Fields to Fords", 90-115.

73. "Ford Acts to Aid Debt Ridden Workers," *New York Times,* December 16, 1931.

74. Lindsey, "Fields to Fords," 74.

75. "Reminiscences of Ernest Liebold," 1424.

76. Ibid.

77. "Reminiscences of H. S. Ablewhite," 12.

78. "Ford Acts to Aid Debt Ridden Workers," *New York Times,* December 16, 1931.

79. "Reminiscences of Ernest Liebold," 1420.

80. Ibid., 1427.

81. Ibid., 1425.

82. Lindsey, "Fields to Fords," 86; on Ford and Carver, see Douglas Brinkley, *Wheels for the World: Henry Ford, His Company and a Century of Progress, 1903–2003* (New York: Penguin, 2003), 444–45.

83. Swenson memorandum, November 25, 1942, cited in Lewis, "Negro Employment," 35.

84. "Reminiscences of Mr. Willis Ward and Supplemental Reminiscences," Accession 65, BFRC, 80, 15–17.

85. "Summary of Welfare Projects at Inkster and Garden City, January 20, 1936, Records Vault, Ford Motor Company Administration Building," cited in Lewis, "Negro Employment," 36.

86. "Henry Ford Spruces Up Inkster," *Atlanta World,* January 22, 1932, A4; Thomas, *Life for Us,* 275–77.

87. "Mr. Ford Speaks," *Pittsburgh Courier,* June 4, 1932, 10.

88. Townsend Boyer, "Reconstruction and the Negro Race: South Tries to Forgot the Troubles That Followed Its Rehabilitation," *Dearborn Independent,* May 15, 1926, 7.

89. Stuart Kinzie, "Mr. Ford Lends a Hand," *Scribner's Commentator,* April 1941, 22.

90. Ibid., 21.

91. Nevins and Hill, *Ford: Expansion and Challenge,* 356.

92. "Reminiscences of Dr. C. F. Holton," Accession 65, BFRC, 12.

93. David Abraham, *The Collapse of the Weimar Republic: Political Economy and Crisis* (Princeton, NJ: Princeton University Press, 1981); Joseph Borkin, *The Crime and Punishment of I. G. Farben* (New York: Free Press, 1978). On the links to Ford, see chapter 2 herein.

94. Howard Watson Ambruster, *Treason's Peace: German Dyes and American Dupes* (New York: Beechhurst Press, 1947), 218–19; "The History of World War Two Medicine: The Use of Atabrine to Fight Malaria During World War II," home.att.net/~steinert/wwii.htm.

95. See home.att.net/~steinert/wwii.htm.

96. Ibid.

97. "Reminiscences of Dr. C. F. Holton," 12.

98. Ibid., 14.

99. Ibid., 18–19. Holton wrote to the Boston owners of the enterprise in Savannah, requesting permission to put a clinic there where they would treat "syphilitic individuals" daily with compounds of arsenic and bismuth, then the treatment for syphilis.

100. Ibid., 21.

101. "Reminiscences of E. D. Mitchum," Accession 280, BRFC (1955), 14. Mitchum recalled, "Some of the best moonshine liquor ever made was made right here in Bryan County. Old whisky dealers up and down the coast will tell you that."

102. Ibid., 26.

103. Brinkley, *Wheels for the World,* 444–45.

104. "Reminiscences of H. S. Ablewhite," 90.

105. "Reminiscences of E. D. Mitchum," 37.

106. Robert P. Moses and Charles E. Cobb, "Quality Education Is a Civil Rights Issue," *Harvard Education Letter* (May–June 2001).

107. "Reminiscences of Mr. H. G. Cooper," Accession 65, BFRC, 7.

108. Ibid..

109. Joseph R. Thomas, "A Study in Social Trends Where the 'Old Order Changeth,'" Accession 587, Box 3, Folder "Richmond Hill, BFRC, 587.

110. Accession 587, Box 3, Folder "Richmond Hill."

111. Thomas, "Study in Social Trends," 67.

112. Ann Laura Stoler, "Tense and Tender Ties: The Politics of Comparison in North American History and (Post)Colonial Studies," *Journal of American History* 88 (December 2001): 829–65.

4. BREEDING RUBBER, BREEDING WORKERS

1. "The Ford Rubber Plantations," 1941, Vertical File, *Pamphlets,* BFRC.

2. Diego Rivera with Gladys March, *My Art, My Life: An Autobiography* (New York: Dover Press, 1991), 116. Rivera is said to have based the white face on his assistant Lucienne Bloch while the black face was based on the housekeeper of the Palms Hotel where Rivera and Kahlo lived while in Detroit.

3. George F. Pierrot, *An Illustrated Guide to the Diego Rivera Frescoes* (Detroit: Detroit Institute of Arts, 1934).

4. On the idea of "in-betweenness" in a U.S. context see James R. Barrett and David Roediger, "Inbetween Peoples: Race, Nationality and the New Immigrant Working Class," *Journal of American Ethnic History* 13 (Spring 1997): 3–44.

5. "Untitled Report, December 16, 1940," Vertical Files, *Rubber Plantations,* BFRC. The term concession dates from the 1650s and means "a right or privilege granted by the government." Most familiar to U. S. historians of labor would be the Firestone concession in Liberia. Interesting that a word whose use today tends to describe an admission of powerlessness (as in a concession speech) was globally used in parsing out and privatizing huge swaths of formerly sovereign land.

6. Andrew Herod, "Social Engineering through Spatial Engineering: Company Towns and the Geographical Imagination," in *Company Towns in the Americas: Landscape, Power and Working Class Communities*, ed. Oliver Dinius and Angela Vergara (Athens: University of Georgia Press, 2011), 21–44.

7. See Ann Laura Stoler, "Tense and Tender Ties: The Politics of Comparison in North American History and (Post)Colonial Studies," *Journal of American History* 88 (December 2001): 53–54.

8. Greg Grandin, *Fordlandia: The Rise and Fall of Henry Ford's Forgotten Jungle City* (New York: New Press, 2009). Fordlandia was not quite as "forgotten" as Grandin's subtitle implies. See Elizabeth Esch, "Shades of Tarzan! Ford on the Amazon," *Cabinet: A Quarterly Journal of Art and Culture* 7 (Summer 2002): esp. 76–79, and Elizabeth D. Esch, "Fordtown: Managing Race and Nation in the American Empire, 1925–1945" (unpublished PhD diss., New York University, 2003). The 2005 film *Amazon Adventures,* distributed by the Arts and Entertainment Network for the History Channel, prefigures the argument Grandin presents as his own about the significance of the sawmill and timber production at Fordlandia and for the company more broadly; Susanna B. Hecht and Alexander Cockburn, *The Fate of the Forest: Developers, Destroyers, and Defenders of the Amazon* (Chicago: University of Chicago Press, 2010, originally 1990), 87–128.

9. John Finley, "Race Development by Industrial Means among the Moros and Pagans in the Southern Philippines," *Journal of Race Development* 3 (January 1913): 343–68; on international relations and "race development," see Robert Vitalis, "The Noble American Science of Imperial Relations and Its Laws of Race Development," *Comparative Studies in Society and History* 52 (October 2010): 909–38. See also Ellsworth Huntington, "The Adaptability of the White Man to Tropical America," *Journal of Race Development* 5 (October 1914): 185–211; Daniel Bender, *American Abyss: Savagery and Civilization in the Age of Industry* (Ithaca, NY: Cornell University Press, 2009); David R. Roediger and Elizabeth D. Esch, *The Production of Difference: Race and the Management of Labor in U. S. History* (New York: Verso, 2012), 98–135.

10. Philip Ainsworth Means, "Race Appreciation and Democracy," *Journal of Race Development* 9 (October 1918): 182 and 180–84; G. Stanley Hall, "The Point-of-View toward Primitive Races," *Journal of Race Development* 1 (July 1910): 5, 6–12.

11. See Jerry Davila, *Diploma of Whiteness: Race and Social Policy in Brazil, 1917–1945* (Durham, NC: Duke University Press 2003); Barbara Weinstein, "Racializing Regional Difference: São Paulo versus Brazil, 1932," in *Race and Nation in Modern Latin America,* ed. Nancy Applebaum, Karin Alejandro Rosenblatt, and Peter Wade (Chapel Hill: University of North Carolina Press 2007).

12. Within a few years of its implementation the British restriction plan was scrapped, owing largely to the refusal of Dutch growers to be cartel-ized. American firms continued to pursue rubber production, however. See John Galey, "Industrialist in the Wilderness: Henry Ford's Amazon Venture," *Journal of Interamerican Studies and World Affairs* 21, no. 2 (1979): 263.

13. Special Report No. 744, "Summary of Activities of Certain Shipping Vessels Sold to Ford Motor Company, Statistical Department, Fleet Corporation, Washington D.C.," cited in Ford Richardson Bryan, *Beyond the Model T: The Other Ventures of Henry Ford* (Detroit: Wayne State University Press, 1997), 148.

14. Unlabeled folders containing the *Ormoc's* provision lists, Accession 74, Box 4, BFRC.

15. "Ford Motor Company of Brazil," Vertical Files, *Ford Motor Company of Brazil,* July 1929.

16. "Untitled Report, December 16, 1940," Vertical files, *Rubber Plantations,* BFRC.

17. Alan I. Marcus, "Physicians Open a Can of Worms: American Nationality and Hookworm in the United States, 1893–1909," *American Studies Journal* 30 (Fall 1989), 103–21.

18. Letter from J.C. Alves de Lima, Brazil Consular, Inspector, April 9, 1923, Vertical Files, *Rubber Plantation,* BFRC.

19. "Articles of Association of Joint Stock Company, Companhia Ford Industrial do Brasil," Chapter IV, "Of the Object and Purposes of the Company," Article 10, Box 1, "1927–1945, Minute Book, Correspondence," Accession 301, BFRC.

20. "Reminiscences of Oz Ide," Accession 65, p. 39. Also see letter from Ide to Detroit, Villares cable to Longley, and letter from J.C. Alves de Lima, April 9, 1923, Folder "Brazil," Box 2, "1927–1945 CFIDB Papers, Correspondence, Stock Certificates," Accession 301, BFRC.

21. "The Irradiating Center of Civilization," *Time Magazine,* June 1941, n.p.

22. On the history of *os confederados* in their several Brazilian settlements see Alan M. Tigay, "The Deepest South," *American Heritage* 49 (April 1998): 84–95; Eugene C. Harter, *The Lost Colony of the Confederacy* (Oxford: University Press of Mississippi, 2000); Judith MacKnight Jones, *Soldado Descansa! Uma Epopeia Norte Americana Sob Os Ceus Do Brasil* (Brasilia: Jarde, 1967, reprinted by Fraternidade Descendencia Americana, 1998). Jones, who is a descendant of a *confederados* family, includes references to about 400 families in her book. There is no archival evidence that the existence of the Santarém confederate colony influenced Ford but it is an interesting juxtaposition. On the work in Pará and later in the world for Ford of David Riker, a descendant of the original Riker Confederate emigrant family, see Grandin, *Fordlandia,* 190–91.

23. Letter from H.F. Firestone to Henry Ford, February 17,1923, Vertical File, "Rubber Plantation," BFRC.

24. Ibid.

25. Contemporary scandals about slave labor in Firestone's Liberian plantations made Ford's public commitment to "progress" strategic and, apparently at least,

heartfelt. See I. K. Sundiata, *Black Scandal: America and the Liberian Labor Crisis, 1929–1936* (Philadelphia: Institute for the Study of Human Issues, 1980).

26. The most far-reaching and thoughtful analysis of rubber tapping in this period comes from Barbara Weinstein, *The Amazon Rubber Boom, 1850–1920* (Palo Alto: Stanford University Press, 1983). See also Galey, "Industrialist in the Wilderness," 261–89.

27. Galey, "Industrialist in the Wilderness," 7.

28. Mark Jacobson, "Manaus Moment," *Travel and Leisure Magazine,* April 2006, online edition, n. p.

29. Ibid.

30. Jacobson, "Manaus Moment," writes: "By the end of World War I, Manaus was well on its way to becoming a backwater once more, the mansions of the erstwhile barons rotting away in the sodden air. Eduardo Ribeiro would not live to see the deterioration of his beloved opera house. He committed suicide in 1900."

31. "CFIDB, General, 1933," Vertical Files, BFRC.

32. Weinstein, *Amazon Rubber Boom,* 212.

33. Grandin, *Fordlandia,* 155–57, 189; cf. Roediger and Esch, *Production of Difference,* 99, 102, and 133 for similar dynamics in British Honduras, Nueva Grenada, Panama, and the Philippines.

34. John Tully, *The Devil's Milk: A Social History of Rubber* (New York: Monthly Review Press, 2012), 185.

35. Weinstein, *Amazon Rubber Boom,* 219. A hectare equals about 2.5 acres. The "thief" is "adventurer" Henry Wickham, who was supported while in the region by the first generation of confederate settlers in Santarém, the Riker family, who provided him a base from which to smuggle the seeds out of Brazil in 1876. After Ford's arrival in the region Wickham come to be known colloquially as "Henry the First." The seed snatch led to the development of rubber seedlings for plantation development at London's Kew Gardens. The realization of those investments, when rubber cultivated and harvested in British colonies in Asia became available, dealt a staggering blow to indigenous production and was integrally connected to global price fluctuation. In spite of Brazil's longtime position as the world's supplier of rubber, investment (that is, money) went instead to other regions. Thus while British holdings in Asia increased astonishingly, from 5,342,000 hectares under cultivation in 1905, to 46,174,000 in 1910, to 101,696,000 in 1915, the Amazon region continued to harvest wild rubber at about the same pace as always. On this scandalous history see Howard Wolf and Ralph Wolf, *Rubber: A Story of Glory and Greed* (New York: Covici Friede, 1936), 151–68.

36. Carl LaRue, "Living Conditions in the Amazon Valley," May 6, 1927, Vertical File, *Rubber Plantation,* BFRC, 6.

37. Ibid., 1, 4.

38. LaRue as quoted in Hecht and Cockburn, *Fate of the Forest,* 97.

39. Anthony Marx, *Making Race and Nation: A Comparison of South Africa, the United States and Brazil* (Cambridge: Cambridge University Press, 1998); Nancy Stepan, *"The Hour of Eugenics": Race, Gender and Nation in Latin America* (Ithaca,

NY: Cornell University Press, 1991); Carl Degler, *Neither Black nor White: Slavery and Race Relations in Brazil and the United States* (Madison: University of Wisconsin Press, 1991); Angello Rossi, *Brasil, integracao de races e nacionalidades* (São Paulo: Companhia Ilimitada, 1991); Maria Luiza Tucci Carneiro, *O racismo na historica do Brasil: Mito e realidade* (São Paulo: Editoria Atica, 1994); Frances Winddance Twine, *Racism in a Racial Democracy: The Maintenance of White Supremacy in Brazil* (New Brunswick, NJ: Rutgers University Press, 1997).

40. LaRue, "Living Conditions in the Amazon Valley," 5.

41. Grandin, *Fordlandia,* 26, 156, 155–57, though (213) some clearing labor was at times done by Indians; on Hoover see Roediger and Esch, *Production of Difference,* 117. On Hoover's cooperation with the U. S. rubber industry responding to the rubber "emergency" ostensibly caused by British policy and on efforts to find new U. S.-controlled sources of rubber, see Joseph Brandes, *Herbert Hoover and Economic Diplomacy: Department of Commerce Policy, 1921–1928* (Pittsburgh: University of Pittsburgh Press, 1962), 18–20; for complexities born in part of Firestone's own aggressively pursued agendas, see Silvano A. Wueschner, "Herbert Hoover, Great Britain, and the Rubber Crisis, 1923–1926," *Essays in Economic and Business History* (2000): 211–21.

42. Grandin, *Fordlandia,* 155–57, 162–63, 302.

43. Barbara Weinstein, *For Social Peace in Brazil: Industrialists and the Remaking of the Working Class in São Paulo, 1920–1964* (Chapel Hill: University of North Carolina Press, 1996), 1–4. See also Joel Wolfe, *Autos and Progress: The Brazilian Search for Modernity* (New York: Oxford University Press, 2010) on the relationships between technology, democracy, and consumerism.

44. Weinstein, *For Social Peace in Brazil,* 5.

45. "With Ford on the Amazon: the Story of the Ford Plantation, an Eye-Witness," *The Planter,* January 1931, 166.

46. Allan Nevins and Frank Ernest Hill, *Ford: Expansion and Challenge, 1915–1933* (New York: Charles Scribner's Sons, 1957), 236. Galey, "Industrialist in the Wilderness," 261–89, says quite clearly that the problem was entirely of Ford's making in that the company sought state, rather than federal, exemptions from taxation.

47. Richard Tucker, *Insatiable Appetite: The United States and the Ecological Degradation of the Tropical World* (Berkeley: University of California Press, 2000), 259.

48. "The Ford Rubber Plantations," n. p., n. d., Vertical File, *Rubber Plantations—Pamphlets,* BFRC.

49. Galey, "Industrialist in the Wilderness," 275. It was not until late 1933 that Ford hired its first botanist. On his recommendation the company abandoned Fordlandia and moved to more usable land upriver.

50. Mira Wilkins and Frank Ernest Hill, *American Business Abroad: Ford on Six Continents* (Detroit: Wayne State University Press, 1964), 128.

51. "Proposed—Rubber Plantation Book—Material Instructions," Accession 74, Box 8, BFRC. The voluminous literature on comparative and transnational

racial systems involving the United States and Brazil centers almost wholly on the Black-white color line. For a recent contribution to the debate, see Michael Hanchard, "Acts of Miscegenation: Transnational Black Politics, Anti-Imperialism and the Ethnocentrisms of Pierre Bourdieu and Louie Wacquant," *Theory, Culture and Society* 20 (August 2003): 5–29. See also Robert Stam and Ella Shohat, *Race in Translation: Culture Wars around the Postcolonial Atlantic* (New York: New York University Press, 2012). The inclusion of indigenous histories means that the Black-white basis of comparison, which is in itself troubling for its reliance on modern racial constructions and therefore limited in its ability to explain how those constructions came into being, will be appropriately decentered.

52. Folder "Proposed—Rubber Plantation Book—Material Instructions," Accession 74, Box 8, BFRC.

53. Cited in Galey, "Industrialist in the Wilderness," 271; for LaRue's understatement, see Hecht and Cockburn, *Fate of the Forest,* 87.

54. Herod, "Social Engineering," 113.

55. This lesson had been learned by Ford from Firestone in Liberia. There, the company had trouble addressing the problem of what it called "absconding," workers leaving before they had repaid what the company had loaned them to get to the plantation. At Fordlandia, contending that what it provided the workers, transportation for example, had a monetary value allowed the company to claim that those men were in debt upon arrival though no money had changed hands.

56. "Weekly Reports, November, December, 1930," Accession 74, Box 2, Folder "Companhia Ford Industrial do Brasil—Progress Reports—1930," BFRC.

57. "South America, 1927 (Blakely File) Carl d. LaRue Data," CFIDB, Accession 4, Box 1, BFRC.

58. E. P. Thompson, "Time, Work-Discipline and Industrial Capitalism," *Past and Present* 38 (December 1967): 56–97; Herbert Gutman, "Work, Culture and Society in Industrializing America, 1815–1919," *American Historical Review* 78 (June 1973): 531–88; A. Mark Smith, *Mastered by the Clock: Time, Slavery and Freedom in the American South* (Chapel Hill: University of North Carolina Press, 1997).

59. See Stepan, "Hour of Eugenics," and Michel Foucault, *The Birth of the Clinic: an Archaeology of Medical Perception,* trans. A. M. Sheridan Smith (New York: Vintage, 1994). On colonial understandings of race and the tropics see Warwick Anderson, "The Natures of Culture: Environment and Race in the Colonial Tropics," in *Nature in the Global South: Environmental Projects in South and Southeast Asia,* ed. Paul Greenough and Anna L. Tsing (Durham, NC, and London: Duke University Press, 2003), 29–46; "Going through the Motions: American Public Health and Colonial Mimicry," *American Literary History* 14, no. 4 (2002): 686–719.

60. "Letter from C. Beaton, Medical Officer, Boa Vista, to R. D. McClure, Henry Ford Hospital, October 1, 1929," Vertical File, *Rubber Plantation,* BFRC. Boa Vista was the name of the area before Ford bought it and named it Fordlandia.

61. Esch, "Shades of Tarzan," 8.

62. Ibid.

63. Jorge Amado, *Tent of Miracles* (New York: Knopf, 1971); Davila, *Diploma of Whiteness.* See LaRue, "Living Conditions," 4; Pierre Bourdieu and Loïc Wacquant, "On the Cunning of Imperialist Reason," *Theory, Culture and Society* 16, no. 1 (1999): 41–58; see also among many acute responses, Hanchard, "Acts of Miscegenation," 5–29.

64. Davila, *Diploma of Whiteness,* 7.

65. "Riot at Boa Vista, December 22, 1930," Accession 74, Box 2, BFRC.

66. Gutman, "Work, Culture and Society."

67. Don Mitchell, "The Scales of Justice: Localist Ideology, Large-Scale Production and Agricultural Labor's Geography of Resistance in 1930s California," in *Organizing the Landscape: Geographical Perspectives on Labor Unionism*, ed. Andrew Herod (Minneapolis: University of Minnesota Press, 1998), 189.

68. Letter from Rogge and Chatfeld to Kennedy; Letter from Kennedy to Carnegie; unsigned report, Accession 74, Box 2, BFRC.

69. Ibid.

70. Nevins and Hill, *Ford: Expansion and Challenge.*

71. Vertical File, *Rubber Plantations.*

72. Radiograms between Jovita and Johnson, "Indian Labor," Accession 74, Box 6, BFRC.

73. "Proposed—Rubber Plantation Book—Material Instructions," Accession 74, Box 8, BFRC.

74. "The Ford Rubber Plantations," n.p. For a thorough synthesis of the rise to power of Getulio Vargas and an analysis of its meaning over time see Robert Levine, *The Father of the Poor? Vargas and His Era* (London: Cambridge University Press, 1998).

75. "Schools," Accession 74, Box 2, BFRC.

76. Photo of time clock in Grandin, *Fordlandia,* 231. Originally appeared in *Time* magazine, 1941.

77. "The Ford Rubber Plantations," 1941, Vertical File, *Rubber Plantations-Pamphlets,* BFRC.

78. Ibid.

79. Vance Simmonds, "Schools of the Amazon," *The Herald,* n.d.

80. Ibid.

81. Here again the important work of Jerry Davila on Vargas-era reform in education is critical to this analysis. See *Diploma of Whiteness,* esp. 133–34.

82. Ibid., esp. 133–34.

83. Du Bois described Reconstruction as a "splendid failure" because of the inability of whites, not of freed African Americans, to build on the promise of formal equality offered by the Thirteenth, Fourteenth, and Fifteenth Amendments and by the potentials of the Freedmen's Bureau. W. E. B. Du Bois, *Black Reconstruction in America, 1860–1880* (New York: Atheneum, 1998, originally 1935), 708.

5. "WORK IN THE FACTORY ITSELF"

1. "Carnegie in South Africa," *Carnegie Corporation Oral History Project,* Columbia University Libraries Oral History Research Office, Butler Library, Columbia University, 1932.

2. John Woodford, "Open Letter from Former Employee of Ford Motor Company, 1983," *Divestment for Humanity: The Anti-Apartheid Movement at the University of Michi*gan, http://michiganintheworld.history.lsa.umich.edu/antiapartheid/items/show/175.

3. Mira Wilkins and Frank Ernest Hill, *American Business Abroad: Ford on Six Continents* (Detroit: Wayne State University Press, 1964), 123. See also Gary Baines, *A History of New Brighton, Port Elizabeth, South Africa, 1903–1953: The Detroit of the Union* (Lewiston, NY: Edwin Mellen Press, 2002). On the local history of Ford see *Ford in South Africa,* www.dyna.co.za/cars/ford.htm. "The first Ford to arrive in South Africa was a 1903 Ford Model A, which was imported by Mr. Arthur Youldon of Johannesburg. In September 1903 Mr Youldon, an importer, was in New York where he saw Henry Ford demonstrate his new car. He immediately placed his order with Henry Ford, who informed him that it would be the first Ford to be sold outside North America. The Ford Motor Company was founded earlier that year, on 16 June 1903." The 1903 Ford is today on display in the Heidelberg Transport Museum near Johannesburg.

4. Print Advertisement, Ford Motor Company South Africa Limited, published by the South African—American Survey, 1948, in author's possession.

5. Letter from Jan Smuts to his mother collected in Jean van der Poel, ed., *Selections from the Smuts Papers, Volumes V—VII* (Cambridge: Cambridge University Press, 2007), 808.

6. Athol Fugard, with John Kani and Winston Ntshona, *Sizwe Bansi Is Dead,* in *Statements* (London: Oxford University Press, 1973), 8.

7. Diary of the Day, "The Ford Idyll," *Eastern Province Herald,* February 11, 1924, holdings in the Port Elizabeth Public Library, Port Elizabeth, South Africa.

8. South Africa called itself the Union of South Africa from 1910 until 1961.

9. Elizabeth W. Adkins, "A History of the Ford Motor Company Archives, with Reflections on Archival Documentation of Ford of Europe's History," on archivists.org, 31–34. Substantial portions of Adkins report were previously published as Elizabeth W. Adkins, "The Development of Business Archives in the United States: An Overview and a Personal Perspective," *American Archivist* 60 (Winter 1997): 8–33. Reprinted here by permission of the Society of American Archivists, www.archivists.org.

10. "The Poor White Problem in South Africa: Report of the Carnegie Commission," *Carnegie Commission of Investigation on the Poor White Question in South Africa* (New York: Carnegie Corporation, 1932, Rare Book and Manuscript Division, Butler Library, Columbia University). Hereafter referred to as the "Poor White Study." The excellent recent work by Tiffany Willoughby-Herard, *Waste of a White Skin: The Carnegie Corporation and the Racial Logic of White Vulnerability* (Berkeley:

University of California Press, 2015), is the most comprehensive examination of the impact of U. S. social science reformers in South Africa.

11. George Fredrickson, *White Supremacy: A Comparative Study in American and South African History* (New York: Oxford University Press, 1981), 236.

12. Belinda Bozzoli, *The Political Nature of a Ruling Class: Capital and Ideology in South Africa, 1890–1933* (London: Routledge, 1981), 4.

13. John S. Saul and Stephen Gelb, *The Crisis in South Africa* (New York: Monthly Review Press, 1986).

14. Luli Callinicos, *Working Life: A People's History of South Africa, Factories, Townships and Popular Culture on the Rand, 1886–1940,* vol. 2 (Johannesburg: Ravan Press, 1987), 108–16.

15. John Higginson, "Privileging the Machines: American Engineers, Indentured Chinese and White Workers in South Africa's Deep-Level Mines, 1902–1907," *International Review of Social History* 52 (2007): 10, 15; see also James T. Campbell, "The Americanization of South Africa," in *"Here, There and Everywhere": The Foreign Politics of American Popular Culture*, ed. Elaine Tyler May and Reinhold Wagnleitner (Hanover, NH: University Press of New England, 2000), 38–41; David R. Roediger and Elizabeth D. Esch, *The Production of Difference: Race and the Management of Labor in U. S. History* (New York: Oxford University Press, 2012), 114–21; N. K. Nkosi, "American Mining Engineers and the Labor Structure of South African Gold Mines," *African Journal of Political Economy* 2 (August 1987): 63–80.

16. Baines, *History of New Brighton,* 18.

17. Glenn Adler, "From the Liverpool of the Cape to the Detroit of South Africa, the Automobile Industry and Industrial Development in the Port Elizabeth-Uitenhage Region," *Kronos* 20 (1993): 17–43.

18. Bozzoli, *Political Nature of a Ruling Class,* 146–47.

19. Jennifer Robinson, *The Power of Apartheid: State, Power and Space in South African Cities* (New York: Oxford University Press, 1996), 96.

20. Baines, *History of New Brighton,* 20. The parenthetical "(White)" is in the original. See also Bozzoli, *Political Nature of a Ruling Class,* 220, on debates about and the gradual recognition of the importance of electrification and other infrastructural development to industry.

21. *Wheels of Progress* (Johannesburg: Felstar), 1977.

22. Adler, "From the Liverpool of the Cape to the Detroit of South Africa," 14–16.

23. "Talk with Love, South African PR Man, May, 1961," Accession 880, Box 4, FMC-Africa," BFRC.

24. Merle Lipton, *Capitalism and Apartheid: South Africa, 1910–1984* (London: Rowman and Allanheld, 1985), 17–19, and Fredrickson, *White Supremacy,* 285.

25. Harold Wolpe, "Capitalism and Cheap Labour Power in South Africa: from Segregation to Apartheid," in *Segregation and Apartheid in Twentieth Century South Africa*, ed. William Beinart and Saul Dubow (London: Routledge, 1995), 71.

26. T. R. H. Davenport, *South Africa: A Modern History* (Toronto and Buffalo: University of Toronto Press, third edition, 1987), 547.

27. Baines, *History of New Brighton*, 95, and photo. Interview with former Port Elizabeth resident Dennis Brutus, June 2001, in author's possession. In the mid-1970s Ford published a pamphlet detailing its commitment to native labor in the new housing it was planning at KwaFord. Margaret Harribene, *Port Elizabeth: A Chronology* (Port Elizabeth: Port Elizabeth Public Library, n. d.), n. p.

28. Baines, *History of New Brighton,* 24–28. The difference between 92 and 60 percent is enormous. Whites never represented more than 50 percent of the population of Port Elizabeth, a number which steadily declined over the years.

29. Robert Morrell, ed., *White but Poor: Essays on the History of Poor Whites in South Africa, 1880–1940* (Pretoria: University of South Africa, 1992). See also G. V. Doxey, *The Industrial Colour Bar in South Africa* (Cape Town: Oxford University Press, 1961), chap. 4.

30. "Has the White Youth Got a Chance?" *Eastern Province Herald*, January 14, 1924.

31. Ibid.

32. See Willoughby-Herard, "'*Waste of a White Skin*."

33. Though Ford's long-standing commitment to South Africa began in these years, it has been largely neglected both by historians who have written about Ford's overseas expansion and by those who have examined South African and American white supremacy in relationship to one another. Business historians Mira Wilkins and Frank Ernest Hill's *American Business Abroad: Ford on Six Continents* (Detroit: Wayne State University Press, 1964) gives brief attention to South Africa in their discussion of Ford of Canada, under whose auspices the plant opened. Allan Nevins and Frank Hill devote a paragraph to it in their three-volume work which, while published in 1957, remains the definitive work on the company. See Allan Nevins and Frank Ernest Hill, *Ford: Expansion and Challenge, 1915-1933* (New York: Charles Scribner's Sons, 1957), 375. In the 1980s a few pathbreaking works of scholarship comparing and contrasting the development of white supremacy in South Africa and the United States appeared, including George Fredrickson, *White Supremacy: A Comparative Study in American and South African History* (New York: Oxford University Press, 1981); John Cell, *The Highest Stage of White Supremacy: The Origins of Segregation in South Africa and the American South* (Cambridge: Cambridge University Press), 1982; Thomas Noer, *Briton, Boer and Yankee: The United States and South Africa, 1870–1914* (Kent, OH: Kent State University Press, 1978); Howard Lamar and Leonard Thompson, *The Frontier in History: North America and Southern Africa Compared* (New Haven, CT: Yale University Press, 1981); Stanley Greenberg, *Race and State in Capitalist Development* (New Haven, CT: Yale University Press, 1980); Anthony Marx, *Making Race and Nation: A Comparison of South Africa, the United States and Brazil* (Cambridge: Cambridge University Press, 1998). A series of papers presented at "The Burden of Race: Whiteness and Blackness in Modern South Africa," History Workshop Conference, July 5–8, 2001, have been extremely useful to me. These include Peter Alexander, "Race, Class Loyalty and the Structure of Capitalism: Coal Miners in Alabama and the Transvaal, 1918–22"; Saul Dubow, "Scientism, Social Research and Limits of 'South Africanism': The Case of

Ernst Gideon Malherbe"; John Hinshaw, "The Politics of Production: Race and Class Conflict in the Iron and Steel Industries of the U.S."; Matthew Pratt Guterl, " 'Domineering Anglo-Saxons and Supple Asians': The Use and Abuse of Chinese Labourers in the Early Twentieth Century Transvaal and Late Nineteenth Century California."

34. The most comprehensive study of U.S. involvement in South Africa remains Noer's *Briton, Boer and Yankee.* Less synthetic but also excellent is James Campbell, *Songs of Zion: The African Methodist Episcopal Church in the United States and South Africa* (New York: Oxford University Press, 1998); see also Campbell, "Americanization of South Africa" 38ff.

35. "The Engineering Requirements of South Africa," *Iron Age* 70 (December 4, 1902): 22, and "More on South Africa," *Iron Age* 70 (December 18, 1902): 66–67; both cited in Noer, *Briton, Boer and Yankee,* 93.

36. Paul Kramer, "Empires, Exceptions and Anglo-Saxons: Race and Rule between the British and United States Empires," *Journal of American History* 88 (March 2002): 1315. See also Jack Temple Kirby, *Darkness at the Dawning: Race and Reform in the Progressive Era South* (Philadelphia: Lippincott, 1972), chap. 6.

37. Kramer, "Empires, Exceptions and Anglo-Saxons," 1315.

38. Jeffrey Stanton, "Disasters, Spectacles and Cycloramas" in *Coney Island,* www.westland.net (revised April 7, 1998).

39. On work that considers the realm of Indian or native policy in the United States and South Africa see Howard Lamar and Leonard Thompson, *Frontier in History;* Richard Hull, *American Enterprise in South Africa: Historical Dimensions of Engagement and Disengagement* (New York: New York University Press, 1990); George M. Fredrickson, *The Comparative Imagination: On the History of Racism, Nationalism, and Social Movements* (Berkeley: University of California Press, 2000).

40. The Witswatersrand, known as "The Rand," is a geographic region in the former Boer Republic of the Transvaal, roughly in the center of South Africa. Johannesburg is its urban center. Gold was discovered on the Rand in 1886 and the "mineral revolution" that expedited the emergence of capitalist relations in the region is considered the earliest beginning of what would become the poor white problem.

41. Sources on the Rand Revolt include Jeremy Krikler's excellent and comprehensive *White Rising: The 1922 Insurrection and Racial Killing in South Africa* (Manchester: Manchester University Press, 2005); Edward Roux, *Time Longer Than Rope: A History of the Black Man's Struggle for Freedom in South Africa* (Madison: University of Wisconsin Press, 1966); Jeremy Krikler, "Women, Violence and the Rand Revolt of 1922," *Journal of Southern African Studies* 22 (September 1996): 349–72 and "White Working Class Identity and the Rand Revolt," paper presented at "The Burden of Race: Whiteness and Blackness in Modern South Africa," History Workshop Conference, University of the Witswatersrand (July 5–8, 2001); Lipton, *Capitalism and Apartheid.*

42. Strike Legal Defence Committee, *The Story of Crime* (Johannesburg, 1924), 6. Quoted in Krikler, "White Working Class Identity and the Rand Revolt," 32.

43. Krikler, "White Working Class Identity and the Rand Revolt," 1.

44. Roux, *Time Longer Than Rope,* 147–48.

45. Krikler, "White Working Class Identity and the Rand Revolt," 30.

46. Ibid., 34.

47. On the idea of racist language being used by white working-class people to distance themselves from their own miseries as workers and poor people see David Roediger, *The Wages of Whiteness: Race and the Making of the American Working Class* (London: Verso, 1991).

48. Morag Bell, "American Philanthropy, the Carnegie Corporation, and Poverty in South Africa," *Journal of African Studies* 26 (September 2000): 484.

49. "Introduction, Joint Findings and Recommendations of the Commission," *The Poor White Study,* Carnegie Corporation, 1932, p. iii.

50. Ann Laura Stoler, "Tense and Tender Ties: The Politics of Comparison in North American History and (Post)Colonial Studies," in *Haunted by Empire: Geographies of Intimacy in North American History,* ed. Ann Laura Stoler (Durham, NC: Duke University Press, 2006).

51. Richard Glotzer, "The Influence of Carnegie Corporation and Teachers College, Columbia, in the Interwar Dominions: The Case for Decentralized Education," *Historical Studies in Education / Revue d'histoire de l'education* 12, nos. 1–2 (Spring / printemps and Fall / automne, 2000): 73–92.

52. Robert S. Patterson, "American Influence on Progressive Education in Canada," *Journal of the Midwest History of Education Society* 2 (Fall 1973): 122–41, as cited in Glotzer, "Influence of Carnegie Corporation," 75.

53. Frederick P. Keppel, *Philanthropy and Learning* (New York: Teachers College Press, 1936), 139–54.

54. Glotzer, 83. Strikingly, artistic representations of Anglo-Saxonists Henry Ford and Frederick Keppel were listed as available for sale in the catalogue for the 1923 *New Society of Artists Fourth Exhibition* (New York: American Society of Painters, Sculptors and Engravers, January 2–27, 1923), holdings in the Frick Art Reference Library, New York, NY. Ford was painted in watercolor by Reynolds Beal and Keppel's head was sculpted in bronze by prominent sculptor-of-elites Paul Manship.

55. Bram D. Fleisch, "The Teachers College Club: American Educational Discourse and the Origins of Bantu Education in South Africa, 1914–1951" (unpublished PhD diss., Teachers College, Columbia University, 1995).

56. Saul Dubow, "Scientism, Social Research and Limits of South Africanism: The Case of Ernst Gideon Malherbe," paper presented at "The Burden of Race: Whiteness and Blackness in Modern South Africa," History Workshop, University of the Witswatersrand, Johannesburg, July 5–8, 2001, unpaginated. See also Bram D. Fleisch, "Social Scientists as Policy Makers: E. G. Malherbe and the National Bureau for Educational and Social Research, 1929–1943," *Journal of Southern African Studies* 21 (1995): 349–72.

57. E. G. Malherbe, *Educational and Social Research in South Africa* (Pretoria: South African Council for Educational and Social Research,1939), 38, cited in

Dubow, "Scientism, Social Research and Limits of South Africanism," unpaginated. See also Bram D. Fleisch, "Social Scientists as Policy Makers: Ernest Malherbe" (unpublished PhD diss., University of the Witswatersrand, 1981). On Thorndike, see Allan Chase, *The Legacy of Malthus: The Social Costs of the New Scientific Racism* (Urbana: University of Illinois Press, 1980), 353–57.

58. Kenyon L. Butterfield, *Report of Dr. Kenyon L. Butterfield on Rural Conditions and Sociological Problems in South Africa* (New York: Carnegie Corporation of New York, 1929).

59. Bell, "American Philanthropy," 492–93.

60. Roberta Balstad Miller, "Science and Society in the Early Career of H.F. Verwoerd," *Journal of Southern African Studies* 19 (December 1993): 634–61.

61. "Letter from Keppel to Malan, January 10, 1928," Carnegie Commission archives, Grant Files, Series 1, Box 295.

62. Ernst Gideon Malherbe, *Never a Dull Moment* (Cape Town: Timmins, 1981), 119; C. Vann Woodward, *Origins of the New South, 1877–1913* (Baton Rouge: Louisiana State University Press, 1999, originally 1951), 109–11, is the classic discussion of the U.S. "poor white." See also Ian Hartman's excellent "From Daniel Boone to the Beverly Hillbillies: Tales of a 'Fallen' Face, 1873–1968" (unpublished PhD diss., University of Illinois, 2011).

63. See Stephen Jay Gould, *The Mismeasure of Man* (New York: W.W. Norton, 1981). Gould offered the sharpest analyses of the a-scientific character of the study of race. He notes that to study race was to assume it, an approach which contradicts the most basic tenets of scientific endeavor. In the case of the poor whites, a decision was made about who was and was not one (or who was in danger of becoming one) before they could be studied.

64. "Dr. Malherbe's Interesting Address: Some Aspects of a Vital Question," *Cape Times*, June 10, 1928.

65. Ibid. See also Kirby, *Darkness at the Dawning*, 117, for comparisons between Boer achievements and the "redemption" of the U.S. South after Reconstruction.

66. "Dr. Malherbe's Interesting Address." It is no coincidence that the figure Malherbe chose to represent was a revolutionary war hero in the United States. For Malherbe, as for Ford, Sorensen, and Liebold, this figure notably represented an "old stock" white American, not a "new" European immigrant and thus a lesser white. In referencing the American Revolution Malherbe also gently reminded his British-descended listeners that their empire was no longer the only model where white civility could be found.

67. "Introduction," *Poor White Study*, v–vi.

68. In a discussion of the need to offer higher wages to white workers the *Eastern Province Herald* (January 14, 1924) stated simply that "when it came to taste the coloured worker fell away. His environment did not make for the aesthetic quality." George Lipsitz's *The Possessive Investment in Whiteness: How White People Profit from Racism* (Philadelphia: Temple University Press, 1998) is an exception to this problem, though Lipsitz deals with the post-WWII world in which both mass consumption and Keynesianism had a stature only being created in the interwar years.

See also Grace Elizabeth Hale, *Making Whiteness: The Culture of Segregation in the South, 1890–1940* (New York: Vintage, 1999).

69. *Eastern Province Herald*, March 17, 1923.

70. *Eastern Province Herald*, March 10, 1923.

71. *Eastern Province Herald*, April 21, 1923.

72. "Introduction," *Poor White Study*, xx.

73. Ibid., xix.

74. Bell, "American Philanthropy," 492; *Report of the Carnegie Commission of Investigation on the Poor White Question in South Africa*, Stellenbosch, 1932, Part V.

75. Joint Findings and Recommendations, xv. "Proceedings of the Third Race Betterment Conference," *National Conference on Race Betterment*, published by the Race Betterment Foundation in 1928. Experimentation with racial improvement through diet was a preoccupation of Ford's, whose Jim Crow plantation in Georgia dedicated in part to the production of soybeans, a food he was certain would revolutionize nutrition and health. See chapter 4 herein.

76. Maria Elizabeth Rothman, "Mother and Daughter in the Poor Family," vol. 5, 206–7, 212.

77. "Is Civilisation to Survive in South Africa?" *Eastern Province Herald*, March 22, 1924.

78. Indeed, there were those who opposed birth control on grounds of competition with Natives. D. F. Malan, Minister of the Interior and Public Health from 1924 to 1934, believed that all white reproduction was equally important and did not wish to control for quality. He proclaimed in Parliament, "We notice in all the countries in the world . . . that the [birth] rate is dropping just with those people who are most highly developed." Quoted in Susanne Klausen, "The Politics of Poor White Fertility within the South African Birth Control Movement, 1929 to 1939," paper presented at "The Burden of Race: Whiteness and Blackness in Modern South Africa," University of the Witswatersrand, July 5–8, 2001. See also Klausen's excellent *Race, Maternity and the Politics of Birth Control in South Africa, 1910–1939* (New York: Palgrave, 2005).

79. Klausen, *Race, Maternity and Politics of Birth Control*, 5.

80. "Union of South Africa," map of "Areas Visited and Studied by the Commission," *Poor White Study*. The map notes, "The degree of heaviness in the shading indicates the relative attention devoted to the area." Cape Town and Port Elizabeth are the only two areas completely shaded.

81. Ibid.

82. Ibid.

83. Ibid., xxiii.

84. Prime Minister Hertzog, Official Circular No. 5 of 1924, as cited in Doxey, *Industrial Colour Bar*, 79.

85. Roux, *Time Longer Than Rope*, 152.

86. "Proposed National Congress on the Poor White Question," NTS 9574, 289 / 400, South African National Archives, Pretoria.

87. Ibid.

88. Letter to P. du Toit from Director of Native Agriculture, December 14, 1933, NTS 9574, 289 / 400, South African National Archives, Pretoria.

89. "Report of the Committee of Mixed Marriages in South Africa," June 2, 1939, K48 vol. 7, National Archive, Pretoria.

90. Rothman, "Mother and Daughter in the Poor White Family," 7.

91. Ibid., 14.

92. See also Virginia Dominguez, *White by Definition: Social Classification in Creole Louisiana* (New Brunswick, NJ: Rutgers University Press, 1997).

93. Ibid., 28.

94. Ibid., 29–30.

95. See chapter 1 herein.

96. Bell, "American Philanthropy," 487.

97. The most important work on the relationship between the spread of American dominance and Ford is Antonio Gramsci's "Americanism and Fordism" from the *Prison Notebooks*. I address Gramsci's argument in the Introduction and chapter 1. Mary Nolan's *Visions of Modernity: American Business and the Modernization of Germany* (New York: Oxford University Press, 1994) is also extremely useful in providing a kind of template for how Fordism and Americanism became interchangeable words in both the workplace and socially.

98. Dubow, "Scientism, Social Research and Limits of 'South Africanism'," unpaginated.

99. Harribene, *Port Elizabeth: A Chronology*, unpaginated. In response to pressures to divest from South Africa the company has made unavailable most of its archived documents that had been kept in the United States and Canada.

CONCLUSION

1. Antonio Gramsci, "Americanism and Fordism," in *Selections from the Prison Notebooks* (New York: International, 1971), 218.

2. Ibid., 221.

3. Robert Vitalis, *White World Order, Black Power Politics: The Birth of International Relations* (Ithaca, NY: Cornell University Press, 2015).

4. Micheline Maynard, "Ford to Cut Up to 30,000 Jobs and 14 Plants in Next 6 Years," *New York Times,* January 23, 2006. For more on *The Way Forward* see Jeffrey McCracken, "Way Forward Requires Culture Shift at Ford," *Wall Street Journal,* January 23, 2006. By comparison, the 1906 slogan the company adopted was "1906 will be a Ford year." See John McDonough and Karen Egolf, eds., *The Advertising Age: Encyclopedia of Advertising* (Chicago: Fitzroy Dearborn, 2002), 605.

5. "Study Points to Large Wage Gaps for Mexican Auto Workers," *Mexico News Daily,* July 2, 2014, http://mexiconewsdaily.com/news/study-points-large-wage-gaps-mexican-auto-workers/#sthash.JVx26mgn.dpuf.

6. *$4 a Day? No Way! Joining Hands across the Border* (Washington, DC: American Labor Education Center, 1991).

7. John Smith, "Imperialism in the Twenty-First Century," *Monthly Review* 67 (July–August 2015), http://monthlyreview.org/2015/07/01/imperialism-in-the-twenty-first-century/, unpaginated; "Why Mexico Works for Automotive?" *Barberbiz*, March 9, 2014, https://deanbarber.wordpress.com/2014/03/09/why-mexico-works-for-automotive/.

8. "Study Points to Large Wage Gaps," *Mexico News Daily.*

9. Lu Zhang, *Inside China's Automobile Factories: The Politics of Labor and Worker Resistance* (New York: Cambridge University Press), 3.

10. Ibid., 40, 91.

11. Ibid., 55–60.

12. Ibid. See also Yu Chen and Jufen Wang, "Social Integration of New-Generation Migrants in Shanghai, China," *Habitat International* 49 (June 2015): 419–25.

13. Peter Alexander and Anita Chan, "Does China Have an Apartheid Pass System?" *Journal of Ethnic and Migration Studies* 30, no. 4 (July 2004): 609–29.

14. Ibid., 619.

15. Zhang, *Inside China's Automobile Factories*, 46–47, 165. Zhang also argues that the presence of growing militancy among more seasoned temporary workers has led management to imagine the possibility of organized resistance despite the many vulnerabilities faced by temporary workers, thus seeing formal workers as a bulwark against labor radicalism and shop floor activism.

16. James R. Healey, "Ford Shows Redone Taurus for China, Not U.S.," *USA Today,* April 19, 2015.

17. Jerry Hirsch, "Ford to Bring Back Continental with Eye on Chinese Market," *Los Angeles Times,* March 30, 2015.

SELECTED BIBLIOGRAPHY

ARCHIVES AND COLLECTIONS CONSULTED

In the United States

Dearborn, Michigan
The Benson Ford Research Library, The Henry Ford, Henry Ford Museum and Greenfield Village
Detroit, Michigan
The Detroit Institute of the Arts
The Detroit Public Library
The Walter Reuther Library, Wayne State University
New York, New York
Tamiment Collection, Bobst Library, New York University
Richmond Hill, Georgia
The Ford Plantation
Richmond Hill Museum
Washington, D. C.
The Library of Congress, College Park, Maryland
The National Archives

In South Africa

Johannesburg
Historical Papers, William Cullen Library
The Johannesburg Public Library
Wits Library of Management, University of the Witswatersrand
Port Elizabeth
Oral Histories
The Port Elizabeth Public Library
The Red District Museum

Pretoria
South African National Archives

In Canada

Windsor, Ontario
The Windsor Public Library

SECONDARY SOURCES

Abraham, David. *The Collapse of the Weimar Republic: Political Economy and Crisis.* New York: Princeton, NJ: Princeton University Press, 1981.

Adams, Mark, ed. *The Wellborn Science: Eugenics in Germany, France, Brazil, and Russia.* New York: Oxford University Press, 1990.

Aglietta, Michel. *A Theory of Capitalist Regulation.* London: Verso, 1987.

Alexander, Peter, and Rick Halpern, eds. *Racializing Class, Classifying Race: Labour and Difference in Britain, the USA and Africa.* New York: St. Martin's Press, 2000.

Amado, Jorge. *Tent of Miracles.* New York: Knopf, 1971.

Ambruster, Howard Watson. *Treason's Peace: German Dyes and American Dupes.* New York: Beechhurst Press, 1947.

Aptheker, Herbert. *The Writings of W. E. B. Du Bois in Periodicals Edited by Others, Volume 4.* Millwood, NY: Kraus-Thomson, 1982.

Arrighi, Giovanni. *The Long Twentieth Century: Money, Power, and the Origins of Our Times.* London: Verso, 1994.

Baines, Gary. *A History of New Brighton, Port Elizabeth, South Africa, 1903–1953: The Detroit of the Union.* Lewiston, NY: Edwin Mellen Press, 2002.

Bak, Richard. *Henry and Edsel: The Creation of the Ford Empire.* New York: Wiley, 2003.

Balderrama, Francisco E., and Raymond Rodríguez. *Decade of Betrayal: Mexican Repatriation in the 1930s.* Albuquerque: University of New Mexico Press, 2006.

Baldwin, Neil. *Henry Ford and the Jews: The Mass Production of Hate.* San Francisco: Public Affairs, 2001.

Ballantyne, Tony. *Orientalism and Race: Aryanism in the British Empire.* Basingstoke, UK: Palgrave, 2002.

Barrett, James R. *Work and Community in the Jungle: Chicago's Packing House Workers, 1894–1922.* Urbana: University of Illinois Press, 1987.

Bates, Beth. *Black Detroit in the Age of Henry Ford.* Chapel Hill: University of North Carolina Press, 2012.

Beard, Charles, ed. *America Faces the Future.* Boston and New York: Houghton Mifflin, 1932.

Beinart, William, and Saul Dubow, eds. *Segregation and Apartheid in Twentieth Century South Africa.* London: Routledge, 1995.

Bender, Daniel. *American Abyss: Savagery and Civilization in the Age of Industry.* Ithaca, NY: Cornell University Press, 2009.

——— and Jana K. Lipman, eds. *Making the Empire Work: Labor and United States Imperialism.* New York: New York University Press, 2015.

Bender, Thomas, ed. *Rethinking American History in a Global Age.* Berkeley: University of California Press, 2002.

———. *A Nation among Nations: America's Place in World History.* New York: Hill and Wang, 2006.

Bennett, Henry, as told to Paul Marcus. *We Never Called Him Henry.* Greenwich, CT: Fawcett Gold Medal Books, 1951.

Beynon, Huw, and Theo Nichols. *The Fordism of Ford and Modern Management: Fordism and Post-Fordism.* Cheltenham, UK: Edward Elgar, 2006.

Borkin, Joseph. *The Crime and Punishment of I. G. Farben.* New York: Free Press, 1978.

Boyle, Kevin. *Arc of Justice: A Saga of Race, Civil Rights, and Murder in the Jazz Age.* New York: MacMillan, 2004.

Bozzoli, Belinda. *The Political Nature of a Ruling Class: Capital and Ideology in South Africa, 1890–1933.* London: Routledge, 1981.

Brandes, Joseph. *Herbert Hoover and Economic Diplomacy: Department of Commerce Policy, 1921–1928.* Pittsburgh: University of Pittsburgh Press, 1962.

Braverman, Harry. *Labor and Monopoly Capital: The Degradation of Work in the Twentieth Century.* New York: Monthly Review Press, 1975.

Brinkley, Douglas. *Wheels for the World: Henry Ford, His Company, and a Century of Progress, 1903–2003.* New York: Penguin Books, 2003.

Bryan, Ford Richardson. *Beyond the Model T: The Other Ventures of Henry Ford.* Detroit: Wayne State University Press, 1997.

———. *Friends, Families and Forays: Scenes from the Life and Times of Henry Ford.* Dearborn, MI: Ford Books, 2002.

Bucci, Federico. *Albert Kahn: Architect of Ford.* New York: Princeton Architectural Press, 1993.

Buff, Rachel Ida, ed. *Immigrant Rights in the Shadow of Citizenship.* New York: New York University Press, 2008.

Bunche, Ralph. *A World View of Race.* Port Washington, NY: Kennikat Press, [1936] 1968.

Callinicos, Luli. *Working Life: A People's History of South Africa, Factories, Townships and Popular Culture on the Rand, 1886–1940,* vol. 2. Johannesburg: Ravan Press, 1987.

Campbell, James T. *Songs of Zion: The African Methodist Episcopal Church in the United States and South Africa.* New York: Oxford University Press, 1998.

———, Matthew Pratt Guterl, and Robert G. Less, eds. *Race, Nation and Empire in American History.* Chapel Hill: University of North Carolina Press, 2007.

Caplan, Jane, ed. *Nazism, Fascism, and the Working Class.* Cambridge: Cambridge University Press, 1995.

Carneiro, Maria Luiza Tucci. *O racismo na historica do Brasil: Mito e realidade.* Sao Paulo: Editoria Atica, 1994.
Casey, Robert. *The Model T: A Centennial History.* Baltimore: Johns Hopkins University Press, 2008.
Catano, James. *Ragged Dicks: Masculinity, Steel and the Rhetoric of the Self-Made Man.* Carbondale: Southern Illinois University Press, 2001.
Cell, John. *The Highest Stage of White Supremacy: The Origins of Segregation in South Africa and the American South.* Cambridge: Cambridge University Press, 1982.
Chalmers, David. *Hooded Americanism: The History of the Ku Klux Klan.* Durham, NC: Duke University Press, 1981.
Chase, Allan. *The Legacy of Malthus: The Social Costs of the New Scientific Racism.* Urbana: University of Illinois Press, 1980.
Chibber, Vivek. *Postcolonial Theory and the Specter of Capital.* New York and London: Verso, 2013.
Cohen, Lizbeth, *A Consumers' Republic: The Politics of Mass Consumption in Post-War America.* New York: Vintage, 2003.
———. *Making a New Deal: Industrial Workers in Chicago, 1919–1939.* Cambridge: Cambridge University Press, 2008.
Commons, John R. *Races and Immigrants in America.* New York: MacMillan, 1907.
Cooper, Frederick. *Colonialism in Question: Theory, Knowledge, History.* Berkeley: University of California Press, 2005.
——— and Ann Laura Stoler. *Tensions of Empire: Colonial Cultures in a Bourgeois World.* Berkeley: University of California Press, 1997.
Cowie, Jefferson. *Capital Moves: RCA's Seventy-Year Quest for Cheap Labor.* Ithaca, NY: Cornell University Press, 1999.
Cruden, Robert. *The End of the Ford Myth.* New York: International, 1933.
Davenport, T.R.H. *South Africa: A Modern History,* third edition. Toronto and Buffalo: University of Toronto Press, 1987.
Davila, Jerry. *Diploma of Whiteness: Race and Social Policy in Brazil, 1917–1945.* Durham, NC: Duke University Press, 2003.
Davis, Mike. *Prisoners of the American Dream.* London: Verso, 1986.
De Grazia, Victoria. *Irresistible Empire: America's Advance through 20th Century Europe.* Cambridge, MA: Harvard University Press, 2006.
Degler, Carl. *Neither Black nor White: Slavery and Race Relations in Brazil and the United States.* Madison: University of Wisconsin Press, 1991.
Delton, Jennifer. *Racial Integration in Corporate America, 1940–1990.* Cambridge: Cambridge University Press, 2009.
Denby, Charles. *Indignant Heart: A Black Worker's Journal.* Detroit: Wayne State University Press, [1952] 1978.
Dickerson, Dennis C. *Black Steelworkers in Western Pennsylvania, 1875–1980.* Albany: State University of New York Press, 1986.
Diggins, John P. *Mussolini and Fascism: The View from America.* Princeton, NJ: Princeton University Press, 1972.

Dillard, Angela. *Faith in the City: Preaching Radical Social Change in Detroit*. Ann Arbor: University of Michigan Press, 2007.
Dinius, Oliver, and Angela Vergara, eds. *Company Towns in the Americas: Landscape, Power and Working Class Communities*. Athens: University of Georgia Press, 2011.
Dominguez, Virginia. *White by Definition: Social Classification in Creole Louisiana*. Rutgers, NJ: Rutgers University Press, 1986.
Downs, Linda Bank. *Diego Rivera: The Detroit Industry Murals*. Detroit: Detroit Institute of Art, 1999.
Doxey, G. V. *The Industrial Colour Bar in South Africa*. Cape Town: Oxford University Press, 1961.
Dubofsky, Melvyn. *We Shall Be All: A History of the Industrial Workers of the World*. Urbana: University of Illinois Press, 2000.
Du Bois, W. E. B. *The Souls of Black Folk*. Mineola, NY: Dover, [1903] 1994.
———. *Black Reconstruction in America, 1860–1880*. New York: Atheneum, [1935] 1998.
Dunn, Robert. *Labor and Automobiles*. New York: International, 1929.
Eugenides, Jeffrey. *Middlesex*. New York: Farrar, Straus, and Giroux, 2002.
Feldman, Herman. *Racial Factors in American Industry*. New York: Harper & Brothers, 1931.
Ferguson, Roderick. *The Reorder of Things: The University and Its Pedagogies of Minority Difference*. Minneapolis: University of Minnesota Press, 2012.
Fields, Karen E., and Barbara J. Fields. *Racecraft: The Soul of Inequality in American Life*. New York: Verso, 2012.
Ford, Henry, with Samuel Crowther. *My Life and Work*. Garden City, NY: Doubleday and Page, 1922.
Ford, Henry. *Today and Tomorrow*. New York: Scribner, 1926.
———. *My Life and Work: An Autobiography of Henry Ford*. New York: Classic House Books, 2009.
Foster, William Trufant, and Waddill Catchings. *The Road to Plenty*. Boston and New York: Houghton Mifflin, 1928.
Foucault, Michel. *The Birth of the Clinic: An Archaeology of Medical Perception*. Translated by A. M. Sheridan Smith. New York: Vintage, 1994.
Fredrickson, George M. *White Supremacy: A Comparative History of American and South African History*. New York: Oxford University Press, 1981.
———. *The Comparative Imagination: On the History of Racism, Nationalism, and Social Movements*. Berkeley: University of California Press, 2000.
Fugard, Athol, with John Kani and Winston Ntshona. "Sizwe Bansi Is Dead." In Athol Fugard, John Kani, and Winston Ntshona, *Statements: Sizwe Bansi Is Dead, the Island, Statements after an Arrest under the Immorality Act/3 Plays*. New York: Theatre Communications Group, 1974.
Gartman, David. *Auto Slavery: The Labor Process in the American Automobile Industry, 1897–1950*. New Brunswick, NJ: Rutgers University Press, 1986.

———. *From Autos to Architecture: Fordism and Architectural Aesthetics in the Twentieth Century.* New York: Princeton Architectural Press, 2009.
Genovese, Eugene. *Roll, Jordan, Roll: The World the Slaves Made.* New York: Vintage, 1974.
Gould, Stephen Jay. *The Mismeasure of Man.* New York: W. W. Norton, 1981.
Gramsci, Antonio. "Americanism and Fordism." In *Selections from the Prison Notebooks.* New York: International, 1971.
Grandin, Greg. *Fordlandia: The Rise and Fall of Henry Ford's Forgotten Jungle City.* New York: New Press, 2009.
Grant-Thomas, Andrew, and Gary Orfield, eds. *Twenty-First Century Color Lines: Multiracial Change in Contemporary America.* Philadelphia: Temple University Press, 2009.
Greenberg, Stanley. *Race and State in Capitalist Development: Comparative Perspectives.* New Haven, CT: Yale University Press, 1980.
Greene, Lorenzo J., and Carter G. Woodson. *The Negro Wage Earner.* Washington, DC: Association for the Study of Negro Life and History, 1930.
Greenough, Paul, and Anna L. Tsing, eds. *Nature in the Global South: Environmental Projects in South and Southeast Asia.* Durham, NC, and London: Duke University Press, 2003.
Guerin, Daniel. *Fascism and Big Business.* New York: Pathfinder Press, 1994.
Haber, Samuel. *Efficiency and Uplift: Scientific Management in the Progressive Era, 1890–1920.* Chicago: University of Chicago Press, 1964.
Hale, Grace Elizabeth. *Making Whiteness: The Culture of Segregation in the South, 1890–1940.* New York: Vintage, 1999.
Hamilton, Charles V., ed. *Beyond Racism: Race and Inequality in Brazil, South Africa, and the United States.* London: Lynne Rienner, 2001.
Hardt, Michael, and Antonio Negri. *Empire.* Cambridge, MA: Harvard University Press, 2001.
Harribene, Margaret. *Port Elizabeth: A Chronology.* Port Elizabeth: Port Elizabeth Public Library, n. d.
Harter, Eugene C. *The Lost Colony of the Confederacy.* Oxford: University Press of Mississippi, 2000.
Hartmann, Edward George. *The Movement to Americanize the Immigrant.* New York: Columbia University Press, 1948.
Harvey, David. *The Condition of Postmodernity.* London: Blackwell, 1990.
Hayes, Peter. *Industry and Ideology: I. G. Farben in the Nazi Era.* Cambridge: Cambridge University Press, 2001.
Hecht, Susanna B., and Alexander Cockburn. *The Fate of the Forest: Developers, Destroyers, and Defenders of the Amazon,* updated edition. Chicago: University of Chicago Press, [1990] 2010.
Herod, Andrew, ed. *Organizing the Landscape: Geographical Perspectives on Labor Unionism.* Minneapolis: University of Minnesota Press, 1998.
Hill, Herbert. *Black Labor and the American Legal System: Race, Work and the Law.* Madison: University of Wisconsin Press, 1985.

Hong, Grace Kyungwon. *The Ruptures of American Capital: Women of Color Feminism and the Culture of Immigrant Labor.* Minneapolis: University of Minnesota Press, 2006.

Hounshell, David. *From the American System to Mass Production, 1800–1932.* Baltimore: Johns Hopkins University Press, 1984.

Hull, Richard. *American Enterprise in South Africa: Historical Dimensions of Engagement and Disengagement.* New York: New York University Press, 1990.

Huxley, Aldous. *Brave New World.* London: Chatto and Windus, 1932.

Jackson, Kenneth. *The Ku Klux Klan in the City.* New York: Oxford University Press, 1967.

———. *Crabgrass Frontier: The Suburbanization of the United States.* New York: Oxford University Press, 1985.

James, C. L. R. *American Civilization.* Edited by Anna Grimshaw and Keith Hart. Cambridge, MA, and Oxford: Blackwell, 1993.

Jeansonne, Glen. *Gerald L. K. Smith: Minister of Hate.* Baton Rouge: Louisiana State University Press, 1997.

Johnson, Walter. "Time and Revolution in African America: Temporality and the History of Atlantic Slavery." In *Rethinking American History in a Global Age,* edited by Thomas Bender. Berkeley: University of California Press, 2002.

Jones, Judith MacKnight. *Soldado Descansa! Uma Epopeia Norte Americana Sob Os Ceus Do Brasil.* Brasilia: Jarde, 1967, reprinted by Fraternidade Descendencia Americana, 1998.

Joseph, Michael Gilbert, Catherine Carlisle LeGrand, and Ricardo Donato Salvatore, eds. *Close Encounters of Empire: Writing the Cultural History of U. S.–Latin American Relations.* Chapel Hill, NC: Duke University Press, 1998.

Jung, Moon-Kie. *Reworking Race: The Making of Hawaii's Interracial Labor Movement.* New York: Columbia University Press, 2006.

Kabeer, Naila. *The Power to Choose: Bangladeshi Women and Labour Market Decisions in London and Dhaka.* London: Verso, 2000.

Kazanjian, David. *The Colonizing Trick: National Culture and Imperial Citizenship in Early America.* Minneapolis: University of Minnesota Press, 2003.

Kelley, Robin D. G. "How the West Was One: The African Diaspora and the Re-Mapping of U. S. History." In *Rethinking American History in a Global Age,* edited by Thomas Bender. Berkeley: University of California Press, 2002.

Kelly, Brian. *Race, Class, and Power in the Alabama Coalfields, 1908–1921.* Urbana: University of Illinois Press, 2001.

Keppel, Frederick P. *Philanthropy and Learning.* New York: Teachers College Press, 1936.

Kessler-Harris, Alice. *A Woman's Wage: Historical Meanings and Social Consequences.* Lexington: University Press of Kentucky, 1990.

Kevles, Daniel. *In the Name of Eugenics: Genetics and the Uses of Human Heredity.* Cambridge, MA: Harvard University Press, [1985] 1998.

Kirby, Jack Temple. *Darkness at the Dawning: Race and Reform in the Progressive Era South.* Philadelphia: Lippincott, 1972.

Kirk, Tim. *Nazism and the Working Class in Austria*. Cambridge: Cambridge University Press, 1996.
Klausen, Susanne M. *Race, Maternity and the Politics of Birth Control in South Africa, 1910–1939*. New York: Palgrave, 2005.
Krikler, Jeremy. *White Rising: The 1922 Insurrection and Racial Killing in South Africa*. Manchester: Manchester University Press, 2005.
Kuhl, Stefan. *The Nazi Connection: Eugenics, American Racism, and German National Socialism*. New York: Oxford University Press, 1994.
Lacey, Robert. *Ford: The Men and the Machine*. New York: Little, Brown, 1986.
Lake, Marilyn, and Harry Reynolds. *Drawing the Global Colour Line: White Men's Countries and the International Challenge of Racial Equality*. Cambridge: Cambridge University Press, 2008.
Lamar, Howard, and Leonard Thompson. *The Frontier in History: North America and Southern Africa Compared*. New Haven, CT: Yale University Press, 1981.
Lee, Albert. *Henry Ford and the Jews*. New York: Stein and Day, 1980.
Lens, Sidney. *The Forging of the American Empire: From the Revolution to Vietnam—A History of US Imperialism*. New York: Thomas Crowell, 1971.
Levine, Robert. *The Father of the Poor?: Vargas and His Era*. Cambridge: Cambridge University Press, 1998.
Lewis, David L. *The Public Image of Henry Ford: An American Folk Hero and His Company*. Detroit: Wayne State University Press, 1976.
Lichtenstein, Nelson. "Life at the Rouge: A Cycle of Workers Control." In *Life and Labor: Dimensions of American Working Class History*, edited by Charles Stephenson and Robert Asher. Albany: State University of New York Press, 1986.
———, ed. *Wal-Mart: The Face of Twenty First Century Capitalism*. New York: New Press, 2006.
Lief, Alfred. *The Firestone Story: A History of the Firestone Tire and Rubber Company*. New York: McGraw Hill, 1951.
Linebaugh, Peter, and Marcus Rediker. *The Many Headed Hydra: The Hidden History of the Revolutionary Atlantic*. Boston: Beacon Press, 2000.
Lipsitz, George. *The Possessive Investment in Whiteness: How White People Profit from Racism*. Philadelphia: Temple University Press, 1998.
Lipton, Merle. *Capitalism and Apartheid: South Africa, 1910–1984*. London: Rowman and Allanheld, 1985.
Loewen, James W. *Sundown Towns: A Hidden Dimension of American Racism*. New York: New Press, 2005.
Longmore, Paul K., and Lauri Umansky, eds. *The New Disability History: American Perspectives*. New York: New York University Press, 2001.
Lowe, Lisa. *Immigrant Acts: On Asian American Cultural Politics*. Chapel Hill, NC: Duke University Press, 1996.
Lowy, Michael. *Politics of Combined and Uneven Development: Theory of Permanent Revolution*. London: Verso, 1987.
——— and Jarius Banaji. *Theory as History*. Chicago: Haymarket, 2011.
Makalani, Minkah. *In the Cause of Freedom: Radical Black Internationalism from*

Harlem to London, 1917–1939. Chapel Hill: University of North Carolina Press, 2011.
Malherbe, Ernst Gideon. *Educational and Social Research in South Africa.* Pretoria: South African Council for Educational and Social Research, 1939.
———. *Never a Dull Moment.* Cape Town: Timmins, 1981.
Marquis, Samuel S. *Henry Ford: An Interpretation.* Detroit: Wayne State University Press, [1923] 2007.
Marx, Anthony. *Making Race and Nation: A Comparison of South Africa, the United States and Brazil.* Cambridge: Cambridge University Press, 1998.
Marx, Karl. *Capital: A Critique of Political Economy,* three volumes. Chicago: Charles H. Kerr, 1906.
———. *Pre-Capitalist Economic Formations.* New York: International, 2000.
——— and Friedrich Engels. *Manifesto of the Communist Party.* Oxford: Oxford University Press, 1992.
May, Elaine Tyler, and Reinhold Wagnleitner, eds. *Here, There, and Everywhere: The Foreign Politics of American Popular Culture.* Hanover, NH: University of New England Press, 2000.
McCormick, Thomas J. *America's Half-Century: United States Foreign Policy in the Cold War and After.* Baltimore: Johns Hopkins University Press, 1995.
McDonough, John, and Karen Egolf, eds. *The Advertising Age: Encyclopedia of Advertising.* Chicago: Fitzroy Dearborn, 2002.
McKiven, Henry M., Jr. *Iron and Steel: Class, Race and Community in Birmingham, Alabama, 1875–1920.* Chapel Hill: University of North Carolina Press, 1995.
Meier, August, and Elliott Rudwick. *Black Detroit and the Rise of the UAW.* New York: Oxford University Press, 1979.
Meyer, Stephen. *The Five Dollar Day: Labor Management and Social Control at the Ford Motor Company, 1908–1921.* Albany: State University of New York Press, 1981.
———. *Manhood on the Line: Working Class Masculinities in the American Heartland.* Urbana: University of Illinois Press, 2016.
Mitchell, Don. "The Scales of Justice: Localist Ideology, Large-Scale Production and Agricultural Labor's Geography of Resistance in 1930s California." In *Organizing the Landscape: Geographical Perspectives on Labor Unionism,* edited by Andrew Herod. Minneapolis: University of Minnesota Press, 1998.
Montgomery, David. *The Fall of the House of Labor: The Workplace, the State, and American Labor Activism, 1865–1925.* Cambridge: Cambridge University Press, 1987.
Morrell, Robert, ed. *White but Poor: Essays on the History of Poor Whites in South Africa, 1880–1940.* Pretoria: University of South Africa, 1992.
Nelson, Bruce. *Divided We Stand: American Workers and the Struggle for Black Equality.* Princeton, NJ: Princeton University Press, 2001.
Nelson, Daniel. *Managers and Workers: Origins of the Twentieth-Century Factory System in the United States, 1880–1920.* Madison: University of Wisconsin Press, 1996.
Nevins, Allan, and Frank Ernest Hill. *Ford: Expansion and Challenge, 1915–1933.* New York: Charles Scribner's Sons, 1957.

Ngai, Mae. *Impossible Subjects: Illegal Aliens and the Making of Modern America.* Princeton, NJ: Princeton University Press, 2004.

Noer, Thomas. *Briton, Boer and Yankee, the United States and South Africa, 1870–1914.* Kent, OH: Kent State University Press, 1978.

Nolan, Mary. *Visions of Modernity: American Business and the Modernization of Germany.* New York: Oxford University Press, 1994.

Northrup, Herbert R. *Organized Labor and the Negro Worker.* New York: Harper & Brothers, 1944.

Parker, Mike, and Jane Slaughter, eds. *Choosing Sides: Unions and the Team Concept.* Boston: South End Press, 1988.

Peck, Gunther. *Reinventing Free Labor: Padrones and Immigrant Workers in the North American West, 1880–1930.* Cambridge: Cambridge University Press, 2000.

Peterson, Joyce Shaw. *American Automobile Workers, 1900–1933.* Albany: State University of New York Press, 1987.

Phillips, Michael. *White Metropolis: Race, Ethnicity, and Religion in Dallas, 1841–2001.* Austin: University of Texas Press, 2006.

Pierrot, George F. *An Illustrated Guide to the Diego Rivera Frescoes.* Detroit: Detroit Institute of Arts, 1934.

Postone, Moishe. *Time, Labor, and Social Domination: A Reinterpretation of Marx's Critical Theory.* Cambridge: Cambridge University Press, 1993.

Powers, Richard Gid. *Not without Honor: The History of American Anticommunism.* New Haven, CT: Yale University Press, 1998.

Quinn, Bill. *How Walmart Is Destroying America (and the World): And What You Can Do about It.* New York: Crown, 2005.

Reed, Touré. *Not Alms but Opportunity: The Urban League and Politics of Racial Uplift.* Chapel Hill: University of North Carolina Press, 2008.

Rivera, Diego, with Gladys March. *My Art, My Life: An Autobiography.* New York: Dover Press, 1991.

Roberts, David. *In the Shadow of Detroit: Gordon M. McGregor, Ford of Canada, and Motoropolis.* Detroit: Wayne State University Press, 2006.

Robinson, Jennifer. *The Power of Apartheid: State, Power and Space in South African Cities.* New York: Oxford University Press, 1996.

Rodgers, Daniel T. "An Age of Social Politics." In *Rethinking American History in a Global Age,* edited by Thomas Bender. Berkeley: University of California Press, 2002.

Roediger, David R. *The Wages of Whiteness: Race and the Making of the American Working Class.* London: Verso, 1991.

———. *Working toward Whiteness: How America's Immigrants Became White: The Strange Journey from Ellis Island to the Suburbs.* New York: Basic Books, 2005.

——— and Philip S. Foner. *Our Own Time: A History of American Labor and the Working Day.* London: Verso, 1989.

——— and Elizabeth D. Esch. *The Production of Difference: Race and the Management of Labor in the United States.* New York: Oxford University Press, 2012.

Rosenberg, Emily. *Spreading the American Dream: American Economic and Cultural Expansion, 1890–1945*. New York: Hill and Wang, 1982.

———. *Financial Missionaries to the World: The Politics and Culture of Dollar Diplomacy, 1900–1930*. Cambridge, MA: Harvard University Press, 1999.

Rossi, Angello. *Brasil, Integracao de races e Nacionalidades*. Sao Paulo: Companhia Ilimitada, 1991.

Roux, Edward. *Time Longer than Rope: A History of the Black Man's Struggle for Freedom in South Africa*. Madison: University of Wisconsin Press, 1966.

Rupert, Mark. *Producing Hegemony: The Politics of Mass Production and American Global Power*. Cambridge: Cambridge Studies in International Relations, no. 38, 1995.

Rydell, Robert W., and Rob Kroes. *Buffalo Bill in Bologna: The Americanization of the World, 1869–1922*. Chicago: University of Chicago Press, 2005.

Saul, John S., and Stephen Gelb. *The Crisis in South Africa*. New York: Monthly Review Press, 1986.

Saxton, Alexander. *The Indispensable Enemy: Labor and the Anti-Chinese Movement in California*. Berkeley: University of California Press, 1975.

Scott, James C. *Seeing Like a State: How Certain Schemes to Improve the Human Condition Have Failed*. New Haven, CT: Yale University Press, 1998.

Segal, Howard. *Recasting the Machine Age: Henry Ford's Village Industries*. Amherst: University of Massachusetts Press, 2008.

Seldes, George, with Helen Seldes. *Facts and Fascism*. New York: In Fact, 1943.

Seltzer, Mark. *Bodies and Machines*. London: Routledge, 1992.

Shurtleff, William, and Akiko Aoyagi, eds. *History of Soy Yogurt, Soy Acidophilus Milk and Other Cultured Soymilks*. Lafayette, CA: Soy Info Center, 2012.

Sinclair, Upton. *The Flivver King: A Story of Ford-America*. Detroit: United Automobile Workers of America, 1937.

Smith, A. Mark. *Mastered by the Clock: Time, Slavery and Freedom in the American South*. Chapel Hill: University of North Carolina Press, 1997.

Smith, Neil. *Uneven Development: Nature, Capital and the Production of Space*. New York: Basil Blackwell, 1991.

Snow, Richard. *I Invented the Modern Age: The Rise of Henry Ford*. New York: Scribner, 2013.

Spiro, Jonathan. *Defending the Master Race: Conservation, Eugenics, and the Legacy of Madison Grant*. Lebanon, NH: University Press of New England, 2009.

Stam, Robert, and Ella Shohat. *Race in Translation: Culture Wars around the Postcolonial Atlantic*. New York: New York University Press, 2012.

Stepan, Nancy. *"The Hour of Eugenics": Race, Gender, and Nation in Latin America*. Ithaca, NY: Cornell University Press, 1991.

Stephenson, Charles, and Robert Asher, eds. *Life and Labor: Dimensions of American Working Class History*. Albany: State University of New York Press, 1986.

Stoler, Ann Laura. *Carnal Knowledge and Imperial Power: Race and the Intimate in Colonial Rule*. Berkeley: University of California, 2002.

———, ed. *Haunted by Empire: Geographies of Intimacy in North American History.* Durham, NC: Duke University Press, 2006.

Sundiata, Ibrahim. *Black Scandal: America and the Liberian Labor Crisis, 1929–1936.* Philadelphia: Institute for the Study of Human Issues, 1980.

Sward, Keith. *The Legend of Henry Ford.* New York: Rinehart, 1948.

Takaki, Ronald. *Pau Hana: Plantation Life in Hawaii, 1835–1920.* Honolulu: University of Hawaiʻi Press, 1983.

Tarbell, Ida. *All in the Day's Work: An Autobiography.* Urbana: University of Illinois Press, [1939] 2003.

Thomas, Richard W. *Life for Us Is What We Make It: Building Black Community in Detroit, 1915–1945.* Bloomington: Indiana University Press, 1992.

Tucker, Richard. *Insatiable Appetite: The United States and the Ecological Degradation of the Tropical World.* Berkeley: University of California Press, 2000.

Tully, John. *The Devil's Milk: A Social History of Rubber.* New York: Monthly Review Press, 2012.

Twine, Frances Winddance. *Racism in a Racial Democracy: The Maintenance of White Supremacy in Brazil.* New Brunswick, NJ: Rutgers University Press, 1997.

Van der Poel, Jean, ed. *Selections from the Smuts Papers, Volumes V–VII.* Cambridge: Cambridge University Press, 2007.

Vargas, Zaragosa. *Proletarians of the North: A History of Mexican Industrial Workers in Detroit and the Midwest, 1917–1933.* Chapel Hill: University of North Carolina Press, 1993.

Vitalis, Robert. *White World Order, Black Power Politics: The Birth of International Relations.* Ithaca, NY: Cornell University Press, 2015.

Wallace, Max. *The American Axis: Henry Ford, Charles Lindbergh, and the Rise of the Third Reich.* New York: St. Martin's Press, 2003.

Wallerstein, Immanuel. The *Modern World System II: Mercantilism and the Consolidation of the European World-Economy, 1600–1750.* New York: Academic Press, 1980.

Watts, Steven. *The People's Tycoon: Henry Ford and the American Century.* New York: Vintage, 2005.

Weinstein, Barbara. *The Amazon Rubber Boom, 1850–1920.* Palo Alto, CA: Stanford University Press, 1983.

———. *For Social Peace in Brazil: Industrialists and the Remaking of the Working Class in Sao Paulo, 1920–1964.* Chapel Hill: University of North Carolina Press, 1996.

———. "Racializing Regional Difference: São Paulo versus Brazil, 1932." In *Race and Nation in Modern Latin America*, edited by Nancy Applebaum, Karin Alejandro Rosenblatt, and Peter Wade. Chapel Hill: University of North Carolina Press, 2007.

Widick, B. J. *Detroit: A City of Race and Class Violence.* Detroit: Wayne State University Press, [1972] 1989.

Wilkins, Mira, and Frank Ernest Hill. *American Business Abroad: Ford on Six Continents.* Detroit: Wayne State University Press, 1964.

Williams, Raymond. *Keywords: A Vocabulary of Culture and Society.* New York: Oxford University Press, 1983.
Willoughby-Herard, Tiffany. *Waste of a White Skin: The Carnegie Corporation and the Racial Logic of White Vulnerability.* Berkeley: University of California Press, 2015.
Wilson, Edmund. *The American Jitters: A Year of the Slump.* New York: Charles Scribner's Sons, 1932.
Wilson, Joan Hoff. *Herbert Hoover: Forgotten Progressive.* Long Grove, IL: Waveland Press, 1992.
Wolcott, Victoria. *Remaking Respectability: African American Women in Interwar Detroit.* Chapel Hill: University of North Carolina Press, 2001.
Wolf, Howard, and Ralph Wolf. *Rubber: A Story of Glory and Greed.* New York: Covici-Friede, 1936.
Wolfe, Joel. *Autos and Progress: The Brazilian Search for Modernity.* New York: Oxford University Press, 2010.
Wood, Gregory. *Retiring Men: Labor and Growing Old in America, 1900–1960.* Lanham, MD: University Press of America, 2012.
Woodward, C. Vann. *Origins of the New South, 1877–1913.* Baton Rouge: Louisiana State University Press, [1951] 1999.
Young, Marilyn B. "The Age of Global Power." In *Rethinking American History in a Global Age,* edited by Thomas Bender. Berkeley: University of California Press, 2002.
Zhang, Lu. *Inside China's Automobile Factories: The Politics of Labor and Worker Resistance.* New York: Cambridge University Press, 2015.
Zimmerman, Andrew. *Alabama in Africa: Booker T. Washington, the German Empire and the Globalization of the New South.* Princeton, NJ: Princeton University Press, 2010.
Zunz, Olivier. *The Changing Face of Inequality: Urbanization, Industrial Development, and Immigrants in Detroit, 1880–1920.* Chicago: University of Chicago Press, 1982.

INDEX

AMERICAN CROSSROADS

Edited by Earl Lewis, George Lipsitz, George Sánchez, Dana Takagi, Laura Briggs, and Nikhil Pal Singh

1. *Border Matters: Remapping American Cultural Studies,* by José David Saldívar
2. *The White Scourge: Mexicans, Blacks, and Poor Whites in Texas Cotton Culture,* by Neil Foley
3. *Indians in the Making: Ethnic Relations and Indian Identities around Puget Sound,* by Alexandra Harmon
4. *Aztlán and Viet Nam: Chicano and Chicana Experiences of the War,* edited by George Mariscal
5. *Immigration and the Political Economy of Home: West Indian Brooklyn and American Indian Minneapolis, 1945–1992,* by Rachel Buff
6. *Epic Encounters: Culture, Media, and U. S. Interests in the Middle East since 1945,* by Melani McAlister
7. *Contagious Divides: Epidemics and Race in San Francisco's Chinatown,* by Nayan Shah
8. *Japanese American Celebration and Conflict: A History of Ethnic Identity and Festival, 1934–1990,* by Lon Kurashige
9. *American Sensations: Class, Empire, and the Production of Popular Culture,* by Shelley Streeby
10. *Colored White: Transcending the Racial Past,* by David R. Roediger
11. *Reproducing Empire: Race, Sex, Science, and U. S. Imperialism in Puerto Rico,* by Laura Briggs
12. *meXicana Encounters: The Making of Social Identities on the Borderlands,* by Rosa Linda Fregoso
13. *Popular Culture in the Age of White Flight: Fear and Fantasy in Suburban Los Angeles,* by Eric Avila
14. *Ties That Bind: The Story of an Afro-Cherokee Family in Slavery and Freedom,* by Tiya Miles
15. *Cultural Moves: African Americans and the Politics of Representation,* by Herman S. Gray
16. *Emancipation Betrayed: The Hidden History of Black Organizing and White Violence in Florida from Reconstruction to the Bloody Election of 1920,* by Paul Ortiz

17. *Eugenic Nation: Faults and Frontiers of Better Breeding in Modern America*, by Alexandra Stern
18. *Audiotopia: Music, Race, and America,* by Josh Kun
19. *Black, Brown, Yellow, and Left: Radical Activism in Los Angeles*, by Laura Pulido
20. *Fit to Be Citizens? Public Health and Race in Los Angeles, 1879–1939,* by Natalia Molina
21. *Golden Gulag: Prisons, Surplus, Crisis, and Opposition in Globalizing California*, by Ruth Wilson Gilmore
22. *Proud to Be an Okie: Cultural Politics, Country Music, and Migration to Southern California*, by Peter La Chapelle
23. *Playing America's Game: Baseball, Latinos, and the Color Line*, by Adrian Burgos, Jr.
24. *The Power of the Zoot: Youth Culture and Resistance during World War II*, by Luis Alvarez
25. *Guantánamo: A Working-Class History between Empire and Revolution*, by Jana K. Lipman
26. *Between Arab and White: Race and Ethnicity in the Early Syrian-American Diaspora,* by Sarah M. A. Gualtieri
27. *Mean Streets: Chicago Youths and the Everyday Struggle for Empowerment in the Multiracial City, 1908–1969,* by Andrew J. Diamond
28. *In Sight of America: Photography and the Development of U. S. Immigration Policy,* by Anna Pegler-Gordon
29. *Migra! A History of the U. S. Border Patrol,* by Kelly Lytle Hernández
30. *Racial Propositions: Ballot Initiatives and the Making of Postwar California,* by Daniel Martinez HoSang
31. *Stranger Intimacy: Contesting Race, Sexuality, and the Law in the North American West,* by Nayan Shah
32. *The Nicest Kids in Town:* American Bandstand, *Rock 'n' Roll, and the Struggle for Civil Rights in 1950s Philadelphia,* by Matthew F. Delmont
33. *Jack Johnson, Rebel Sojourner: Boxing in the Shadow of the Global Color Line,* by Theresa Rundstedler
34. *Pacific Connections: The Making of the U. S.-Canadian Borderlands*, by Kornel Chang

35. *States of Delinquency: Race and Science in the Making of California's Juvenile Justice System,* by Miroslava Chávez-García
36. *Spaces of Conflict, Sounds of Solidarity: Music, Race, and Spatial Entitlement in Los Angeles,* by Gaye Theresa Johnson
37. *Covert Capital: Landscapes of Denial and the Making of U. S. Empire in the Suburbs of Northern Virginia,* by Andrew Friedman
38. *How Race Is Made in America: Immigration, Citizenship, and the Historical Power of Racial Scripts,* by Natalia Molina
39. *We Sell Drugs: The Alchemy of U. S. Empire,* by Suzanna Reiss
40. *Abrazando el Espíritu: Bracero Families Confront the U. S.-Mexico Border,* by Ana Elizabeth Rosas
41. *Houston Bound: Culture and Color in a Jim Crow City,* by Tyina L. Steptoe
42. *Why Busing Failed: Race, Media, and the National Resistance to School Desegregation,* by Matthew F. Delmont
43. *Incarcerating the Crisis: Freedom Struggles and the Rise of the Neoliberal State,* by Jordan T. Camp
44. *Lavender and Red: Liberation and Solidarity in the Gay and Lesbian Left,* by Emily K. Hobson
45. *Flavors of Empire: Food and the Making of Thai America,* by Mark Padoongpatt
46. *The Life of Paper: Letters and a Poetics of Living beyond Captivity,* by Sharon Luk
47. *Strategies of Segregation: Race, Residence, and the Struggle for Educational Equality,* by David G. García
48. *Soldiering through Empire: Race and the Making of the Decolonizing Pacific,* by Simeon Man
49. *American Language: The History of Spanish in the United States,* by Rosina Lozano
50. *The Color Line and the Assembly Line: Managing Race in the Ford Empire,* by Elizabeth D. Esch
51. *Confessions of a Radical Chicano Doo-Wop Singer,* by Rubén Funkahuatl Guevara